INTERNET OF THINGS

AUTHOR

Dr. Sujata Pal
Associate Professor
Department of Computer Science and Engineering
Indian Institute of Technology Ropar
Punjab, India

REVIEWER

Prof. Maitreyee Dutta
Professor
Department of Information Management and
Emerging Engineering, NITTTR Chandigarh
Chandigarh, India

KHANNA BOOK PUBLISHING CO. (P) Ltd.
4C/4344, Ansari Road, Darya Ganj,
New Delhi, India

All India Council for Technical Education
Nelson Mandela Marg, Vasant Kunj,
New Delhi, India

Dear Readers,

To prevent the piracy, this book is secured with HIGH SECURITY HOLOGRAM on the front title cover. In case you don't find the hologram on the front cover title, please write us to at contact@khannabooks.com or whatsapp us at +91-99109 09320 and avail special gift voucher for yourself.

Specimen of Hologram on front Cover title:

Moreover, there is a SPECIAL DISCOUNT COUPON for you with EVERY HOLOGRAM.

How to avail this SPECIAL DISCOUNT:

Step 1: Scratch the hologram

Step 2: Under the scratch area, your "coupon code" is available

Step 3: Logon to www.khannabooks.com

Step 4: Use your "coupon code" in the shopping cart and get your copy at a special discount

Step 5: Enjoy your reading!

ISBN: 978-93-5538-495-9

Book Code: DIP497EN

Internet Of Things

by Dr. Sujata Pal

First Edition: 2026

Originally Published by:

All India Council for Technical Education, Ministry of Education, GOI

Exclusively Published & Distributed by:

Khanna Book Publishing Co. (P) Ltd.
4C/4344, Ansari Road, Daryaganj,
New Delhi (INDIA)

Visit us at: **www.khannabooks.com**
Write us at: **contact@khannabooks.com**

To view complete list of books, Please scan the QR Code: KPH

Printed in Bharat.

प्रो. टी. जी. सीताराम
अध्यक्ष
Prof. T. G. Sitharam
Chairman

सत्यमेव जयते

आज़ादी का अमृत महोत्सव

अखिल भारतीय तकनीकी शिक्षा परिषद्
(भारत सरकार का एक सांविधिक निकाय)
(शिक्षा मंत्रालय, भारत सरकार)
नेल्सन मंडेला मार्ग, वसंत कुंज, नई दिल्ली–110070
दूरभाष : 011–26131498
ई–मेल : chairman@aicte-india.org

ALL INDIA COUNCIL FOR TECHNICAL EDUCATION
(A STATUTORY BODY OF THE GOVT. OF INDIA)
(Ministry of Education, Govt. of India)
Nelson Mandela Marg, Vasant Kunj, New Delhi-110070
Phone : 011-26131498
E-mail : chairman@aicte-india.org

FOREWORD

Engineers are the backbone of any modern society. They are the ones responsible for the marvels as well as the improved quality of life across the world. Engineers have driven humanity towards greater heights in a more evolved and unprecedented manner.

The All India Council for Technical Education (AICTE), have spared no efforts towards the strengthening of the technical education in the country. AICTE is always committed towards promoting quality Technical Education to make India a modern developed nation emphasizing on the overall welfare of mankind.

An array of initiatives has been taken by AICTE in last decade which have been accelerated now by the National Education Policy (NEP) 2020. The implementation of NEP under the visionary leadership of Hon'ble Prime Minister of India envisages the provision for education in regional languages to all, thereby ensuring that every graduate becomes competent enough and is in a position to contribute towards the national growth and development through innovation & entrepreneurship.

One of the spheres where AICTE had been relentlessly working since past couple of years is providing high quality original technical contents at Under Graduate & Diploma level prepared and translated by eminent educators in various Indian languages to its aspirants. For students pursuing 2nd year of their Engineering education, AICTE has identified 87 books, which shall be translated into 12 Indian languages - Hindi, Tamil, Gujarati, Odia, Bengali, Kannada, Urdu, Punjabi, Telugu, Marathi, Assamese & Malayalam. In addition to the English medium, books in different Indian Languages are going to support the students to understand the concepts in their respective mother tongue.

On behalf of AICTE, I express sincere gratitude to all distinguished authors, reviewers and translators from the renowned institutions of high repute for their admirable contribution in a record span of time.

AICTE is confident that these outcomes based original contents shall help aspirants to master the subject with comprehension and greater ease.

(Prof. T. G. Sitharam)

DEDICATION

This book is dedicated to my students Vidushi, Arshi, Kavitha and my son, Soham.

ACKNOWLEDGEMENT

The authors are grateful to the authorities of AICTE, particularly Prof. (Dr.) T G Sitharam, Chairman; Dr. Abhay Jere, Vice-Chairman, Prof. Rajive Kumar, Member-Secretary, Dr. Sunil Luthra, Director, and Reena Sharma, Hindi Officer Training and Learning Bureau for their planning to publish the books on Internet of Things. We sincerely acknowledge the valuable contributions of the reviewer of the book Prof. Maitreyee Dutta, Department of Information Management and Emerging Engineering, NITTTR Chandigarh.

I would like to express my warm appreciation to my PhD students, Dr. Vidushi Agarwal, Ms. Arshi Zameer, and Ms. M. Kavitha, for their invaluable support in helping me complete this book. I am deeply thankful to my husband, Mr. Anup, my son, Soham, my students, friends, colleagues, and family members for their understanding and patience throughout the writing process. A special thank you to my mother, Mrs. Bulu Pal, for her unwavering encouragement to write this book. Lastly, I dedicate this work to the memory of my late father, Mr. Gouranga Chand Pal, whose inspiration and guidance continue to shape my journey.

This book is the result of numerous insights and suggestions from AICTE members, experts, and authors who shared their perspectives on advancing engineering education in our country. I am grateful to the contributors and all those involved in this field whose published works, review articles, papers, photographs, footnotes, references, and other invaluable resources significantly enriched the content during the writing process.

Dr. Sujata Pal

PREFACE

The Internet of Things (IoT) brought about a new way of interactions with surroundings. From smart homes and wearable gadgets to industrial automation and smart cities, IoT is redefining connectivity, efficiency, and innovation in many aspects of life. This book, Internet of Things (IoT) aims to provide a thorough grasp of the fundamental ideas, technologies, and applications of IoT.

This book, intended for students, educators, and practitioners, combines theoretical insights with practical knowledge, allowing readers to understand both the "what" and the "how" of IoT systems. It covers a wide range of topics, including the principles of IoT, communication protocols, device integration, domain-specific applications, and the crucial aspects of security and challenges in IoT systems.

One of the core philosophies driving this book is the adoption of an Outcome-Based Education (OBE) framework. By aligning the content with clear Program Outcomes (POs) and Course Outcomes (COs), the book ensures a focused approach to learning, with measurable objectives. Each chapter concludes with exercises to reinforce concepts, while real-world case studies illustrate the practical applications of IoT in diverse domains.

Key highlights of the book include:

- A deep dive into IoT architectures and protocols.
- Insights into the integration of sensors, actuators, and cloud services to create efficient IoT solutions.
- Practical examples of IoT applications across industries, healthcare and agriculture.
- Discussions on emerging trends, ethical concerns, and security challenges in IoT.

This book was created by the collective efforts of numerous individuals. I am grateful to the reviewers and writers whose insights increased the content. I am very grateful to my students and colleagues, whose inquiries and excitement prompted me to dive deeper into this topic. My heartfelt gratitude goes out to my family for their patience and support throughout this journey.

As the Internet of Things evolves, I hope that this book will provide a solid platform for readers to explore, create, and contribute to this dynamic subject. This book is designed with you in mind, whether you are a student just starting out in the Internet of Things, an instructor searching for teaching tools, or a professional looking to use IoT solutions.

Welcome to the wonderful world of the Internet of Things!!

Dr. Sujata pal

OUTCOME BASED EDUCATION

For the implementation of an outcome based education the first requirement is to develop an outcome based curriculum and incorporate an outcome based assessment in the education system. By going through outcome based assessments evaluators will be able to evaluate whether the students have achieved the outlined standard, specific and measurable outcomes. With the proper incorporation of outcome based education there will be a definite commitment to achieve a minimum standard for all learners without giving up at any level. At the end of the programme running with the aid of outcome based education, a student will be able to arrive at the following outcomes:

PO1. Engineering Knowledge: Use your knowledge of IoT principles, technologies, and frameworks to analyze and solve real-world engineering challenges.

PO2. Problem Analysis: Identify and analyze IoT-related challenges, drawing on theoretical and practical knowledge to suggest viable solutions.

PO3. Design/development of solutions: Create IoT-based solutions by developing efficient systems, devices, and networks that satisfy specific functional needs.

PO4. Engineering Tools and Experimentation and Testing: Use contemporary IoT tools, protocols, and frameworks to efficiently design and test IoT systems.

PO5. Engineering practices for society, sustainability and environment: Integrate sustainability concepts and ethical issues into IoT projects, focusing on societal impact.

PO6. Project Management: Work together to effectively manage IoT projects, ensuring seamless communication and execution.

PO7. Lifelong Learning: Commit to continuous learning by remaining current on emerging IoT technology and breakthroughs.

COURSE OUTCOMES

After completion of the course the students will be able to:

CO-1: Explain the principles of the Internet of Things, including its evolution and essential building blocks such as sensors, actuators, and networks.

CO-2: Showcase the use of IoT communication protocols and frameworks while creating IoT systems.

CO-3: Create useful IoT solutions by combining sensors, actuators, and cloud services.

CO-4: Evaluate the performance, scalability, and security of IoT systems in real-world scenarios.

CO-5: Evaluate IoT applications across multiple sectors, focusing on their potential for innovation and societal benefits.

Mapping of Course Outcomes with Programme Outcomes to be done according to the matrix given below:

Course Outcomes	Expected Mapping with Programme Outcomes *(1- Weak Correlation; 2- Medium correlation; 3- Strong Correlation)*						
	PO-1	**PO-2**	**PO-3**	**PO-4**	**PO-5**	**PO-6**	**PO-7**
CO-1	3	2	3	2	3	2	1
CO-2	3	2	1	3	2	2	1
CO-3	3	2	3	3	3	3	2
CO-4	1	2	3	3	1	1	1
CO-5	1	1	3	2	3	1	1

GUIDELINES FOR TEACHERS

To implement Outcome Based Education (OBE), the knowledge level and skill set of the students should be enhanced. Teachers should take a major responsibility for the proper implementation of OBE. Some of the responsibilities (not limited to) for the teachers in OBE system may be as follows:

- Within reasonable constraints, they should maneuver time to the best advantage of all students.
- They should assess the students only upon certain defined criterion without considering any other potential ineligibility to discriminate against them.
- They should try to grow the learning abilities of the students to a certain level before they leave the institute.
- They should try to ensure that all the students are equipped with quality knowledge as well as competence after they finish their education.
- They should always encourage the students to develop their ultimate performance capabilities.
- They should facilitate and encourage group work and team work to consolidate newer approaches.
- They should follow Bloom's taxonomy in every part of the assessment.

Bloom's Taxonomy

Level	Teacher should Check	Student should be able to	Possible Mode of Assessment
Create	Students ability to create	Design or Create	Mini project
Evaluate	Students ability to justify	Argue or Defend	Assignment
Analyse	Students ability to distinguish	Differentiate or Distinguish	Project/Lab Methodology
Apply	Students ability to use information	Operate or Demonstrate	Technical Presentation/ Demonstration
Understand	Students ability to explain the ideas	Explain or Classify	Presentation/Seminar
Remember	Students ability to recall (or remember)	Define or Recall	Quiz

GUIDELINES FOR STUDENTS

Students should take equal responsibility for implementing the OBE. Some of the responsibilities (not limited to) for the students in OBE system are as follows:

- Students should be well aware of each UO before the start of a unit in each and every course.
- Students should be well aware of each CO before the start of the course.
- Students should be well aware of each PO before the start of the programme.
- Students should think critically and reasonably with proper reflection and action.
- Learning of the students should be connected and integrated with practical and real life consequences.
- Students should be well aware of their competency at every level of OBE.

ABBREVIATIONS AND SYMBOLS

List of Abbreviations

General Terms	
Abbreviations	**Full form**
6LoWPAN	IPv6 over Low Power Wireless Personal Area Networks
6TiSCH	IPv6 over the TSCH
AMQP	Advanced Message Queuing Protocol
BLE	Bluetooth Low Energy
CoAP	Constrained Application Protocol
DARPA	Defense Advanced Research Projects Agency
HTTP	Hypertext Transfer Protocol
IPv4	Internet Protocol Version 4
IPv6	Internet Protocol Version 6
LoRaWAN	Long Range Wide Area Network
LTE	Long-Term Evolution
LWM2M	Lightweight Machine-to-Machine Protocol
MAC	Media Access Control
MQTT	Message Queuing Telemetry Transport
NBIoT	Narrowband Internet of Things
PHY	Physical Layer
PLC	Programmable Logic Controller
RFID	Radio Frequency Identification
RPi	Raspberry Pi
TSCH	Time-Slotted Channel Hopping
WAN	Wide Area Network
WiFi	Wireless Fidelity

LIST OF FIGURES

UNIT 1

UNIT 2

UNIT 3

AICTE'S LIST OF PRESCRIBED TEXTBOOKS

As Per Model Curriculum & Outcome Based Education
aligned with
NATIONAL EDUCATION POLICY 2020

UNDERGRADUATE COURSE BOOKS

S.No.	ISBN	Book Name	Author
1	9789355382160	Advanced Electrical Machines: Theory and Practicals	Bharat Singh Rajpurohit
2	9789355382139	Analog Electronic Circuits: Theory and Practical	Venu Sonti, Sachin Jain
3	9789355383808	Analog Electronic Devices: Theory and Practicals	N. B Balamurugan
4	9789391505158	Basic Electrical Engineering (with Lab Manual)	S.K. Sahdev
5	9789355388087	Basic of Electronics	Brijesh Iyer
6	9789355387127	Basics of Electrical Machines: Theory and Practicals	D. K. Palwalia, U. K. Kalla, R. K. Kumawat
7	9789355389381	Basics of Mechanics	Shubhankar Bhowmick, N. Venkata Swamy Naidu
8	9789355386250	Basics of Thermodynamics	Parmod Kumar, Atul Dhar
9	9789355386984	Biology for Engineers	Annamma Odaneth
10	9789391505141	Chemistry-I	Manisha Agarwal
11	9789355384843	Civil Engineering Societal and Global Impact	Shakuntala Acharya
12	9789355382184	Computer Aided Civil Engineering Drawing	D. Chandra Mouli, B. Swathi
13	9789355382580	Computer Aided Design & Analysis	Hari Kumar Voruganti
14	9789355387592	Computer Architecture	D. Vaithiyanathan
15	9789355385093	Computer Networks	Hari Prabhat Gupta
16	9789355385307	Construction Engineering & Management	Sparsh Johari
17	9789355388728	Control Systems	S.N. Deepa
18	9789355385420	Data Structure and Algorithms	Ranbir Singh Sanasam
19	9789355386700	Design and Analysis of Algorithms	Hari P. Gupta, Rahul Mishra
20	9789355388872	Digital Electronics and System	Abhishek Bhatt
21	9789355386571	Digital Signal Processing	Sanjeev Sharma
22	9789355383396	Disaster management	Pradeep K. Goyal, Anil K. Gupta
23	9789355385222	Discrete Mathematical Structures	Narendra S. Chaudhari, Sharmila S. P.
24	9789355387868	Effective Technical Communication	Pritee Sharma, Sanchita Verma
25	9789355383389	Electrical Circuit Analysis and Network Theory	Shouri Chatterjee
26	9789355388957	Electromagnetic Waves	Uttam M. Pal, Srijith K.
27	9789355384652	Electronic Communication	Vimal Bhatia
28	9789355388711	Embedded Systems	Santanu Chattopadhyay
29	9789355385147	Energy Science and Engineering	M. Rizwan, Majid Jamil
30	9789355387929	Engineering Economics, Estimation & Costing	Yogesh C. Joshi
31	9789355384669	Engineering Geology	R. N. Khare, Ketan Chourasia
32	9789391505066	Engineering Graphics & Design	Pradeep Jain
33	9789391505097	English (with Lab Manual)	Kulbhushan Kumar
34	9789355385963	Environmental Engineering	Chandra Sekhar Matli
35	9789355388117	Fluid Mechanics	Shreenivas N. Londhe, Pradnya R. Dixit
36	9789355388377	Fluid Mechanics & Fluid Machines	R.P. Saini
37	9789355387103	Geotechnical Engineering	Paramita Bhattacharya

UNDERGRADUATE COURSE BOOKS

S.No.	ISBN	Book Name	Author
38	9789355385130	Hydraulic Engineering	Sayantan Ganguly
39	9789355385550	Hydrology & Water Resources Engineering	Mitthan Lal Kansal, P.K. Agarwal
40	9789355389688	Information Technology Workshop in MATLAB	Hari Prabhat Gupta
41	9789355383235	Instrumentation for Civil Engineering Applications	Ashim Kanti Dey, Manita Das
42	9789355387042	Introduction to Civil Engineering	Manabendra Saharia, Nagendra R. Velaga
43	9789355384805	Introduction to Database Systems	Vikram Singh
44	9789355387509	Machine Element & System Design	Sabah Khan
45	9789355385383	Machine Learning	Himanshu Mittal
46	9789355388414	Manufacturing Automation	Chitragupt Swaroop Chitransh
47	9789355387233	Manufacturing Processes	Dheerendra Kumar Dwivedi
48	9789355389886	Materials Engineering	Dheerendra Kumar Dwivedi
49	9789391505172	Mathematics - I Calculus and Linear Algebra [For Non-Computer Science Engineering Branches]	Reena Garg
50	9789391505271	Mathematics - I Calculus and Linear Algebra [For Computer Science Engineering Branches]	Reena Garg
51	9789355384607	Measurements & Metrology	V.P. Chandramohan
52	9789355383730	Mechanics of Materials	Arvind Vyavahare
53	9789355383358	Mechatronics, Robotics & Control	J. Srinivas
54	9789355385116	Microprocessor and Microcontroller	Saurabh Chaudhury, Risha Mal
55	9789355386083	Microprocessors	Yogendra Kumar Gupta
56	9789355389169	Mobile Communication and Networks	Vimal Bhatia
57	9789355385475	Operating Systems	Sukomal Pal
58	9789355385604	Operating Systems	Sanjaya Kumar Panda
59	9789391505134	Physics (Oscillations, Waves and Optics) With lab manual	A.B. Bhattacharya, Atanu Nag
60	9789391505257	Physics (Quantum Mechanics for Engineers) With lab manual	A.B. Bhattacharya, Atanu Nag
61	9789391505165	Physics (Introduction to Electromagnetic Theory) (with Lab Manual)	A.B. Bhattacharya, Atanu Nag
62	9789391505059	Physics (Introduction to Mechanics) (with Lab Manual)	A.B. Bhattacharya, Atanu Nag
63	9789355385956	Power Electronics: Theory and Practicals	Lalit Chandra Saikia
64	9789355384942	Power Systems-I	Suresh Mikkili
65	9789355386236	Power Systems-II	Arun Rahul S, Manas K. Jena
66	9789355383754	Product Innovation & Entrepreneurship	Vigneswaran C
67	9789355384584	Production & Operation Management	Navin Kumar Dev
68	9789391505219	Programming for Problem Solving (with Lab Manual)	R.S. Salaria
69	9789355385451	Signals and Systems	Sanjay L. Nalbalwar
70	9789355386021	Strength of Materials	Uday Shanker Dixit, Nelson Muthu, S. M. Kamal
71	9789355383792	Structural Engineering	T.D. Gunneswara Rao, D. Ravi Prasad
72	9789355387004	Surveying and Geomatics	P. K. Garg
73	9789355384317	Testing & Evaluation of Civil Engineering Materials	Sandeep Chaudhary, Kashyap A Patel
74	9789355382306	Theory of Computation	Debi Prasanna Acharjya
75	9789355384928	Transportation Engineering	A.K. Raji
76	9789355385208	VLSI Design	Mahendra Sakare, Shonal Chouksey
77	9789391505332	Workshop / Manufacturing Practices (with Lab Manual)	Veeranna D.K.

DIPLOMA COURSE BOOKS

S.No.	ISBN	Book Name	Author
1	9789355382481	Aanandam An Act of Community Service	Shuchi Sharma
2	9789355385567	Advanced Manufacturing Processes	Ranjeet Kumar Sahu, Devendra Laxman Kamble
3	9789355385109	Advanced Surveying: Theory & Practice	Ramakant Agrawal, Parshottam Sarathe
4	9789355384546	Algorithms	Piyoosh P, Arnab Sarkar
5	9789391505448	Applied Chemistry (with Lab Manual)	Anju Rawlley, Devdatta Vinayakrao Saraf
6	9789391505431	Applied Physics-I (with Lab Manual)	Vinod Kumar Yadav, Mina Talati
7	9789391505578	Applied Physics-II (with Lab Manual)	Hussain Jeevakhan
8	9789355387530	Basic Mechanical Engineering	Dharmendra Singh, Chandra Shekhar Rajoria
9	9789355387394	Building Construction	Rinku Kumar, Sandeep Panchal
10	9789355383280	Building Electrification	Arnab Ghosh
11	9789355384379	Building Planning and Drawing	Aparna Dwivedi
12	9789391505493	Communication Skills in English	Anjana Tiwari
13	9789355383570	Computer Aided Machine Drawing Practice	Kanak Kalita
14	9789355388964	Computer Networking and Data Communication	Sanjaya Shankar Tripathy
15	9789355382986	Computer Networks: Theory & Practicals	Brijendra Pratap Singh, Manoj Madhava Gore
16	9789355382672	Computer Programming: Theory and Practicals	Satyendra Singh Chouhan
17	9789355387714	Computer System Organization	Sonal Yadav
18	9789355382658	Concrete Technology: Theory and Practice	Sasankasekhar Mandal, Vishwajit Anand, Sushil K. Agarwala
19	9789355383334	Construction Materials and Testing	Vanita Aggarwal
20	9789355383501	Consumer Electronics	Amit M. Joshi, Maulin M. Joshi, Urvashi Prakash Shukla
21	9789355387684	Data Structures: Theory & Practicals	NB Venkateswarlu
22	9789355388513	Design of Machine Elements	A. Kumaravel, M. Kathirselvam
23	9789355388360	Design of Steel and RCC Structure	Sparsh Johari
24	9789355383303	Digital Communication	Muralidhar Kulkarni, K. S. Shivaprakasha
25	9789355387295	Digital Electronics	Menka Yadav
26	9789355389435	Electric Circuits and Networks	Jamuna K., Nilanjan Tewari
27	9789355388452	Electric Motors and Transformers (Theory and Practicals)	Sanjay B. Bodkhe
28	9789355385901	Electric Power Transmission and Distribution	Sudhir Sharma
29	9789355389466	Electrical & Electronics Measurements and Instrumentation	Sudarsan Sahoo, Vipin Chandra Pal, Sudipta Chakraborty
30	9789355382696	Electronic Communication	M. D. Selvaraj, P. Nagaradjane
31	9789355387202	Electronic Devices and Circuits	Ankesh Jain
32	9789355386373	Electronic Equipment Maintenance	Chanchal Sharma
33	9789355384690	Embedded Systems	Deepa M, G. Santhanamari, Susithra. N
34	9789355384867	Energy Conservation and Audit	M. Rizwan, Majid Jamil
35	9789391505509	Engineering Graphics	Sharad K. Pradhan, K.K. Jain
36	9789391505608	Engineering Mechanics (with Lab Manual)	Bhankhar Bharat, Gokaldas Vandana Somkuwar

DIPLOMA COURSE BOOKS

S.No.	ISBN	Book Name	Author
37	9789391505516	Engineering Workshop Practice	A. K. Sarathe
38	9789391505653	Environmental Science	Subrat Roy
39	9789355384966	Estimating, Costing and valuation	Sandeep Panchal
40	9789355389510	Fluid Mechanics & Hydraulic Machinery	Suman Chakraborty, Sourav Mitra, Aditya Bandopadhyay
41	9789391505592	Fundamentals of Electrical and Electronics Engineering (with Lab Manual)	Susan S. Mathew, Saji T. Chacko
42	9789355387240	Fundamentals of Power Electronics	Soumitra Kumar Mandal
43	9789355389602	Geotechnical Engineering (Theory & Practicals)	Neelima Satyam
44	9789355386137	Induction, Synchronous, and Special Electrical Machines	K. Selvajyothi, S. Tamilselvi, Sarat Kumar Sahoo
45	9789355382290	Industrial Engineering & Management	A. Manimaran
46	9789355384959	Internet of Things	Sujata Pal
47	9789355388650	Introduction to DBMS: Theory & Practicals	Myneni Madhu Bala
48	9789355384294	Introduction to e-Governance	Kamal Kant Verma
49	9789355386564	Introduction to Electric Generation Systems	Lalit Chandra Saikia, Nalin Behari, Deb Choudhury
50	9789391505585	Introduction to IT Systems (with Lab Manual)	Prashant Joshi
51	9789355382900	Linear Integrated Circuit	B. T. Krishna
52	9789355388148	Manufacturing Engineering	Santosh Kumar
53	9789355383877	Material Science & Engineering	Vinod Kumar, Nisheeth k. Prasad
54	9789391505424	Mathematics-I	Deepak Singh
55	9789391505523	Mathematics-II	Garima Singh
56	9789355385994	Measurements and Metrology	A. Gnanavelbabu, M. Santhana kumar, R. Saranraj
57	9789355388131	Mechanics of Materials and their Testing	R. Velmurugan, Pragathi
58	9789355385048	Microcontroller Applications	Ritula Thakur
59	9789355385062	Microcontrollers and Applications	Santanu Chattopadhyay
60	9789355388100	Mobile and Wireless Communication	Maulin Joshi, Urvashi P. Shukla
61	9789355387790	Production & Operations Management	Mayank Kumar Agrawal
62	9789355388704	Public Health Engineering	Rinku Kumar
63	9789355387455	Python Programming	Rupesh Nasre
64	9789355387189	Renewable Energy Technologies	Sanjay Agrawal, Rajeev K. Mishra
65	9789355387479	Software Engineering	Salman Abdul Moiz
66	9789355389749	Theory of Machines & Mechanisms	G. C. Mohan Kumar
67	9789355387332	Theory of Structures	Arunachalam Subramanian Balu
68	9789355389015	Thermal Engineering - I	V. Raghavan
69	9789355389831	Thermal Engineering - II	Parvesh Antil
70	9789355386779	Transportation Engineering (Theory & Practice)	A.K. Raji, K.K. Babu
71	9789355384287	Water Resource Engineering (Theory & Practice)	Prakash C. Swain, Dillip K. Ghose
72	9789355383051	Web Technologies: Theory & Practical	Raman Dugyala

UNIT 4

UNIT 5

LIST OF TABLES

CONTENTS

1 FUNDAMENTALS OF INTERNET OF THINGS

UNIT SPECIFICS

In this unit, the following aspects will be discussed:

- Introduction to the Internet of Things, including its significance and evolution.
- Sensors, actuators, communication devices, and computation devices are essential components of the Internet of Things.
- IoT designs, including the oneM2M and IoT World Forum models, and their applications.
- RFID, WSN, and Cloud Computing play important roles in enabling technology.
- Use cases and applications for smart cities, healthcare, and industrial automation.

Examples of real-world IoT applications are explored to help students understand the concepts more practically. Visual aids, such as diagrams and tables, are used to improve conceptual clarity.

This section has exercises with long and short-term questions, multiple-choice questions, and practical projects that reinforce learning through application. Students can use additional resources, like web pages or QR codes, to investigate advanced topics independently.

RATIONALE

This unit gives the fundamental ideas of the Internet of Things (IoT), offering a thorough knowledge of its evolution and role in converting traditional systems into interconnected ecosystems. The major aspects of IoT, such as sensors, actuators, communication devices, and compute devices, are explored to help students understand their roles in smart systems. IoT designs, including oneM2M and IoT World Forum models, are thoroughly explained to demonstrate their appropriateness for a variety of applications. Enabling technologies such as RFID, Wireless Sensor Networks, and Cloud Computing are investigated to demonstrate their importance in IoT ecosystems. This lesson establishes the foundations for students to build a solid conceptual foundation and piques their interest in the subject through examples and application cases.

PRE-REQUISITES

No prerequisites are required for studying this unit.

UNIT OUTCOMES

The list of outcomes of this unit is as follows:

U1-O1: Understand IoT's meaning and evolution

U1-O2: Explore the role of IoT components like sensors and actuators

U1-O3: Analyze IoT architectures like oneM2M and IoTWF

U1-O4: Examine the importance of enabling technologies (RFID, WSN)

U1-O5: Evaluate IoT use cases and applications

Unit Outcomes	Expected Mapping with Course Outcomes (1- Weak Correlation; 2- Medium correlation; 3- Strong Correlation)				
	CO-1	CO-2	CO-3	CO-4	CO-5
U1-O1	3	2	1	1	2
U1-O2	3	3	2	1	3
U1-O3	3	3	3	1	2
U1-O4	2	2	3	1	2
U1-O5	2	3	3	1	3

1.1 Beginner's Idea for IoT

The Internet of Things, or IoT, is like giving the internet to everyday objects, making them "smart". Imagine things like lamps, watches, thermostats, or even cars that can communicate, receive instructions, and send information over the Internet. These objects are fitted with sensors and software that allow them to collect data and act on it without human intervention as shown in Figure 1.1. For example, a smart thermostat can learn your schedule and adjust the temperature in your home before you arrive, or a fitness tracker on your wrist can monitor your heart rate and send that information to an app on your phone. The figure shows everyday objects like a coffee maker, a lamp, and a thermostat, all connected to a smartphone, demonstrating how they can be controlled and monitored through the internet to make daily life more convenient.

1.2 Definition of IoT

IoT can be defined as a network that extends the power of the internet beyond computers and smartphones to a whole range of other objects, processes, and environments. These objects, from everyday household items to advanced industrial tools, have unique identifiers and the ability to automatically transfer data over a network without requiring human-to-human or human-to-computer interaction.

Figure 1.1: An illustration of basic elements in IoT

The essence of IoT lies in transforming the internet into a vast, global network that connects not only servers, computers, and mobile devices but also embeds intelligence into physical objects around us. These objects become capable of sensing, communicating, and interacting with other devices and the environment, thereby enabling a wide range of new and enhanced services. This concept has evolved significantly with initial steps marked by the use of identity communication devices such as Radio Frequency Identification Devices (RFID), which enable objects to be identified, tracked, and managed remotely via the internet. IoT extends its capabilities to various applications, including GPS-based device management, machine-to-machine (M2M) communication, connected vehicles, and the interaction among wearable technology, thus playing a crucial role in the rise of smart ecosystems.

1.3 Evolution of IoT

The advancement of IoT has been an evolutionary process over several years marked by significant milestones.

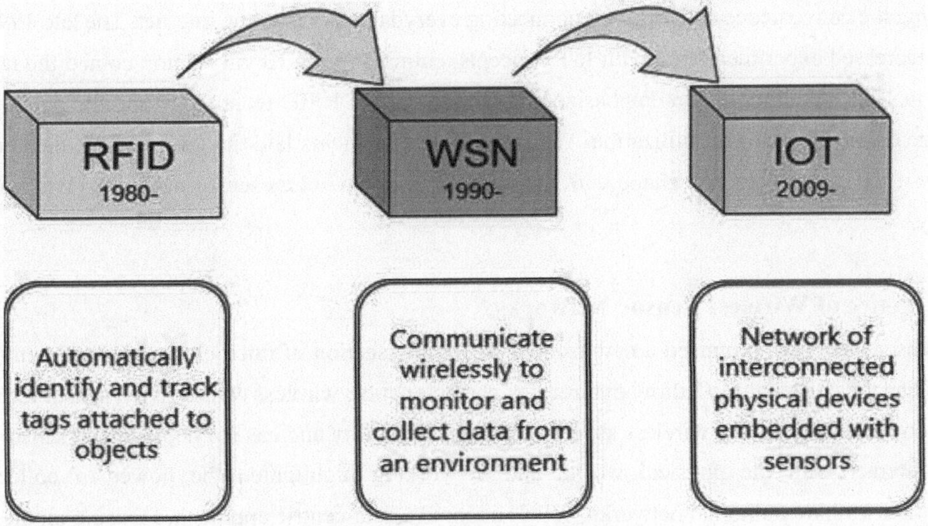

Figure 1.2: Evolution of IoT

Figure 1.2 illustrates the evolution of IoT, including RFID and WAN technologies. RFID, which was created in the 1940s and was widely used in the 1980s, transitioned from short-range to long-range tracking. WANs have evolved from slow dial-up connections to high-speed fiber-optic networks, enabling worldwide connectivity. IoT, which emerged in the 2000s, has progressed from simple sensor networks to complex, interconnected systems in industries such as healthcare and transportation. Together, these technologies now enable global tracking and data interchange.

1.3.1 Origin and Conceptual Foundations:

The conceptual foundation of IoT can be traced back to the early visions of a networked world. In 1962, J.C.R. Licklider of DARPA imagined a globally interconnected set of computers, facilitating data exchange and enhancing communication. This vision materialized as ARPANET in 1969, which eventually evolved into the commercial internet by 1980. Although this period did not see the creation of IoT devices per se, it established the infrastructure and the idea of a connected world, paving a path for IoT's development.

1.3.2 The Advent of IoT Devices:

The practical inception of IoT is marked by innovative solutions to everyday problems. Notably, in 1989, a group of Carnegie Mellon University students devised a method to check the status of a Coca-Cola vending machine over the Internet, thereby creating one of the first instances of a smart device. This was followed by the Internet Toaster in 1991, which showcased the ability to control appliances remotely. These early instances of IoT were characterized by their novelty and the practical benefits they offered, highlighting the potential for a future where everyday objects could be monitored and controlled via the Internet.

1.3.3 Milestones in IoT Evolution:

A significant milestone in the evolution of IoT was the development of the first online webcam at the University of Cambridge in 1993. Aimed at monitoring a coffee pot, this simple application had a profound impact, demonstrating the convenience and utility of connecting everyday objects to the internet. The late 1990s and early 2000s saw increased experimentation with IoT concepts, culminating in Kevin Ashton coined the term "Internet of Things" in 1999. Ashton's vision emphasized the importance of RFID technology and the potential of IoT to revolutionize data collection and utilization. While these developments laid the groundwork, the concept of IoT as we know it today began to take shape with the introduction of wireless sensor networks (WSNs) in the early 21st century.

1.3.4 Emergence of Wireless Sensor Networks:

Wireless Sensor Networks promised a new frontier in the intersection of microelectronics and communications. They embodied the concept of IoT through three key characteristics: wireless connectivity, sensor technology, and networked communication. The wireless aspect emphasized mobility and ease of deployment, sensors provided a means to interact with the physical world, and networking highlighted the power of collective device communication. Unlike traditional networks, WSNs adopted a data-centric approach, focusing on the information being exchanged rather than the specific endpoints involved in the communication.

1.3.5 Mainstream Adoption and Commercialization:

The early 2000s marked the transition of IoT from experimental projects to mainstream applications. LG's smart refrigerator announcement in 2000 showcased the potential for smart appliances, while the deployment of RFID technology in the US Army and Walmart's global operations illustrated the scalability of IoT solutions. Media coverage in the mid-2000s by mainstream publications further highlighted IoT's significance, signaling its growing impact on society and industry. The launch of the iPhone in 2007 by Apple was a pivotal moment, popularizing smart technology and highlighting the importance of internet connectivity in everyday devices. The proliferation of connected devices soon led to the emergence of smart cities, wearable technology, and industrial applications, showcasing the versatility and wide-ranging impact of IoT.

1.3.6 Infrastructure Development and Global Initiatives:

The formation of the IPSO Alliance in 2008 and the approval of the white space spectrum by the FCC marked significant milestones in standardizing and expanding IoT's infrastructure. The launch of IPv6 in 2011 addressed the need for a larger address space, accommodating the explosive growth of IoT devices. Furthermore, educational and commercial initiatives by major IT companies played a critical role in advancing IoT technologies and increasing widespread adoption.

1.4 Conceptual Framework of IoT

At its most basic, IoT can be thought of as:

- **Physical Object:** Anything from an umbrella to a streetlight.
- **Controller, Sensor, and Actuators:** Little helpers that gather information, make decisions, and act on them. For example, a sensor on your umbrella might detect rain.
- **Internet:** The superhighway that connects everything, allowing your umbrella to receive weather updates.

This setup allows your umbrella to warn you when it's going to rain, by gathering data (like weather forecasts) from the internet.

1.4.1 How It Works:

- **Gathering Data:** Just like humans use the senses to understand their surroundings, IoT devices use sensors. These sensors can detect all sorts of things, like temperature, motion, or even how full a container is.
- **Making Sense of Data:** Once the data is collected, it needs to be understood. This is done using controllers that are visualized as mini-computers that decide what the data means. For example, if the data says it's raining, the controller decides it's time to alert you.
- **Acting on the Data:** After the controller decides what to do, actuators come into play. They are the movers and shakers. If the decision is to alert you about rain, an actuator might be what triggers your umbrella to send a notification to your phone.
- **Communication:** For all this to happen, these devices need to communicate with each other and the internet. They use various technologies like WiFi, Bluetooth, or cellular networks to send and receive information.
- **Managing and Analyzing:** To handle all this data and processing, cloud servers are employed where data is sent, stored, and analyzed. This can help understand patterns (like when it's most likely to rain) and improve how devices work.

Example 1.1: Smart Street Lights

Imagine a city with smart streetlights. Each streetlight has sensors that detect when it gets dark or when someone is nearby. They gather this data (it's dark, or someone's there) and use a controller to decide what to do (turn on the light). They act on this decision using actuators (the part that physically turns the light on). All streetlights are connected to the internet, allowing them to receive updates (like weather conditions) and be managed remotely (city workers can turn them on or off as needed).

1.4.2 From Simple to Complex Frameworks:

At the most basic level, the IoT framework involves gathering data through sensors, making decisions through controllers, and acting through actuators, all connected by the internet.

As we move to more complex systems, like a whole city's lighting system or a factory, the framework expands. Here, data is not just gathered but also enriched (made more useful, like identifying exactly which streetlight needs maintenance). It's streamed to central systems, managed in terms of device health and security, and analyzed for insights (which areas need more light based on usage patterns).

The main goal of the IoT is to collect information from our surroundings to analyze it, control various devices, and take appropriate actions based on the data collected. IoT devices exchange data through the internet, using a combination of different technologies such as Wireless Sensor Networks (WSN) and Radio Frequency Identification (RFID). These technologies allow IoT to include smart objects that can be identified, located, addressed, and controlled remotely. By pairing IoT with cloud computing, these technologies also help overcome limitations like storage and processing power. These technologies are described in more detail as follows:

1.4.3 Radio Frequency Identification (RFID)

RFID is a system that uses electronic tags (RFID tags) to automatically identify and track objects. These tags, which store a unique Electronic Product Code for each object, can be read by an RFID reader without needing the tag and reader to be in direct sight of each other. The RFID reader acts as a bridge to the internet, sending the object's identity and location to a computer system that manages a large database. This technology is particularly useful in logistics for tracking packages, managing supply chains, and in healthcare. There are two main types of RFID tags:

- **Active RFID Tags:** These come with their own power source (a battery).
- **Passive RFID Tags:** These don't have a built-in power source and get their energy from the reader's signal.

1.4.4 Wireless Sensor Networks (WSN)

WSNs are crucial in today's world, consisting of many sensor nodes spread out to collect and transmit data among themselves. These networks benefit from advancements in small-scale technology, allowing for the creation of compact, smart devices (sensor nodes). Each sensor node has a sensor, a wireless communication controller, and a microcontroller, capable of measuring various environmental factors. WSNs remain functional as long as some nodes are active and can maintain a connection to a base station. These networks are used in transport monitoring, military operations, and weather forecasting, thanks to their ability to manage network dynamics and topology effectively.

1.4.5 Cloud Computing

Cloud computing offers almost limitless processing and storage capabilities, providing services on-demand over the Internet as shown in Figure 1.3. The cloud delivers infrastructure, platforms, and software applications via the Internet, making computing resources more affordable, reliable, and accessible than ever. With rapid advancements in technology and the internet, cloud computing has significantly impacted the IT industry. Big companies like Amazon, Google, IBM, and Microsoft are leveraging cloud technology to enhance their business strategies, offering more efficient and cost-effective services. Therefore, the cloud acts as a new business model, integrating existing technologies to offer innovative solutions.

Figure 1.3: An illustration of Cloud Computing

1.5 IoT Elements

IoT relies on several key elements to function efficiently, each playing a crucial role in the architecture and operation of these systems.

1.5.1 Identifiers

At the foundation of IoT functionality are identifiers, which provide unique identities to each device within the network. Identifiers are crucial because they enable devices to be distinctly recognized and interacted with. There are two main aspects of identifiers in the IoT:

- **Naming:** This involves assigning a human-readable name or title to devices. While names can be duplicated, the identifier system ensures each device can still be uniquely recognized.
- **Addressing:** In contrast to naming, addressing refers to the assignment of a unique address to each device, which is crucial for network communications. Initially, IPv4 addressing was used, but due to its limited capacity, it was unable to accommodate the burgeoning number of IoT devices. Consequently, IPv6 has been adopted, utilizing a 128-bit addressing system to vastly increase the number of unique addresses available, thus enabling the expansive growth of IoT networks.

1.5.2 Sensing Devices

Sensing devices are essential for collecting environmental data, which can be used to adjust conditions in smart homes or optimize industrial processes. These devices vary widely, ranging from RFID tags, which facilitate tracking and identification without direct contact, to actuators that perform actions based on processed data. Portable and smart sensors, capable of moving or processing data immediately, transmit the gathered information to local or cloud-based storage systems for further analysis.

1.5.3 Communication Devices

The backbone of IoT is its communication devices, which ensure the seamless transmission of data between devices and central processing systems. Technologies such as Bluetooth and NFC are ideal for short-range communication in consumer devices, while Wi-Fi and LTE provide broader coverage suitable for home and industrial applications. RFID technology plays a crucial role in automated inventory and supply chain management by enabling efficient tracking and management.

1.5.4 Compute Devices

Compute devices process the data collected by sensors and execute necessary actions. These devices range from simple microcontrollers in household gadgets to complex servers that process data from numerous industrial sensors. Devices like Raspberry Pi and Arduino are popular for their versatility and capability in handling data processing tasks. They run on operating systems like Lite OS, Riot OS, and Android, which manage the data processing and responsiveness of IoT applications.

1.5.5 IoT Services

IoT systems offer various services that enhance functionality and user experience. It offers four primary services:

- **Identity Services:** These services manage the identification details of the devices connected to the network.
- **Information Aggregation Services:** They compile data from various sources, enhancing the decision-making process.
- **Cooperative Services:** This involves devices working together to make decisions and respond to environmental changes.
- **Pervasive Services:** They ensure that IoT services are available across different devices and locations without restrictions related to time or place.

1.5.6 Semantics

Semantics play a pivotal role in the functionality of IoT by interpreting the data collected to make intelligent decisions. This component acts as the brain of IoT, processing information and enabling devices to respond autonomously based on the insights gained. It enhances the efficiency and effectiveness of IoT applications, allowing for autonomous operations and improved responsiveness.

1.6 Architecture of IoT

IoT has diverse architectures that aim to standardize and streamline the deployment and management of IoT devices and applications. Among these, the architectures developed by oneM2M and the IoT World Forum (IoTWF) stand out as two of the most popular frameworks. This section describes these architectures in detail, highlighting their structure, objectives, and impact on the IoT ecosystem.

1.6.1 The oneM2M IoT Architecture

The European Telecommunications Standards Institute (ETSI) initiated efforts in 2008 to harmonize machine-to-machine (M2M) communications, leading to the formation of oneM2M in 2012. This global initiative aimed to develop a universal IoT service layer, enabling efficient communication across various devices and platforms. The oneM2M architecture introduces a vendor-independent software middleware, known as the IoT Service Layer, strategically positioned between the processing/communication hardware and IoT applications. This middleware provides essential functions required by IoT applications, ensuring seamless interaction and data exchange as shown in Figure 1.4.

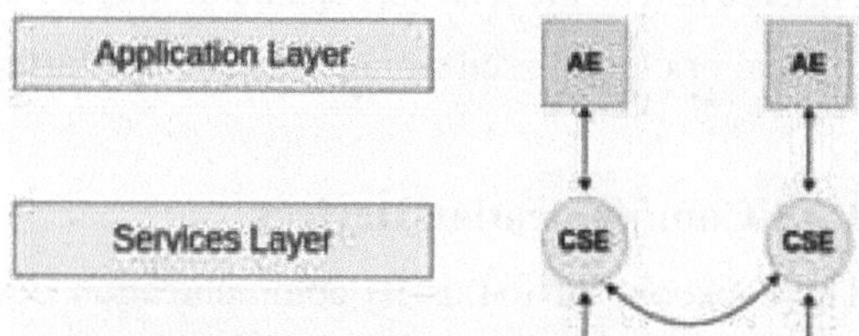

Figure 1.4: OneM2M functional architecture

Key Components of oneM2M Architecture:

Application Layer: This layer is at the forefront of the oneM2M architecture, interfacing directly with IoT applications. It standardizes the application-layer protocols and northbound API definitions, facilitating interaction with various business intelligence systems. Given the industry-specific nature of applications, this layer is tailored to accommodate diverse data models.

Services Layer: Acting as a unifying framework across various industry applications, this layer comprises the foundational network and its management protocols, alongside the physical hardware. It includes both the infrastructure for backhaul communications (such as cellular networks, MPLS, and VPNs) and a common services layer that introduces middleware and APIs for third-party services integration. oneM2M's ambition to create a common M2M service layer aims at bridging the vast array of devices with application servers located in cloud or data center environments, enabling collaboration across sectors like healthcare, industrial automation, and smart homes. This layer introduces the Common Service Functions (CSFs), offering functionalities like device management, data aggregation, and end-to-end encryption. These functions are crucial for ensuring the interoperability and efficient operation of IoT systems.

Network Layer: This domain is dedicated to the connectivity of IoT devices, including both the devices and the communication networks that bind them. It covers various forms of wireless and wired communication technologies, from mesh networks (IEEE 802.15.4) to power line communications (IEEE 1901) and more. Additionally, it includes gateway devices that serve as a channel between the device and network layers, facilitating upward communication into the core network. It addresses the complexities of diverse communication technologies and protocols, ensuring devices can reliably transmit and receive data.

oneM2M Common Service Functions (CSFs):

CSFs are the foundation of oneM2M Service Layer, offering a comprehensive suite of functionalities:

- **Identification and Authentication:** Ensuring users and applications are properly identified and authenticated.
- **Data Security:** Providing end-to-end encryption to safeguard data integrity and privacy.
- **Device Management:** Facilitating remote provisioning, service activation, and comprehensive management of devices.
- **Connectivity Management:** Establishing and scheduling data transmission, crucial for maintaining efficient network communication.
- **Data Processing:** Encompassing data aggregation and buffering, ensuring data consistency, especially in scenarios of intermittent connectivity.
- **Group and Discovery Services:** Enabling effective management of device groups and facilitating the discovery of applications and data.

These CSFs, accessible via globally standardized APIs, abstract the complexities of underlying connectivity technologies, allowing application developers to concentrate on delivering value through their IoT solutions.

Application Entities (AEs) and Nodes:

AEs, or Application Entities, are the dynamic elements within the oneM2M architecture that execute the application logic across various nodes, categorized as follows:

- **Application Service Node (ASN):** An ASN is a versatile node equipped with at least one CSE and one or more AEs, positioned within the Field Domain, which is essentially the operational environment of IoT devices. ASNs can be deployed on a wide array of devices, from those with limited resources to more sophisticated systems. This flexibility allows ASNs to cater to various IoT applications, from gathering data through sensors to executing complex server tasks.

- **Application Dedicated Node (ADN):** An ADN is characterized by hosting at least one AE but lacks a CSE, making it more suitable for devices with constrained resources, such as limited storage or processing capabilities. Positioned within the Field Domain, ADNs are typically embodied in simpler devices like basic sensors or actuators, focusing on specific tasks without the need for the full suite of services provided by a CSE.
- **Middle Node (MN):** MNs are key components within the Field Domain, housing a CSE and potentially multiple AEs. These nodes often serve as M2M Gateways, facilitating the connection and communication between various devices and the broader IoT system. MNs play a critical role in structuring the network, enabling the hierarchical organization of data across different levels, from individual buildings to entire regions.
- **Infrastructure Node (IN):** Each oneM2M Service Provider operates exactly one IN within the Infrastructure Domain, which is the backbone of the IoT system. INs are comprehensive nodes that contain a CSE and can also host AEs, serving as central hubs for processing, managing, and distributing IoT data and services across the network.
- **Non-oneM2M Node (NoDN):** NoDNs are nodes that do not incorporate oneM2M-specific entities like AEs or CSEs. These nodes might host non-oneM2M IoT solutions or legacy technologies, which can still integrate with the oneM2M system through interworking proxies. This allows for the inclusion and interoperability of a wide range of devices and technologies within the oneM2M framework, even those not natively designed to comply with oneM2M standards.

This stratification ensures that applications, whether operating on a small sensor or a cloud platform, interact seamlessly with the oneM2M Service Layer, benefiting from the uniform APIs to utilize the CSFs.

<u>Benefits of oneM2M:</u>

- **Interoperability:** By providing a common framework for IoT deployments, oneM2M aims to foster interoperability among devices and systems, reducing the fragmentation that has historically plagued the IoT industry.
- **Scalability:** The modular nature of the oneM2M architecture allows for scalable IoT solutions that can grow and evolve with changing requirements and technological advancements.
- **Security:** A strong emphasis on security is embedded within the architecture, offering robust mechanisms for authentication, authorization, and encryption to protect IoT data and devices.

1.6.2 The IoT World Forum (IoTWF) Architecture

Recognizing the need for a unified architectural framework to navigate the complexities of IoT implementations, the IoT World Forum (IoTWF), led by industry giants like Cisco, IBM, and Rockwell Automation, introduced a comprehensive seven-layer reference model in 2014 as shown in Figure 1.5. This model not only simplifies the understanding of IoT but also addresses critical aspects like edge computing, data storage, and accessibility, embedding security across all levels. This model divides IoT architecture into seven distinct layers, each serving specific functions described as follows:

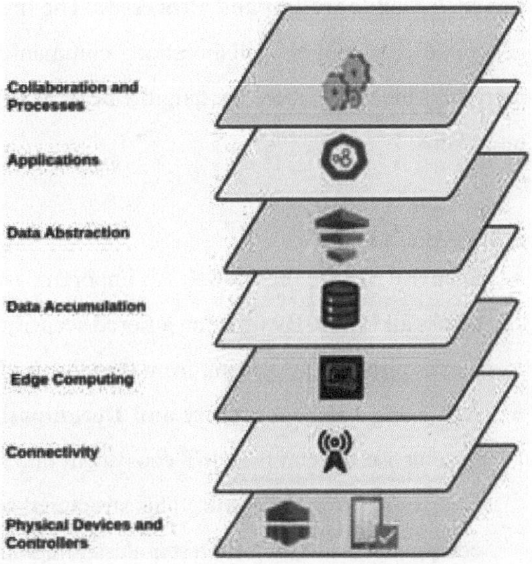

Figure 1.5: IoT World Forum Reference Model

Layer 1: Physical Devices and Controllers

At the base of the IoT architecture lies the physical devices and controllers layer. This foundational layer hosts the "things" in IoT—ranging from tiny sensors embedded in wearable devices to large-scale industrial machinery. The primary role of these devices is to generate data through sensing the environment, respond to control signals, and execute actions as dictated by higher layers.

Layer 2: Connectivity

Moving up, the connectivity layer ensures the seamless transmission of data collected by physical devices to other parts of the IoT framework. It consists of all networking elements necessary for data communication, including but not limited to last-mile connections, gateways, and broader network infrastructures. Key functions include device-to-network communication, reliable data delivery, protocol translation, and maintaining network security.

Layer 3: Edge Computing

The edge computing layer, or the "fog" layer, focuses on processing data at or near the source of data generation. This approach minimizes latency, reduces bandwidth usage, and supports real-time processing by analyzing and filtering data before it's transmitted to centralized data centers. It works on the principle of initiating data processing as close to the edge as possible, streamlining the flow of information to upper layers for further analysis.

Upper Layers (4-7): Data to Decision

The upper layers transition from handling raw data to generating actionable insights and facilitating collaboration and processes based on IoT data.

Layer 4: Data Accumulation: This layer acts as a repository, capturing and storing data for access and processing. It transitions event-based data into a format suitable for query-based processing.

Layer 5: Data Abstraction: Serving as the middle ground for data formats, this layer standardizes and consolidates data from diverse sources, ensuring consistent semantics and preparing data sets for application-level processing.

Layer 6: Applications: At the applications layer, software interprets the processed data to monitor, control, and report on various aspects of the IoT system. This layer houses the logic for making sense of the data and applying it to real-world applications.

Layer 7: Collaboration and Processes: The highest level of IoT architecture, this layer, leverages the insights generated to facilitate collaboration, communicate information, and potentially alter business processes. It represents the layer where the tangible benefits of IoT are realized, enabling innovative services and transforming operations.

Benefits of IoTWF:

- **Security Across the Model:** An important aspect of the IoTWF reference model is the embedding of security across all layers. By utilizing a tiered security model, the architecture ensures that data remains protected as it moves through the system, from the edge to the cloud.
- **Achieving Interoperability and Decomposition:** One of the strengths of the IoTWF model is its ability to decompose the complex IoT ecosystem into manageable segments, identifying relevant technologies at each layer and how they interact. This structured approach facilitates interoperability between diverse systems and components, allowing for a seamless integration of solutions provided by different vendors. Furthermore, the model outlines a process for defining interfaces, essential for achieving system-wide interoperability and security.
- **Flexibility and Scalability:** By defining distinct layers within the architecture, the model allows for flexibility in the choice of technologies and scalability of IoT solutions.
- **Enhanced Data Management:** The emphasis on local data processing (edge computing) and structured data storage and analysis supports efficient data management practices, crucial for deriving value from IoT deployments.

1.7 Sensing and Actuation in IoT

Sensing and actuation are the fundamental blocks in the IoT ecosystem. They enable multiple devices to interact with their environment, gather data, and perform actions. With Sensing and actuation, we can imagine a future where we can have automated lighting, precision farming with soil moisture sensors and automated irrigation, or traffic management and autonomous vehicles.

They come under the class of transducers. Sensors collect multiple forms of energy and convert them into electrical signals while actuators convert electrical signals into various forms of energy. IoT applications can involve them in one form or the other to transform industries.

1.7.1 Sensors and actuators for IoT

Sensors and actuators work together to form embedded systems. We can use them to control the mechanism of the systems. Sensor is used to collect the data from the environment while actuator will work on that collected data. Both the devices are needed to work the system properly. We will first study them separately and then check how they will work with ioT.

Sensors

Sensors that are connected to IoT devices can collect data from the environment to measure various aspects of the physical world, like temperature, humidity, and health related information. This data can be converted into a human-readable display and sent across a network for additional processing. For example, a temperature sensor can measure temperature of the body to enable informed decision-making and proactive maintenance. We can classify sensors in two categories:

1. Active Sensors
2. Passive Sensors

Active sensors need a continuous power supply while passive sensors don't require a continuous power supply.

Actuators

Actuators are devices responsible for moving or controlling a mechanism or system. They are a critical component in various applications, converting energy into physical outputs. They enable automation and precise control in various fields. Their design and selection depend on the specific requirements of the application, such as the type of motion needed, the environment, and the level of control required.

The starting point for any actuator is its energy source. Actuators receive an input signal from a control system. The input signal dictates the desired motion or position of the actuator. The internal mechanism of an actuator translates the input signal into mechanical movement. The actuator's output motion is the result of the conversion process, where the actuator produces a specific motion, force, or displacement. This motion is used to perform work, such as moving a robotic arm, opening a valve, or shifting a load.

Embedding of sensors and actuators

IoT sensors are utilized to capture and track data and information from processes and equipment. Conversely, actuators are employed to automate workplace tasks, thereby reducing the need for human labor. Together, these components create efficient IoT solutions. Figure 1.5 illustrates the working of sensors and actuators.

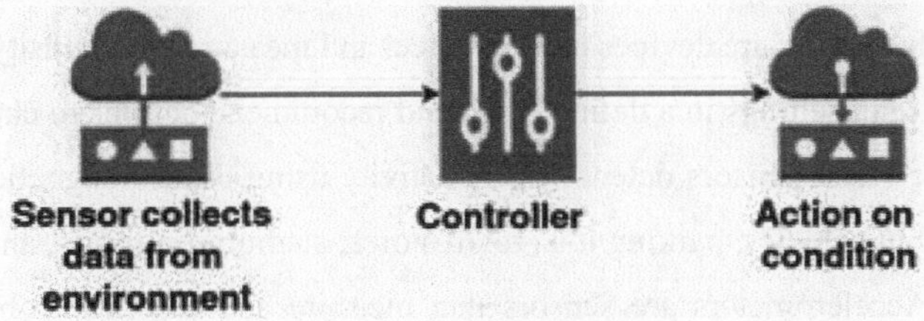

Figure 1.6: Embedding of Sensors and Actuators.

1.7.2 Types of sensors and actuators

Sensors play an important role in the IoT ecosystem by collecting data from the physical world and transforming it into digital information. These digital signals are then analyzed and utilized for process optimization, predictive maintenance, and overall system efficiency. In this section, we will explore some of the most commonly used sensors in industrial applications. Figure 1.7 shows the Types of sensors in common.

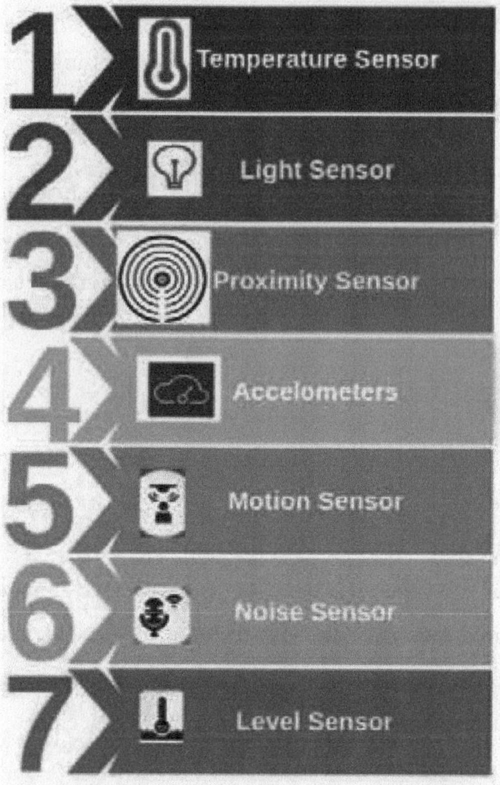

Figure 1.7: Types of Sensors

a) **Temperature Sensor:** Temperature sensors are devices used to measure the temperature of an object or environment. This information can be used to take the desired action, like changing the temperature to optimal settings. The same can be automated according to some specific environmental conditions and settings.

b) **Light Sensor:** Light sensors are devices used to detect and measure the intensity of light. They record and assess the ambient light settings in a defined area and recommend actions to change the same.

c) **Proximity Sensor:** These sensors detect nearby activity using electromagnetic waves, such as infrared. They are employed in vehicles, parking lots, retail stores, stadiums, airports, and many other locations

d) **Accelerometers:** Accelerometers are sensors that measure and record an object's acceleration. These sensors capture the rate at which an object's speed changes over time and can also detect changes in gravitational force.

e) **Motion Sensors:** Motion sensors are commonly integrated into security systems to identify unauthorized movements. These sensors detect activity through variations in heat or weight and trigger an alarm, which then sends alerts to the connected people.

f) **Noise Sensors:** Noise sensors monitor the sound levels in various environments, such as a city, room, or car. In IoT applications, these sensors are utilized to create safe working and living conditions for individuals.

g) **Level Sensors:** Level sensors measure the quantity or level of various substances. They are particularly beneficial in organizations.

Additionally, there are various types of actuators listed below:

1. **Hydraulic Actuators:** These actuators utilize hydraulic power to execute mechanical tasks and operations Typically, they are driven by a cylinder or fluid motor as shown in Figure 1.8 .

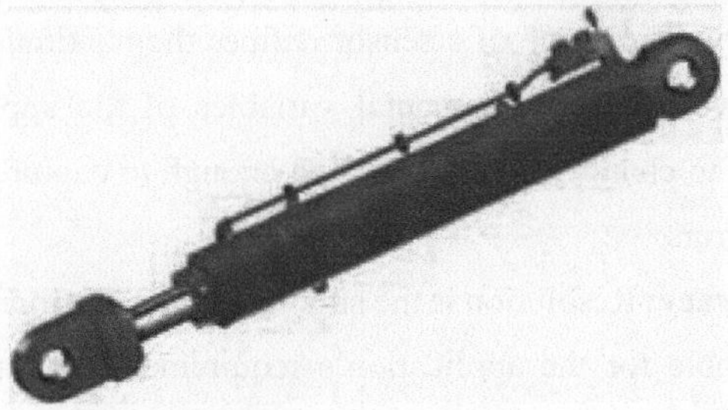

Figure 1.8: Hydraulic Actuator

2. **Electrical Actuators:** In these actuators, a motor transforms electrical energy into mechanical motion. Powered by electricity, they offer precise control and are extensively utilized in industrial environments to automate mechanical processes as shown in Figure 1.9.

Figure 1.9: Electrical Actuator

3. **Thermal Actuators:** Thermal actuators contain a thermal-sensitive material that generates linear motion in response to temperature changes as shown in Figure 1.10. As their name suggests, these actuators operate based on temperature variations.

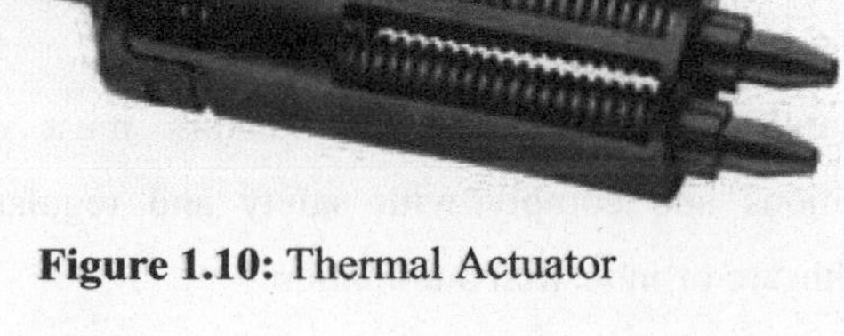

Figure 1.10: Thermal Actuator

1.7.3 Selection criteria for sensors and actuators

Selecting the right sensors and actuators is crucial when building effective and efficient IoT systems. Each component should be chosen after a thorough examination of its features and how well it fits the specific needs of the application. This careful selection process is key to successfully launching and maintaining IoT solutions that serve a variety of industries and keep up with technological progress.

Sensor Selection Criteria

The choice of sensors in an IoT application depends on several critical factors that determine the sensor's effectiveness in real-world conditions:

- **Range and Sensitivity:** The range of a sensor defines the maximum and minimum values it can detect, which should align with the environmental variables of the application. Sensitivity, indicating how responsive a sensor is to changes, should be high enough to capture necessary data but not so high as to introduce noise and errors.
- **Resolution and Accuracy:** Resolution is the smallest detectable incremental change the sensor can detect, and it should be suitable for the application's requirements. Accuracy, which describes how close a sensor's readings are to the true values, is crucial for reliability. High accuracy reduces the error margin, enhancing the trustworthiness of sensor data.
- **Precision and Calibration:** Precision refers to the reproducibility of the sensor readings under the same conditions, which is vital for consistent data collection. Sensors should maintain precision over time and conditions. Regular calibration is necessary to maintain accuracy and precision, and should be easy to perform.
- **Error and Response Time:** The error margin should be minimized to ensure data reliability. Response time, which is the delay between the input and sensor's output, should be as low as possible to allow real-time monitoring and control.
- **Signal-to-Noise Ratio and Environmental Robustness:** The sensor should have a high signal-to-noise ratio to enhance data integrity. It should also be robust against environmental factors such as temperature fluctuations, humidity, and electromagnetic interference, which might otherwise skew the sensor data.
- **Cost, Size, and Power Consumption:** Cost-effectiveness is key in large-scale deployments. Sensors should also be compact and energy-efficient, especially in battery-powered or remote applications. The trade-off between cost and functionality needs to be balanced according to the project requirements.

Actuator Selection Criteria

Key selection criteria for actuators include:

- **Operating Conditions and Compliance:** Actuators must operate reliably under the defined environmental conditions and comply with safety and regulatory standards, especially in critical applications like healthcare or industrial automation.

- **Functional Requirements:** The actuator's performance in terms of force, torque, speed, and range of motion should meet the application's demands. Different applications may require actuators with specialized capabilities to perform precise movements or to exert significant force.
- **Powering Methods and Integration:** It is crucial to consider how actuators will be powered, especially in terms of energy efficiency and compatibility with existing power sources. Integration with the overall system, without the need for additional power supplies, simplifies installation and reduces complexity.
- **Spatial Considerations and Control Interface:** The physical size of the actuator should fit within the allocated space of the device architecture. Additionally, the control interface should enable easy and precise control through the system's PLC or management software, ensuring effective actuation and feedback.
- **Cost and Environmental Considerations:** Like sensors, actuators must balance cost against performance. Environmental durability is also vital, as actuators often face mechanical wear and exposure to harsh conditions.

Example 1.2: Select a sensor for Home Security System

Let's explore how we can apply the criteria discussed above to select the appropriate temperature sensor for our application. In the context of selecting the right motion sensor for a home security system, two common options are the *Passive Infrared (PIR) sensor* and *the Ultrasonic sensor.*

The PIR sensor detects motion by sensing changes in infrared radiation emitted by warm objects within its field of view, which typically extends up to 12 meters with a 120-degree angle. This sensor is ideal for identifying human presence because it reacts instantaneously and consumes very little power, which is beneficial for battery-operated devices. Additionally, it is less prone to false alarms from non-living moving objects and is generally more cost-effective than ultrasonic sensors.

On the other hand, the Ultrasonic sensor operates by emitting sound waves and measuring the reflection off moving objects to determine their distance. It can detect objects up to 4 meters away but with a narrower detection angle compared to the PIR sensor. While offering precise information about the location or movement of an object, ultrasonic sensors require more power and are typically more expensive. They may also trigger more false alarms since they respond to any movement, not just thermal signatures.

When deciding between these two sensors for a home security system, considerations include the environmental conditions, which are usually controlled in a home setting, making both sensors suitable. The choice depends on the specific security needs: if basic human detection suffices, PIR sensors are preferred for their simplicity and efficiency. However, for more detailed spatial monitoring, such as determining the exact position of an intruder, ultrasonic sensors may be the better choice despite their higher cost and power demands. This decision-making process highlights the importance of matching sensor capabilities with the specific requirements of the application, taking into account factors like budget, power availability, and desired accuracy.

1.8 Summary

This chapter provides a comprehensive introduction to the IoT, beginning with basic concepts and definitions. It describes the evolution of IoT from its origins and conceptual foundations, highlighting key developments such as the advent of IoT devices, milestones in IoT evolution, the emergence of wireless sensor networks, and mainstream adoption. The chapter also details the conceptual framework of IoT, explaining how it operates and transitions from simple to complex frameworks. It then explains the architecture of IoT, outlining two important models: the oneM2M and IoT World Forum architecture. Finally, the chapter covers the roles of sensing and actuation in IoT, describing various sensors and actuators, their types, and the criteria for their selection, providing a foundational understanding of IoT networking.

1.9 Exercise

A. Multiple Choice Questions

1. What does IoT stand for?

a) Internet of Things

b) Internet of Technology

c) Integration of Tools

d) Information on Technology

2. Which of the following is NOT a basic element of IoT?

a) Sensors

b) Actuators

c) Internet connection

d) USB storage

3. Which of the following technologies is often used for object identification in IoT?

a) RFID

b) Bluetooth

c) Wi-Fi

d) Ethernet

4. Which IoT protocol is most suitable for resource-constrained devices?

a) HTTP

b) CoAP

c) SMTP

d) SNMP

5. What is the main function of actuators in IoT systems?

a) Collecting data

b) Processing information

c) Storing data

d) Performing actions based on data

6. Who coined the term "Internet of Things"?

a) J.C.R. Licklider

b) Tim Berners-Lee

c) Kevin Ashton

d) Vint Cerf

7. Which type of IoT devices are used for collecting environmental data?

a) Actuators

b) RFID tags

c) Sensors

d) Controllers

8. Which of the following protocols is used for Machine-to-Machine (M2M) communication in IoT?

a) HTTP

b) MQTT

c) FTP

d) POP3

9. Which of the following is an example of an early IoT device?

a) The Internet Toaster

b) Smart Watch

c) Smart Refrigerator

d) Google Nest

10. Which layer in the IoT architecture is responsible for processing data collected by sensors?

a) Application Layer

b) Network Layer

c) Device Layer

d) Service Layer

11. What is the primary use of RFID technology in IoT?

a) Communication between devices

b) Tracking and identifying objects

c) Data processing

d) Cloud storage

12. Which IoT architecture is developed by oneM2M?

a) Cloud-based architecture

b) Peer-to-peer architecture

c) Functional architecture

d) Client-server architecture

13. What does the abbreviation "WSN" stand for in the context of IoT?

a) Web Services Network

b) Wireless Sensor Network

c) Wide Spread Network

d) Wired Security Network

14. Which of the following is an advantage of using IPv6 in IoT?

a) Higher data transmission speed

b) Unlimited address space

c) Better encryption

d) Higher storage capacity

15. Which of the following is an example of a smart city application in IoT?

a) E-commerce website

b) Smart street lights

c) Personal fitness tracker

d) Virtual reality headset

16. What is the main function of cloud computing in IoT?

a) Connecting devices over short-range networks

b) Processing and storing large volumes of data

c) Controlling devices remotely

d) Facilitating data transfer between two devices

17. Which of the following is an IoT device with low energy consumption for long-range communication?

a) Zigbee

b) LoRaWAN

c) Bluetooth

d) Wi-Fi

18. Which of these IoT services involves devices working together to make decisions?

a) Information Aggregation Services

b) Cooperative Services

c) Identity Services

d) Pervasive Services

19. What is the role of the Network Layer in the oneM2M architecture?

a) Storing data

b) Providing connectivity between devices

c) Managing device health

d) Providing cloud services

20. Which of these technologies enables devices in IoT to exchange data without requiring a direct internet connection?

a) Ethernet

b) Wi-Fi

c) Bluetooth

d) LoRaWAN

B. Short Answer Questions

1. Define IoT and give one example of its application in daily life.
2. Explain the role of sensors in IoT systems.
3. What is RFID, and how does it contribute to IoT systems?
4. Describe the oneM2M architecture and its importance in IoT.
5. What is the role of actuators in an IoT system?
6. Explain the significance of CoAP in IoT and how it differs from traditional protocols like HTTP.

C. Long Answer Questions

1. Discuss the evolution of IoT from its conceptual foundations to its present-day applications. Include key milestones and technologies.
2. Explain the working of MQTT and its role in IoT communication protocols.
3. What is Cloud Computing in the context of IoT, and how does it benefit IoT devices and applications?
4. Describe the components and functions of a Wireless Sensor Network (WSN) in IoT.
5. Discuss the importance of IPv6 in the expansion and scaling of IoT devices and networks.

Answers of MCQ's

1. a) Internet of Things
2. d) USB storage
3. a) RFID
4. b) CoAP
5. d) Performing actions based on data
6. c) Kevin Ashton
7. c) Sensors
8. b) MQTT
9. a) The Internet Toaster
10. b) Network Layer
11. b) Tracking and identifying objects

12. c) Functional architecture
13. b) Wireless Sensor Network
14. b) Unlimited address space
15. b) Smart street lights
16. b) Processing and storing large volumes of data
17. b) LoRaWAN
18. b) Cooperative Services
19. b) Providing connectivity between devices
20. d) LoRaWAN

REFERENCES

1. L. D. Xu, W. He and S. Li, "Internet of Things in Industries: A Survey," in *IEEE Transactions on Industrial Informatics*, vol. 10, no. 4, pp. 2233-2243, Nov. 2014, doi: 10.1109/TII.2014.2300753.

2 IOT COMMUNICATIONS PROTOCOLS

UNIT SPECIFICS

In this unit, the following aspects will be discussed:

- An overview and importance of IoT communication protocols
- Wireless protocols, such as Wi-Fi, Bluetooth and Zigbee and their uses in IoT
- LoRaWAN, NB-IoT and 6LoWPAN are low-power protocols designed for energy-efficient applications
- Networking protocols such as MQTT, CoAP, HTTP/HTTPS, and their applications in IoT data sharing
- IoT network topologies and their scaling implications

This chapter overviews IoT communication protocol concepts to students. Diagrams and flowcharts are utilized to explain the complicated topics. Standardized protocol formats are proposed.

This subject contains practical activities including establishing MQTT brokers and analyzing IoT security requirements. QR codes and links are used for detailed materials, so that students can explore deeper into specific protocols.

RATIONALE

This section examines the crucial significance of communication protocols in IoT systems. It includes wireless protocols, like Wi-Fi, Bluetooth, and Zigbee, as well as low-power protocols like LoRaWAN and NB-IoT, which are required for energy-efficient communication. Students gain a thorough understanding of data transmission and exchange in IoT systems by discussing networking protocols such as MQTT, CoAP, and HTTP/HTTPS. The effects of network topologies, such as star, mesh, and hybrid setups, on scalability and performance are investigated. Security issues in IoT networks, such as encryption and authentication, are discussed to prepare students for real-world implementations. This unit improves students' technical knowledge by providing them with the skills they need to properly create and protect IoT communication networks.

PRE-REQUISITES

No prerequisites are required for studying this unit.

UNIT OUTCOMES

The list of outcomes of this unit is as follows:

U2-O1: Describe wireless protocols like Wi-Fi, Bluetooth, and Zigbee.

U2-O2: Analyze low-power protocols like LoRaWAN, NB-IoT

U2-O3: Evaluate IoT network topologies and their impact

U2-O4: Explain key networking protocols (MQTT, CoAP)

Unit Outcomes	Expected Mapping with Course Outcomes (1- Weak Correlation; 2- Medium correlation; 3- Strong Correlation)				
	CO-1	CO-2	CO-3	CO-4	CO-5
U2-O1	3	2	3	2	3
U2-O2	3	3	3	2	3
U2-O3	3	3	3	1	3
U2-O4	3	3	3	2	3

2.1 Introduction to IoT Communications Protocols

IoT Networks provide communication frameworks to "smart" devices or "things", which are embedded with microcontrollers, transmitters, receivers and appropriate protocol stacks for communications. These devices can collect, communicate and analyze collected data for doing several operations and also enhance automation in healthcare, transportations, smart cities and agriculture. IoT devices, such as sensors, actuators, etc. collect and transmit data wirelessly or in wired networks for processing, analyzing data for taking different actions and decisions accordingly.

Traditional routing protocols are not ideal for IoT due to challenges with scalability. Therefore, working groups of the Institute of Electrical and Electronics Engineers (IEEE) and the Internet Engineering Task Force (IETF) were to design new communication protocols, which are inline with the constraints and characteristics of low-energy sensing devices and low-rate wireless communications. The layered architecture and the corresponding communication protocols [1] are shown in figure 2.1.

Layers Communication Protocols

Application layer	CoAP
Network layer	IPv6, RPL
Adaptation layer	6LoWPAN
MAC layer	IEEE 802.15.4, IEEE 802.15.4e
Physical layer	IEEE 802.15.4

Figure 2.1: Communication protocols with layered architecture

Physical and MAC layers (IEEE 802.15.4): IEEE 802.15.4 [2] [3] supports low-energy communications at the physical and MAC layers. It sets all the rules of communications for lower layers.

Adaptation layer (6LoWPAN): The 6LoWPAN protocol is developed by applying Ipv6 over MAC and PHY layer of IEEE 802.15.4. IEEE 802.15.4 supports at most 127 bytes and a part of it will be for the header and the minimum value Maximum Transmission unit (MTU) for Ipv6 is 1280 bytes [4] [5] [6]. 6LoWPAN addresses this issue and is present just above the data-link layer. 6loWPAN implements mechanisms for packet fragmentation and reassembly required for IPv6.

Network layer (RPL): Routing Protocol for Low-power and Lossy Networks (RPL) [7] is developed for routing over 6LoWPAN environments. RPL is suitable and adaptable for IoT application domains.

Application layer (CoAP): The Constrained Application Protocol (CoAP) [8] supports application layer communications. CoAP is defined for UDP communications over 6LoWPAN. The CoAP protocol uses a request and response communications model between application endpoints. It supports end-to-end communications at application layer IoT devices and other Internet entities [9].

2.2 IoT Communication Protocols

The Internet of Things (IoT) depends on different communication protocols that allow devices to connect and exchange data. These protocols can be grouped based on their characteristics and usage, including **Wireless Protocols, Low-Power Protocols**, and **Networking Protocols**. Each category serves a distinct purpose and has specific applications depending on the requirements of the IoT system. Table 2.1 shows the key characteristics and typical use cases of the IoT protocols.

Table 2.1: Key characteristics and typical use cases of the IoT network protocols.

Protocol	Type	Range	Data Rate	Typical Use Cases
Bluetooth	Wireless	Short (10-100 m)	Low to Medium	Wearables, Personal devices, Home automation
Ethernet	Wired	N/A	High	Industrial automation, Data centers, Large networks
Wi-Fi	Wireless	Medium (50-100 m)	High	Smart homes, Security cameras, Voice assistants
Zigbee	Wireless	Medium (10-100 m)	Low	Home automation,

Protocol	Type	Range	Data Rate	Typical Use Cases
Thread	Wireless	Medium (10-100 m)	Low	Smart energy, Healthcare Home IoT networks, Smart devices
Cellular (4G/5G)	Wireless	Wide (Kilometers)	High (4G) to Very High (5G)	Fleet tracking, IoT in remote areas
LWM2M	Protocol over IP	Depends on underlying network	Varies	Remote device management, Firmware updates
LoRaWAN	Wireless	Long (2-5 km urban, 15+ km rural)	Low	Environmental monitoring, Smart agriculture, Smart cities

2.2.1 Wireless Protocols

2.2.1.1 Wi-Fi

Wi-Fi is a technology that uses radio waves to provide network connectivity as shown in figure 2.2. A Wi-Fi setup involves a wireless router that transmits data to and from a wired internet connection to devices that are equipped to receive the data. In IoT, Wi-Fi connects devices like security cameras, smart thermostats, and voice assistants to the internet and each other. It's ideal for devices that require high data transmission speeds and are typically operated within the range of a local area network.

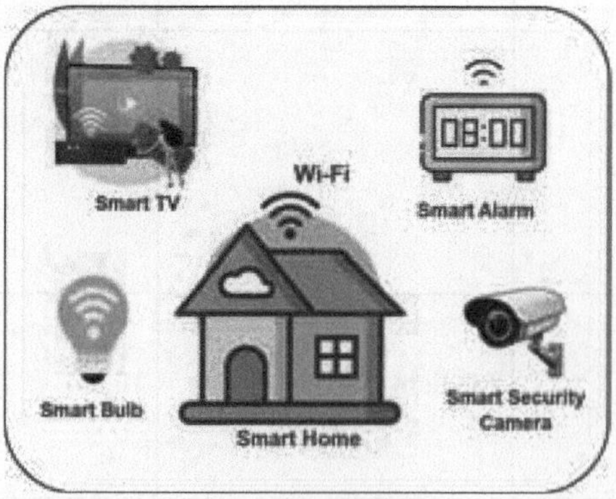

Figure 2.2: IoT devices connected using WiFi

2.2.1.2 Bluetooth

Bluetooth is a wireless technology standard used for exchanging data over short distances as shown in figure 2.3. It uses radio waves and is built into many of the products we use every day, including mobile phones, computers, and headsets. For IoT, Bluetooth is particularly useful for small, battery-operated IoT devices that require low energy consumption. The Bluetooth Low Energy (BLE) variant is especially significant in IoT for applications that need to exchange small amounts of data periodically, like fitness wearables or smart home devices.

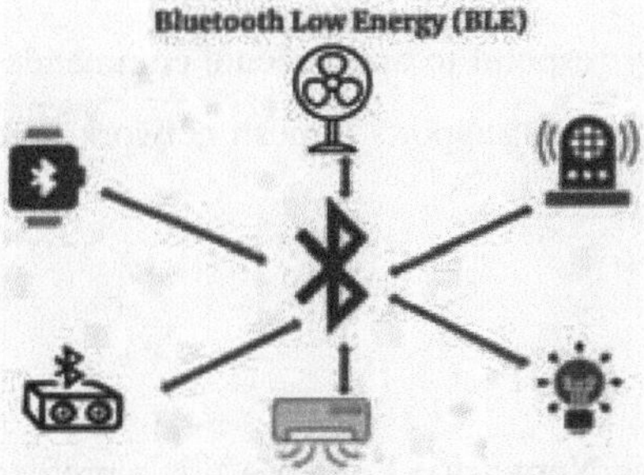

Figure 2.3: Bluetooth Low Energy (BLE)

2.2.1.3 Zigbee

The ZigBee protocol, developed by the ZigBee Alliance, is based on the IEEE 802.15.4 standard for low-power wireless networks. It is designed as a cost-effective solution for high-level communication protocols, enabling the creation of personal area networks (PANs) using small, low-power digital radios that can transmit data over longer distances. ZigBee is particularly suited for applications requiring low data rates, extended battery life, and secure networking. Additionally, ZigBee supports various network topologies, including mesh, star, and tree configurations, making it versatile for different networking needs as shown in figure 2.4. Zigbee is used extensively in home automation, smart energy systems, and healthcare because it can support a large number of nodes in a network and has highly reliable data transfer capabilities.

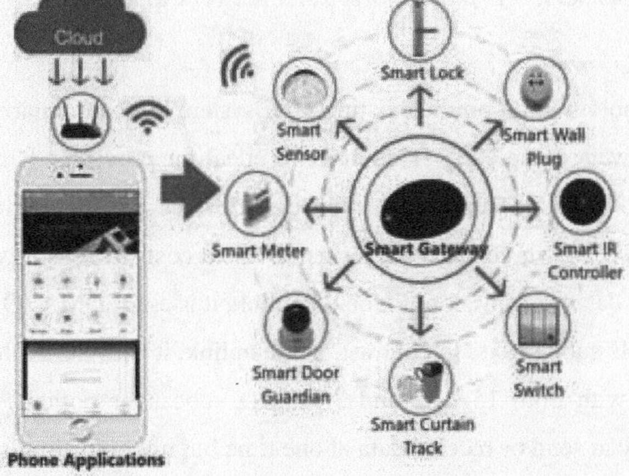

Figure 2.4: Various smart devices uses Zigbee

2.2.1.4 Z-Wave

Z-Wave is a low-power MAC protocol developed by Zensys, primarily used for wireless home automation to connect between 30 to 50 nodes. It has been widely adopted for IoT communication, especially in smart homes and small commercial environments. Z-Wave is optimized for small data packets with communication speeds of up to 100 kbps and a range of 30 meters in point-to-point connections. This makes it ideal for transmitting small messages in IoT applications, such as lighting control, energy management, and healthcare monitoring. The technology operates with two types of devices: controllers and slaves. Slave nodes are low-cost devices that cannot initiate communication; they can only respond to and execute commands from controlling devices that initiate messages within the network. Z-Wave also supports a mesh network topology, enhancing its connectivity and range.

2.2.2 Low-Power Protocols:

2.2.2.1 LoRaWAN

LoRaWAN (Long Range Wide Area Network): LoRaWAN is a protocol for wide-area networks designed to allow low-powered devices to communicate with internet-connected applications over long range wireless connections. It is highly suitable for outdoor IoT applications that need to operate over long distances, such as in agriculture, smart city, and environmental monitoring. LoRaWAN is valued for its ability to provide long-range communication at low power, thereby extending the battery life of devices.

2.2.2.2 Sigfox

SigFox is a low-power wireless communication technology designed for a wide range of low-energy devices, such as sensors and machine-to-machine (M2M) applications. It enables the transmission of small data packets over distances of up to 50 kilometers using Ultra Narrow Band (UNB) technology. SigFox is optimized for low data transfer speeds, ranging from 10 to 1,000 bits per second, and is capable of operating on minimal battery power. It is commonly used in applications like smart meters, patient monitoring, agriculture, security devices, street lighting, and environmental sensors. SigFox supports a star network topology.

2.2.2.3 NB-IoT

(Narrowband IoT) is a technology built on the existing LTE system but uses a narrower band of 200 kHz, which simplifies the design and lowers complexity. This makes it ideal for providing better coverage, reducing device costs, extending battery life, and supporting more connected devices in a given area. Like LTE-M, NB-IoT can work with existing LTE networks, which helps reduce deployment costs by reusing current infrastructure. NB-IoT uses different techniques for data transmission. In the downlink, it uses OFDMA (Orthogonal Frequency Division Multiple Access) with 15 kHz subcarriers. In contrast, in the uplink, it uses SC-FDMA (Single Carrier Frequency Division Multiple Access) with both 15 kHz and 3.75 kHz subcarrier options. It only supports half-duplex communication, meaning it can send or receive data at one time but not both simultaneously.

2.2.2.4 6LoWPAN

6LoWPAN (IPv6 over Low-Power Wireless Personal Area Networks) is a protocol for sending IPv6 data over low-power, low-bandwidth networks such as IEEE 802.15.4, which is widely used in IoT applications. It enables resource-constrained devices to interact across the internet by compressing and fragmenting IPv6 headers to fit inside the small frame sizes and energy limits of low-power networks. This protocol is IPv6 compatible, making IoT devices accessible across the worldwide internet, and it includes header compression to minimize data loads, as well as fragmentation and reassembly to manage bigger packets efficiently. 6LoWPAN is suited for applications such as smart homes, environmental monitoring, and industrial automation, where a large number of small, battery-powered devices run and communicate with low energy consumption, allowing for scalable, long-term IoT deployments.

2.2.2.4 6TiSCH

The IETF 6TiSCH Working Group (WG) was established to standardize the control plane and IP layer adaptation for IPv6 over the IEEE802.15.4 TSCH link layer [11]. 6TiSCH is crucial in delivering IPv6 to industrial low-power wireless environments by connecting TSCH networks with 6LoWPAN networks. This program addressed fundamental issues in adopting IPv6 for low-capacity networks by serving as an integrative layer between different network layers. Its work has also influenced improvements in header compression, IP-in-IP encapsulation, and 6LoWPAN Neighbor Discovery, resulting in more efficient, competent routing systems and improved security management that prioritizes simplicity and efficiency.

2.2.3 Networking Protocols:

2.2.3.1 MQTT (Message Queuing Telemetry Transport)

MQTT is a communication protocol specifically designed for the Internet of Things (IoT) and Machine to Machine (M2M) communication as shown in figure 2.5. Originating from a collaboration between Dr. Andy Stanford-Clark of IBM and Arlen Nipper of Arcom (now Eurotech), MQTT has grown to become one of the cornerstone protocols in the IoT ecosystem due to its simplicity, efficiency, and reliability in constrained environments. Officially becoming an OASIS standard in 2014, MQTT's primary goal is to establish a lightweight messaging framework that supports all levels of network transmission and ensures swift data delivery, even across unreliable networks.

Scan for more on MQTT

Key Characteristics of MQTT:

MQTT is distinguished by several unique features, making it particularly well-suited for IoT applications where network bandwidth and device capabilities are limited:

- **Lightweight Protocol:** Its design minimizes network traffic and resource requirements, making it ideal for devices with limited processing power and memory.

- **Publish-Subscribe Model:** Unlike traditional request-response paradigms, MQTT operates on a publish-subscribe model. This decouples the producer and consumer of messages, allowing devices to publish information to a "topic" without needing to know the consumers.
- **Quality of Service (QoS):** MQTT offers three levels of message delivery assurance: At most once (0), At least once (1), and Exactly once (2), catering to various reliability and performance requirements.
- **Efficient Message Distribution:** It supports one-to-many message distribution efficiently, enabling scenarios such as sensor readings or broadcast commands.
- **Persistent Sessions:** MQTT can maintain persistent sessions, which helps in minimizing the setup overhead for repeated connections and ensures message delivery even when the client is temporarily offline.
- **Security:** Though MQTT itself doesn't define encryption, it supports TLS/SSL for secure network connections and allows for additional authentication mechanisms to be implemented.

Evolution and Versions of MQTT:

MQTT has seen several iterations, with versions 3.1 and 3.1.1 enjoying widespread adoption for their balance of simplicity and functionality. MQTT 5.0, introduced as a significant upgrade, brought enhancements aimed at large-scale deployments and more granular message control, including improved error reporting, message property descriptions, and enhanced topic aliasing capabilities.

MQTT Architecture Components:

Understanding MQTT necessitates familiarity with its core components:

- **Client:** A client is any device that interacts with the MQTT broker, capable of publishing messages to topics or subscribing to topics to receive messages.
- **Broker:** The central figure in the MQTT architecture, the broker, is responsible for receiving all messages, filtering them, deciding who is interested in them, and then publishing those messages to all subscribed clients.
- **Topic:** A simple string that the broker uses to filter messages for each connected client. Topics allow a level of hierarchy, e.g., "home/livingroom/temperature", enabling precise targeting of message recipients.
- **Message:** The data transported between the client and the broker. It consists of a payload (the actual data), and optionally, headers and properties that can contain metadata or attributes about the message.

Example 2.1: Example of MQTT:

Consider a device equipped with a temperature sensor that needs to transmit its readings to a server or broker (figure 2.5). On the other end, a phone or desktop application wants to access this temperature data. Here's how it happens in two key steps:

1. Defining and Publishing the Topic:

The device, acting as the publisher, first establishes a topic, such as "temperature." It then sends the temperature data as a message under this topic. For instance, if the temperature is 22 degrees Celsius, the message "22" is published to the "temperature" topic.

2. Subscribing and Receiving the Message:

Concurrently, the phone or desktop application functions as a subscriber. It subscribes to the "temperature" topic through the same MQTT broker. Once the device publishes the temperature data, the MQTT broker's responsibility is to ensure this message reaches the subscriber.

In this setup, the broker's primary role is to facilitate the delivery of messages from the publisher (the temperature sensor device) to the subscriber (the phone or desktop application), thus completing the communication loop efficiently.

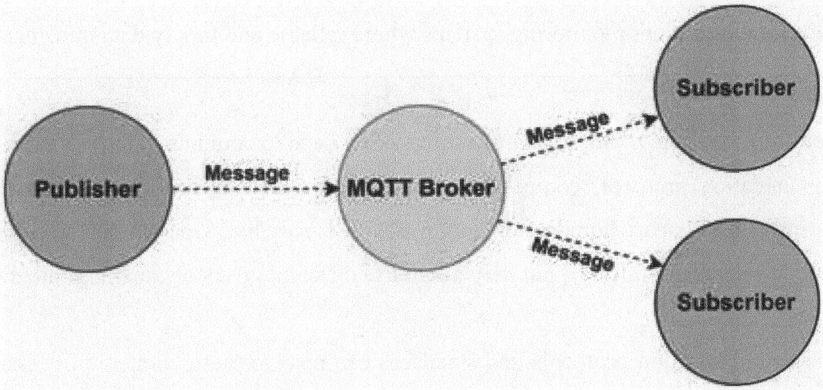

Figure 2.5: Architecture of MQTT

MQTT Message Flow:

The essence of MQTT lies in its simple but powerful message flow as shown in figure 2.6:

1) **Connect:** A client starts by establishing a connection to the broker, optionally specifying a will message to be published if the connection unexpectedly breaks.
2) **Publish:** Once connected, the client can publish messages to a specific topic, which the broker then processes according to the subscriptions it has received.
3) **Subscribe:** A client subscribes to a topic (or topics) to receive messages that other clients have published to the broker under those topics.
4) **Acknowledge:** Depending on the QoS level, messages may require acknowledgments, ensuring the desired delivery assurance.

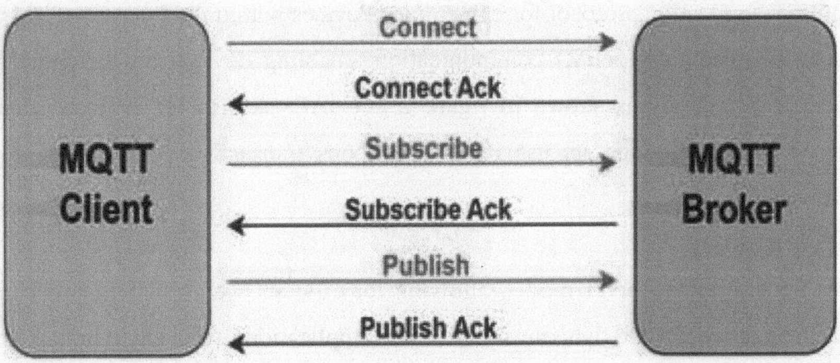

Figure 2.6: MQTT Message Flow

Use Cases and Applications:

MQTT's design and characteristics make it versatile for a wide range of IoT applications, including:

- **Telemetry and Remote Monitoring:** Collecting data from dispersed sensors in real-time, such as in agricultural, environmental, or infrastructure monitoring.
- **Home Automation:** Coordinating smart home devices for enhanced convenience and energy efficiency.
- **Industrial IoT:** Enabling reliable machine-to-machine communication in manufacturing environments for process automation and optimization.
- **Healthcare:** Facilitating patient monitoring systems where reliable and timely data transmission is critical.

Example 2.2:

In an IoT ecosystem, devices from multiple manufacturers often need to communicate with each other. Without a standardized communication protocol, compatibility issues can arise, leading to inefficiencies and limited functionality. For instance, a smart home setup might have devices like smart bulbs, sensors, cameras, and appliances that need to interact seamlessly, but they might use different protocols, making integration difficult.

Solution:

Adopting universal communication protocols and standards can resolve these compatibility issues. Here's how such a solution might look:

i. Adoption of MQTT and CoAP: MQTT is ideal for low-bandwidth, high-latency networks and is great for tasks that require minimal code footprints on devices (like sensors and actuators), while CoAP is designed to easily translate to HTTP for simplified integration with the web.

ii. Implementation of IPv6: Since IoT involves a vast number of devices, IPv6 can provide enough IP addresses for every device to have its own unique address, facilitating easier device communication over the Internet.

iii. Use of Standardized IoT Platforms: Platforms like AWS IoT, Google Cloud IoT, and Microsoft Azure IoT provide standardized ways to connect, monitor, and manage IoT devices at scale. These platforms support various IoT protocols and help ensure different devices can communicate effectively.

2.2.3.2 CoAP (Constrained Application Protocol)

CoAP is an internet application protocol for constrained devices within the Internet of Things (IoT) ecosystem. It facilitates machine-to-machine (M2M) communication, enabling devices on the same network or across the internet to interact seamlessly as shown in figure 2.7. CoAP, akin to HTTP in its operation, is tailored for constrained environments through its use of asynchronous transactions over UDP, significantly optimizing resource utilization.

CoAP's Core Mechanisms:

CoAP operates under a client-server model, allowing for efficient web transfers between devices. Its structure accommodates the lightweight and dynamic nature of IoT applications, from smart homes to industrial automation. Key to CoAP's design is its compatibility with four primary types of information exchange: acknowledgments, confirmable messages, reset messages, and non-confirmable information. This versatility ensures reliable communication tailored to the specific needs of IoT deployments.

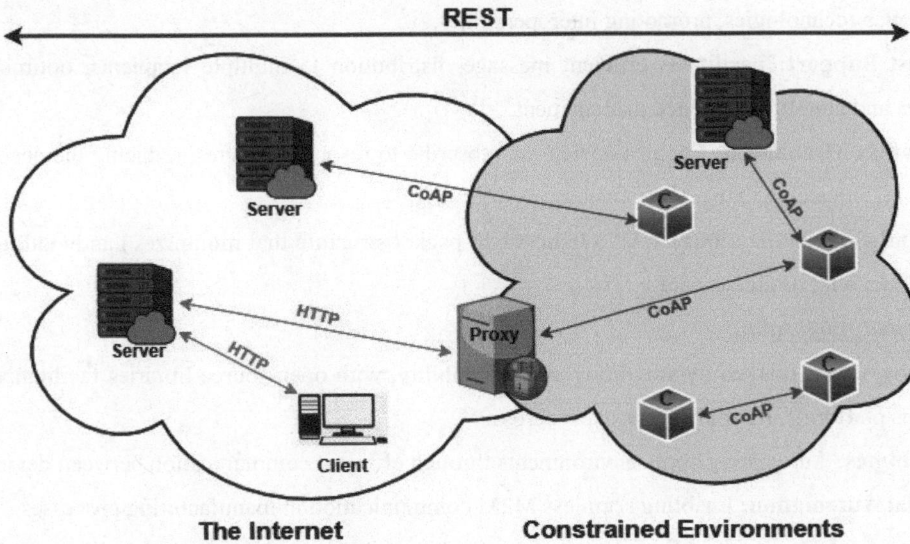

Figure 2.7: CoAP Network

Key Characteristics:

- **Lightweight:** Optimized for devices with limited processing power and memory, CoAP ensures minimal overhead.
- **Asynchronous Communication:** Utilizes UDP for low-latency, efficient data transmission, distinguishing itself from traditional protocols.
- **Highly Secure:** Implements robust security measures including RPK and PSK certification, safeguarding data integrity and confidentiality.

Information Exchange in CoAP:

- **Acknowledgments:** Serve as signals for the successful receipt of messages, ensuring reliability in communication.
- **Confirmable Messages:** Require acknowledgments, guaranteeing message delivery through retries until an acknowledgment is received.
- **Non-Confirmable Messages:** Do not necessitate acknowledgments, used for non-critical data transmission where reliability is not paramount.
- **Reset Messages:** Indicate issues in processing received messages, initiating corrective actions to maintain communication integrity.

CoAP's Role in IoT Communication:

CoAP acts as a bridge, filling the gaps left by HTTP in constrained environments. It enables devices, such as sensors and actuators, to not only exchange data over the internet but also do so with remarkable efficiency. This positions CoAP as a critical enabler in the widespread adoption and growth of IoT technologies.

Features That Define CoAP:

- **Resource-Oriented:** CoAP's web-like, resource-oriented approach allows straightforward integration with existing web technologies, promoting interoperability.
- **Multicast Support:** Facilitates efficient message distribution to multiple recipients, optimizing network resources and simplifying device management.
- **Observation Mechanism:** Enables devices to subscribe to resource updates, reducing the need for constant polling and enhancing network efficiency.
- **Low Bandwidth Utilization:** CoAP's lightweight packet structure that minimizes bandwidth usage, crucial for networks with limited capacity.

Deployment and Application:

CoAP's deployment is marked by simplicity and adaptability, with open-source libraries facilitating integration across various platforms. Its application spans across:

- **Smart Homes:** Automating home environments through efficient communication between devices.
- **Industrial Automation:** Enabling seamless M2M communication in manufacturing processes.
- **Environmental Monitoring:** Facilitating real-time data collection and analysis for climate and agricultural applications.

2.2.3.3 AMQP (Advanced Message Queuing Protocol)

AMQP is a globally recognized, open standard for passing business messages between applications or organizations as shown in figure 2.8. It provides a robust, secure, and interoperable messaging framework. Here's a detailed explanation of AMQP, breaking down its core components, functionality, and benefits.

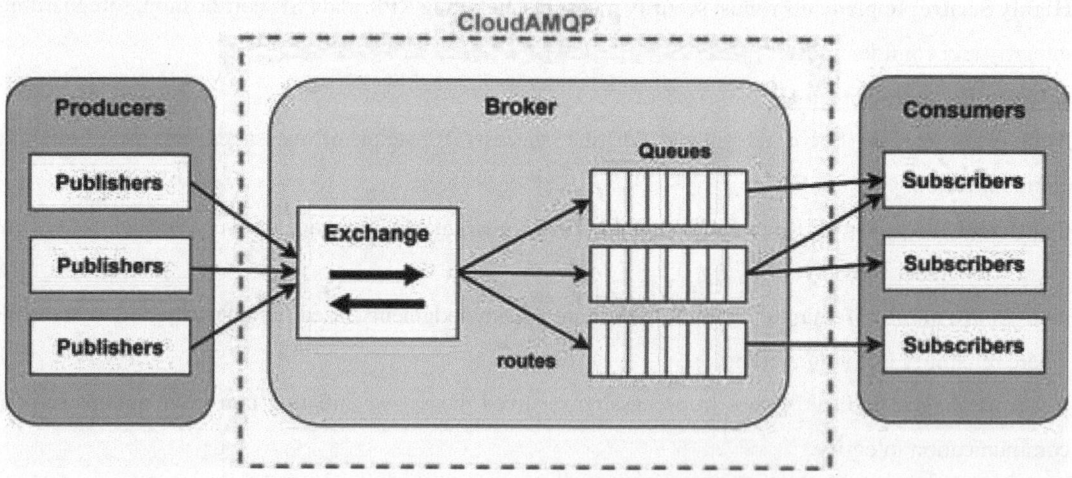

Figure 2.8: AMQP (Advanced Message Queuing Protocol)

Core Principles and Components of AMQP:

- **Broker (Server):** This acts as the middleman in the AMQP protocol. The broker receives messages from producers (publishers) and routes these messages to appropriate consumer queues.

- **Producer (Publisher):** A producer sends messages to an exchange, without knowing the consumers of the message.
- **Consumer:** A consumer subscribes to a queue and processes messages coming from the queue.
- **Exchange:** This component takes messages from producers and routes them to one or more queues based on routing rules. Exchanges can be of different types such as direct, topic, headers, and fanout.
    - **Direct Exchange:** Routes messages to queues based on message routing key.
    - **Topic Exchange:** Routes messages to one or many queues based on matching between a message routing pattern and the pattern used to bind a queue to an exchange.
    - **Fanout Exchange:** Routes messages to all of the queues that are bound to it without any routing criteria.
    - **Headers Exchange:** Routes based on a message header attribute instead of a routing key.
- **Queue:** This is where messages are held until they can be processed by a consumer.
- **Binding:** A binding is a link between a queue and an exchange.

<u>How AMQP Works:</u>

- When a producer wants to send a message, it sends the message to an exchange. The exchange then uses binding rules to route the message to one or more queues.
- The consumers connected to those queues then receive the messages for processing.
- AMQP ensures that messages are not lost by providing features like message acknowledgment, persistence, and durable queues.

<u>Use Cases and Benefits:</u>

- **Reliability:** Messages can be marked as persistent, and are stored on disk, ensuring that they are not lost even if the broker restarts.
- **Flexibility:** Different types of exchanges allow for sophisticated routing schemes.
- **Scalability:** AMQP can handle high-throughput scenarios in various environments, from cloud computing platforms to mobile devices.
- **Interoperability:** As an open standard, AMQP is supported by multiple vendors and platforms, facilitating integration between different systems and technologies.

<u>API Development with AMQP:</u>

AMQP can be used to enhance API capabilities by supporting asynchronous message handling. This is useful for transactions where immediate response is not critical but reliability and eventual consistency are important.

For example, in financial transactions, AMQP can manage messages related to funds transfers where the completion of a transaction can occur after several steps, each managed and acknowledged separately.

DDS (Data Distribution Service)

DDS is a middleware protocol and API standard developed by the Object Management Group (OMG). It's designed to facilitate robust, scalable, and high-performance data exchanges between distributed systems as shown in figure 2.9. DDS is widely used in various sectors, including IoT, autonomous vehicles, industrial automation, aerospace, and defense, due to its ability to handle complex, real-time data flows efficiently.

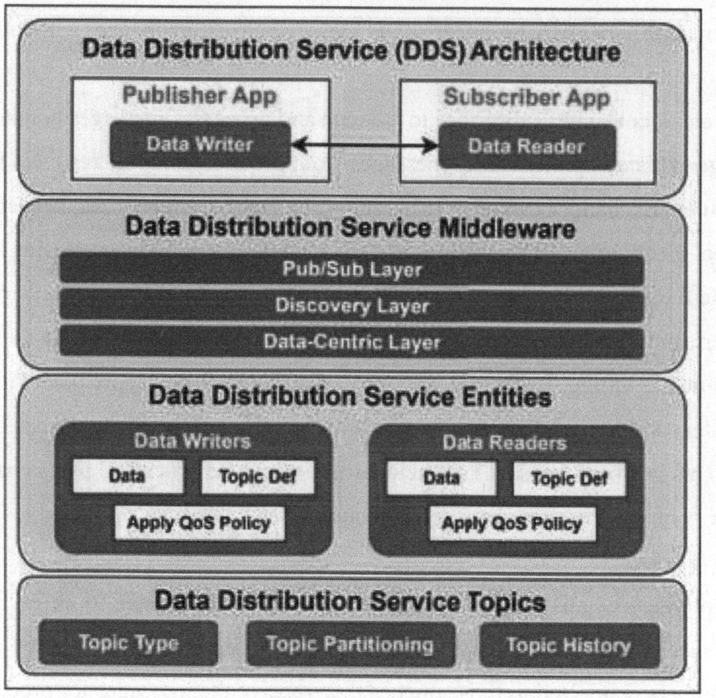

Figure 2.9: DDS Architecture and Components

Key Features of DDS:

DDS is known for its real-time data distribution capabilities, which are critical for applications where delays are unacceptable. It is highly scalable and capable of managing interactions across a vast number of devices. DDS also provides fault tolerance, ensuring reliable data delivery even in challenging network conditions. One of its standout features is the flexible Quality of Service (QoS) policies that allow for detailed customization to meet specific application needs. These policies include settings for data delivery deadlines, reliability, resource limits, and more. Additionally, DDS includes robust security features offering authentication, authorization, and encryption to ensure secure communication channels across distributed systems.

Architecture and Components:

- **DDS Domain:** Defines a virtual space where participants communicate. It isolates communications such that only participants within the same domain can interact.
- **Participants:** Applications or devices that either publish or subscribe to data. Each participant can be both a publisher and a subscriber.
- **Topics:** Named data distributions channels. Publishers and subscribers communicate by publishing or subscribing to Topics.
- **Data Writers and Data Readers:** Interfaces for sending and receiving data. A Data Writer sends data to a Topic, while a Data Reader receives data from a Topic.
- **Pub/Sub Layer:** Manages the publish-subscribe mechanism, enabling decoupled communication between data producers and consumers.

- **Discovery Layer:** Automatically detects and configures entities within the network, facilitating dynamic scalability and configuration changes without manual intervention.
- **Data-Centric Layer:** Focuses on data management, ensuring that data flows are handled according to the QoS policies set by the application.

Benefits of DDS:

- **Increased Productivity:** Simplifies distributed application development by managing complex networking tasks.
- **Improved Responsiveness:** Enables applications to react promptly to real-time data and events.
- **Enhanced Scalability:** Facilitates easy scaling of applications as the number of devices or data volumes increase.
- **Reduced Maintenance Costs:** The self-healing and fault-tolerant nature of DDS reduces downtime and maintenance efforts.

2.2.3.4 A) XMPP (Extensible Messaging and Presence Protocol)

XMPP is a comprehensive communication protocol initially designed for instant messaging, presence information, and contact list management. Over time, its flexibility has allowed it to be extended for voice and video calling, file transfers, and IoT applications.

Benefits of XMPP:

XMPP is fundamentally a decentralized communication framework, which means that it does not rely on a single central server. This architecture enhances security and reduces potential points of failure, making the protocol robust and reliable for real-time communications. Being an open-standard protocol, XMPP fosters widespread adoption and facilitates innovation and collaborative development across various platforms.

Usage of XMPP:

Implementing XMPP requires setting up client and server components. Clients are the end-user applications that interact with the XMPP network, enabling users to send messages, manage presence info, and more. Servers act as the intermediaries that route messages and manage the overall network communications.

Client-Server Communication in XMPP:

XMPP communication is structured around a client-server model:

- **Connection Management:** Clients initiate connections to servers, which respond and manage session continuity.
- **Handshake and Authentication:** Includes negotiating features and authenticating client identities.
- **Message Routing and Presence Management:** Servers handle the distribution of messages and updates about user availability.
- **Roster and Contact List Maintenance:** Servers also manage and synchronize user contact lists across different client instances.

In the given Figure, we observe three principal user nodes identified as Alice, Bob, and Carol. Each node symbolizes an end-user's computing device, capable of sending and receiving XMPP communications. The connections between these user nodes and various server entities indicate the multi-faceted interaction capabilities facilitated by XMPP, supporting both direct user-to-user communications and interactions mediated through server entities. It also indicates the protocol's interoperability, with lines suggesting potential interactions between XMPP and the Hypertext Transfer Protocol (HTTP), which shows XMPP's capability to integrate with web-based technologies.

Stanzas in XMPP:

XMPP uses XML stanzas (structured data formats) for communication, which include:

- Message Stanzas: Used for text messaging between users.
- Presence Stanzas: Indicate a user's online status and availability.
- IQ (Info/Query) Stanzas: Handle data requests and modifications, similar to HTTP's GET and POST methods.

XMPP Features:

- **Asynchronous Push Messaging:**
  XMPP excels in delivering messages asynchronously, which means that the communication doesn't require the receiver or the sender to be actively engaging at the time of message exchange. Messages are sent as XML stanzas, which are structured blocks containing the message body, metadata, and unique identifiers for sender and receiver. This method enables continual message flow without waiting for responses, facilitating a real-time communication experience that is efficient and reduces the need for constant server queries, known as polling. Polling can lead to high bandwidth consumption and delays in message delivery, issues XMPP inherently avoids by pushing messages directly to the server or client as soon as they are available.
- **Client-Server Architecture:**
  XMPP operates on a client-server model where the server acts as an intermediary routing messages to and from clients. Each client connects to the server using a unique identifier, similar to an email address, ensuring messages are directed accurately. This structured routing ensures that XMPP maintains consistent and efficient communication paths between clients and servers.
- **Persistent TCP Connections:**
  Traditionally, XMPP uses persistent TCP connections for data transmission, meaning once a connection is established between a client and a server, it remains open for the duration of the session. This persistent connection facilitates a continuous and free exchange of XML data, which is particularly beneficial for applications requiring real-time updates. Modern implementations of XMPP also incorporate TLS for enhanced security and WebSockets for better integration with web technologies, providing flexible and secure options for developers.
- **Decentralized Hosting:**
  XMPP supports decentralized hosting, allowing anyone to set up and run their own XMPP server. This capability is akin to how email works, where no single central authority controls the communication. Users

can choose to host their servers on the cloud or on-premises, providing flexibility in how they manage and secure their communication infrastructure. This decentralized approach not only enhances privacy and control but also aids in preventing single points of failure, making the system more robust and resilient.

- **Gateways:**
  XMPP gateways enable the protocol to interact with other messaging systems, broadening its application. For example, an XMPP server can connect with an SMS gateway to send messages to mobile phones, or with an SMTP server for email interactions. This interoperability is facilitated by XMPP's flexible architecture, which can accommodate various communication protocols, allowing XMPP to serve as a bridge across different messaging platforms.

B) HTTP (HyperText Transfer Protocol)

HTTP is a cornerstone of data communication in the World Wide Web, enabling the transfer of hypertext and multimedia across the Internet. Developed by Tim Berners-Lee at CERN in the early 1990s, HTTP has evolved from a simple protocol to a complex foundation supporting global information exchange.

HTTP began as a simple protocol (HTTP/0.9) to facilitate raw data transfer. This early version could only handle basic communications and was not extensible. With the explosive growth of the web, there was a pressing need for a more robust and efficient protocol, which led to the development of HTTP/1.0 (RFC 1945) in 1996. This version introduced versioning and a new structure that included method, headers, and a response status code. Improvements continued with HTTP/1.1 (RFC 2616) in 1999, which introduced critical performance optimizations like persistent connections and chunked transfers. This version remained the standard for over a decade. To address performance bottlenecks related to HTTP/1.1, HTTP/2 was standardized in 2015, introducing features such as multiplexing, header compression, and server push. The most recent iteration, HTTP/3, leverages the QUIC transport protocol to improve security and efficiency in connections plagued by latency and packet loss issues.

Features of HTTP:

- **Client-Server Model:** HTTP operates on a client-server model where the client initiates an HTTP request and the server responds. This model is fundamental to all web interactions and defines the operational dynamics of HTTP communications.
- **Stateless Protocol:** Each request is processed independently without any knowledge of previous requests. This makes the protocol suitable for large-scale distributed systems, though it necessitates mechanisms such as cookies to manage states in web applications.
- **Extensibility:** HTTP headers offer a flexible way to extend functionality. These headers provide essential data about the request or response, or about the object sent in the message body.
- **Versatility:** HTTP is not confined to hypertext. It can transfer any type of data as long as both the client and server agree on how to handle the data type, which is generally specified in MIME-type format.

How HTTP Operates:

- **Establishing Connections:** HTTP typically uses TCP (Transmission Control Protocol) to establish connections between the client and the server. The default port used is 80 for HTTP and 443 for HTTPS, the secure version of the protocol that encrypts data using TLS/SSL.
- **Sending an HTTP Request:** Composed of a request line (method, URI, HTTP version), headers, and sometimes a body, the request tells the server what the client wants to do and provides contextual information.
- **Server Response:** After processing the request, the server responds with a status line (HTTP version, status code, descriptive phrase), headers, and often a body containing the requested data as shown in figure 2.10.
- **Connection Management:** Depending on the headers, the connection may be closed after the response, or kept open for further requests, enhancing the efficiency of network resources.

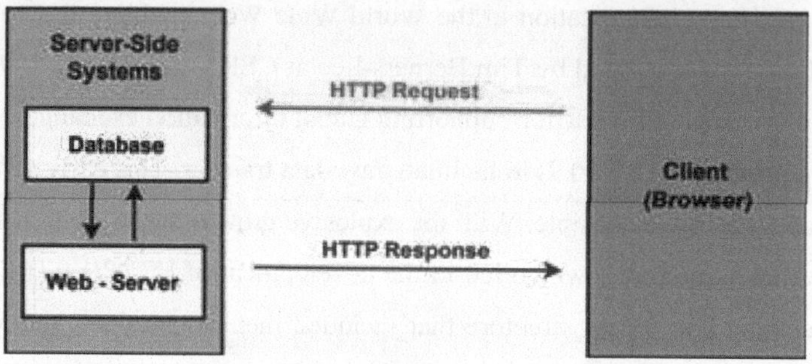

Figure 2.10: HTTP Response

HTTP Methods:

- **GET:** Retrieves information from the server (idempotent).
- **POST:** Submits data to be processed to a specified resource.
- **PUT:** Replaces all current representations of the target resource with the uploaded content (idempotent).
- **DELETE:** Removes specified resources (idempotent).
- **HEAD:** Similar to GET but retrieves headers only, without the body of the response.
- **OPTIONS:** Describes the communication options for the target resource.
- **PATCH:** Applies partial modifications to a resource.

Security Considerations:

While HTTP itself does not provide encryption, HTTPS (HTTP Secure) encapsulates HTTP inside the TLS/SSL protocol, providing encrypted transport. This prevents eavesdropping, tampering, and message forgery, ensuring the security and privacy of data between the client and server.

2.2.3.5 WebSockets

The WebSocket protocol was developed to enable real-time communication between servers and clients. In a TCP connection, both sides can send and receive data in real time. WebSocket is designed for full-duplex communication, meaning data can flow simultaneously in both directions as shown in figure 2.11. It uses HTTP as the transport layer, allowing it to leverage existing infrastructure such as proxies, filters, and authentication mechanisms. Primarily, WebSocket offers an efficient and standardized solution for real-time communication between web browsers and web servers, though it is also used in other applications like IoT. The WebSocket protocol operates in two main phases: *the handshake* and *the data transfer*. The connection is initiated by an HTTP request to establish the handshake, after which data can be exchanged.

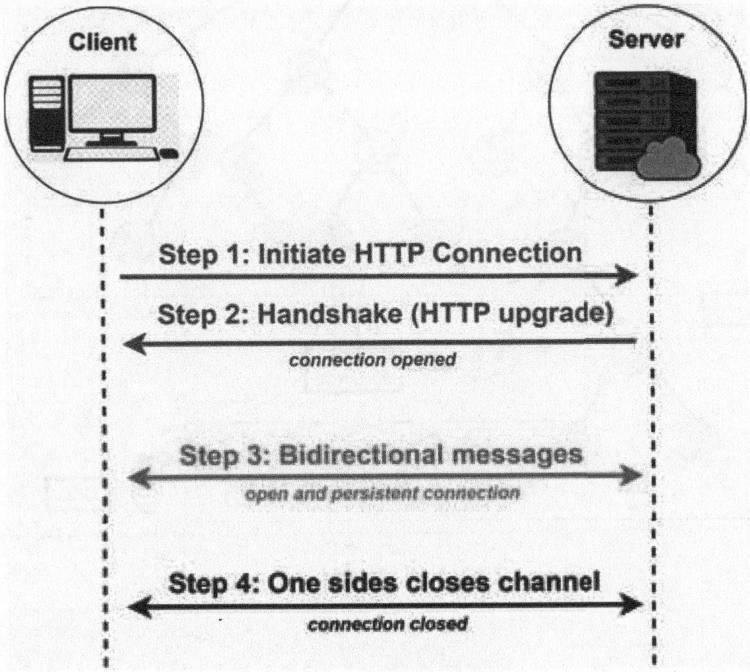

Figure 2.11: WebSockets

2.2.3.6 RPL

The IETF ROLL working group created RPL to provide routing services in Low-Power and Lossy Networks (LLNs), where devices often have limited resources. RPL is a distance vector routing technique that groups network devices into Directed Acyclic Graphs. A DAG connects nodes without forming loops, ensuring that data traffic travels to one or more root nodes. Each DAG may contain one or more Destination-Oriented DAGs (DODAGs); each DODAG has a single root node, which typically serves as the gateway or border router ("6BR") and is where data is largely collected. Multiple RPL instances can run simultaneously within a DAG, allowing different applications to execute independently but concurrently. One or more DODAGs may be included in each RPL instance; they will all share the same RPLInstanceID and adhere to the same Objective Function. Rank is a key statistic for organizing nodes in a Directed Acyclic Graph (DAG). It represents a node's relative position, or "distance" from the DAG root, which guides packet routing and ensures loop-free routes. Figure 2.12 shows an example of a typical RPL-based IoT network that include all essential components: RPL Instances, a Directed Acyclic Graph (DAG), Destination-Oriented DAGs (DODAGs), Rank, and Sub-DODAGs [10].

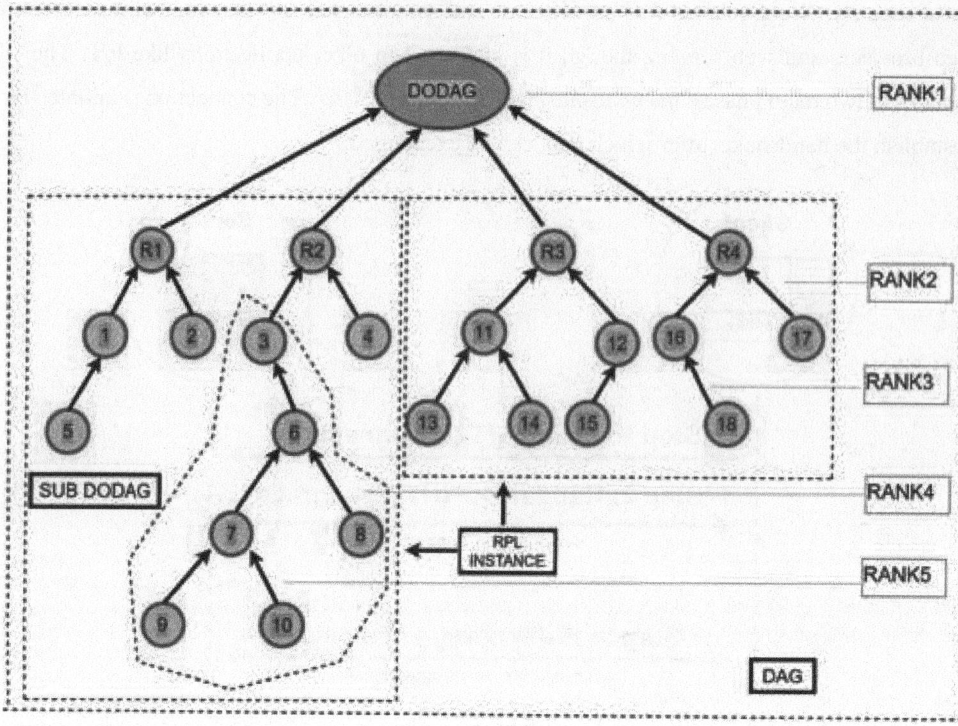

Figure 2.12: RPL-based IoT network

2.3 IoT Network Topologies

The configuration or pattern in which devices connect to create a network is known as network topology. It specifies how various network nodes such as PCs, servers, or other devices are connected to one another and how information moves between them.

2.3.1 Star topology

The server, sometimes referred to as the central node, is connected to every single node in a star topology as shown in figure 2.13. This central server, which processes data from the source node before sending it to the destination, is required for all data exchanges between nodes. Because the central node can effectively control data, this design is frequently employed in both voice and information networks.

Many low-power, wide-area networks (LPWANs), WiFi, and cellular networks also adopt star topology, even though mesh networks are frequently used for low-power Internet of Things applications. The communication topology of these networks is centered on a central router or access point that is connected to every terminal or node.

By focusing communication on the center node, star topology has the important benefit of simplifying network complexity.

The radio link between the end nodes and the central gateway might be rather lengthy, which is a significant disadvantage. Consequently, nodes located further away from the gateway have to expend more energy in order to send messages. However, star nodes can take a break in between transmissions, which reduces their overall energy consumption, in contrast to mesh nodes, which must always be active.

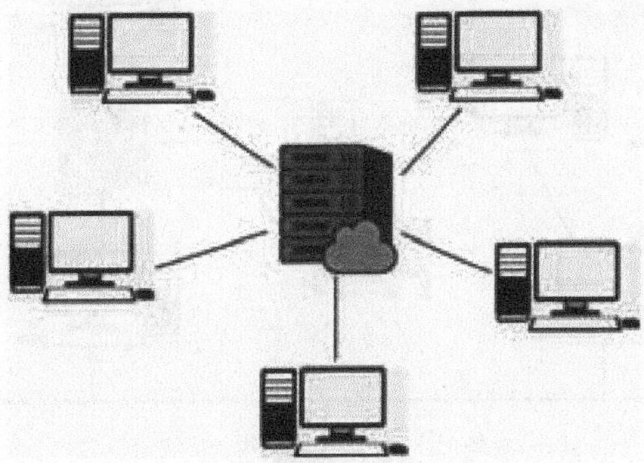

Figure 2.13: Star Topology

2.3.2 Mesh topology

In a mesh topology, devices are interconnected in a point-to-point arrangement, where each network node is connected to every other node as shown in figure 2.14. For *n* devices, a mesh topology requires $n(n-1)/2$ physical channels.

Mesh topology uses two main techniques for data transmission:

1. **Mesh Topology Routing Technique:** In this technique, nodes use routing logic based on network requirements. This logic directs data along the shortest path to its destination and identifies broken links, allowing the network to avoid failed nodes and reconfigure itself as needed.
2. **Mesh Topology Flooding Technique:** In flooding, the same data is sent to all nodes in the network, eliminating the need for routing logic. While this ensures robustness and prevents data loss, it can also cause unnecessary load on the network due to redundant data transmissions.

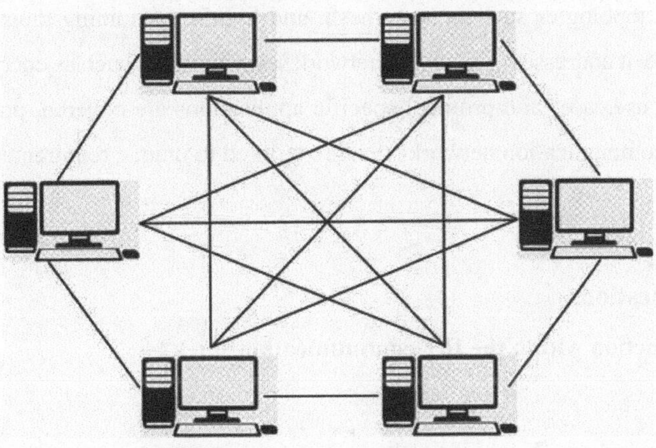

Figure 2.14: Mesh Topology

2.3.3 Hybrid topology

In order to build a more adaptable and effective network structure, a hybrid topology integrates components from two or more distinct topologies, such as mesh, star etc as shown in figure 2.15.

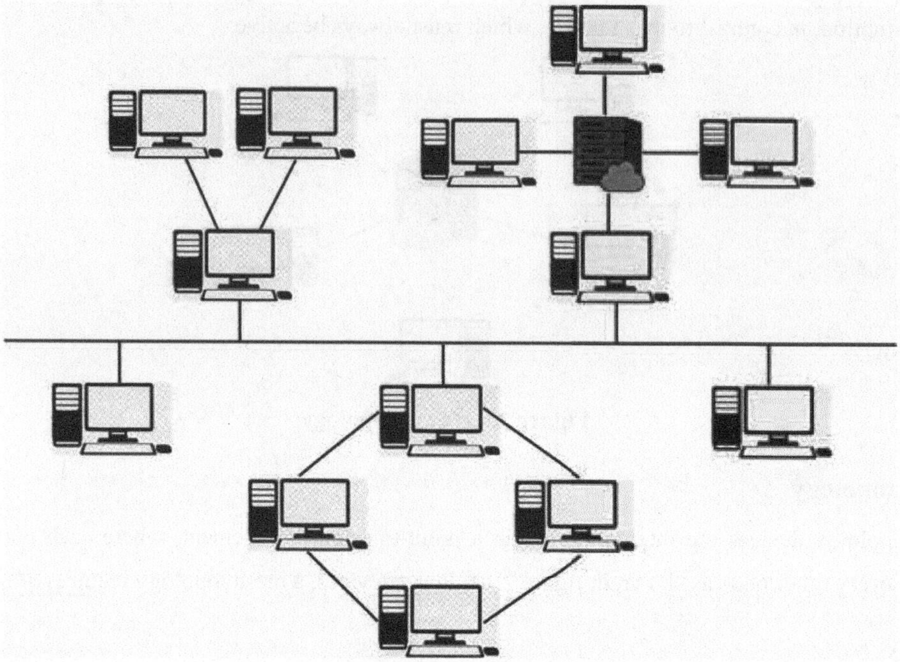

Figure 2.15: Hybrid Topology

2.4 Summary

This chapter focused on the crucial function of communication protocols in IoT systems, which allow objects to communicate and share data seamlessly. It divides communication protocols into three categories: wireless (e.g., Wi-Fi, Bluetooth, Zigbee), low-power (e.g., LoRaWAN, Sigfox, NB-IoT), and networking (e.g., MQTT, CoAP, HTTP/HTTPS), explaining their functionality and suitability for various IoT applications. The unit also investigates IoT network topologies such as star, mesh, and hybrid, examining their effects on scalability and performance. Furthermore, it addresses critical IoT network security issues such as encryption, authentication, and resource limits. Practical use cases and protocol-specific applications are covered, preparing students to design efficient and secure IoT communication networks that are tailored to unique requirements.

2.5 Exercise

A. Multiple-choice Questions

1. Where does CoAP function within the IoT communication stack?

a) Physical layer

b) MAC layer

c) Network layer

d) Application layer

2. What is the primary purpose of the 6LoWPAN protocol?

a) High-speed data transmission

b) Compression and fragmentation of IPv6 headers

c) Secure communication

d) Power optimization

3. Which Internet of Things protocol is publish-subscribe based?

a) MQTT

b) HTTP

c) CoAP

d) RPL

4. What is the main objective of the ZigBee protocol?

a) High bandwidth applications

b) Large-scale industrial automation

c) Low-power, low-data-rate applications

d) Wide area networks

5. What topology links every device to a central node directly?

a) Mesh topology

b) Star topology

c) Hybrid topology

d) Tree topology

6. What is one of LoRaWAN's main advantages?

a) High data rates

b) Long-range communication

c) High energy consumption

d) Real-time communication

7. What MQTT feature makes sure that messages are delivered even when the client is not online?

a) Persistent sessions

b) Publish-subscribe model

c) Lightweight protocol

d) Multicast support

8. In terms of IoT connectivity, what does BLE stand for?

a) Bluetooth Low Energy

b) Broadband Link Extension

c) Binary Link Exchange

d) Base Line Extension

9. In IoT networks, what is the primary drawback of star topology?

a) High complexity

b) High energy consumption for distant nodes

c) Unscalable network

d) Lack of fault tolerance

10. What protocol routes using a Directed Acyclic Graph (DAG)?

a) CoAP

b) RPL

c) MQTT

d) HTTP

B. Long Answer Questions

1. Hybrid Topology in Disaster Management:

   During a natural catastrophe, an IoT-based system is used to monitor environmental variables (such as water levels and air quality) and provide real-time data to emergency response teams.

   a. Create a hybrid topology that combines star and mesh elements to enable consistent data delivery.

   b. Explain how this design will handle rapid changes in network connectivity during a disaster.

2. Bluetooth Low Energy For Wearables:

   A fitness tracking startup is creating a wearable device that constantly analyzes a user's heart rate, step count, and sleep quality. The device must be able to run on a small battery for extended periods.

   a. Explain how Bluetooth Low Energy (BLE) meets the needs of this wearable gadget.

   b. Compare the energy efficiency and range of BLE to other wireless technologies.

3. RPL for Smart Agriculture:

   A large-scale smart agriculture project entails placing sensors throughout many fields to monitor environmental conditions. These sensors send data to a centralized server.

   a. Explain how RPL can be used to develop an effective routing framework for this system.

   b. Discuss how DODAGs and rankings affect the network's reliability and scalability

4. Figure 2.1 (Communication protocols with layered architecture) illustrates the duties of each tier in the IoT communication stack. Explain the significance of protocols such as CoAP, 6LoWPAN, and RPL.

5. Analyze Figure 2.5 (MQTT Architecture) and explain the roles of the client, broker, and topic in MQTT communication. How does the publish-subscribe paradigm function, and how does it vary from conventional request-response models?
6. Using Figure 2.6 (MQTT Message Flow) as a guide, describe the procedures involved in MQTT communication, such as connection formation, publishing, and message subscription. Discuss the significance of QoS levels.
7. Examine Figure 2.7 (CoAP Network) and describe the important characteristics of CoAP, such as its lightweight design, asynchronous communication, and security methods. How can CoAP provide effective communication in constrained environments?
8. Discuss the uses, benefits, and limits of low-power protocols such as LoRaWAN, Sigfox, and NB-IoT in IoT systems.
9. Explain the operation of the MQTT protocol, including its architecture and message flow. How does it differ from other IoT protocols, such as COAP?
10. Compare and contrast wireless technologies including Wi-Fi, Zigbee, Bluetooth, and Z-Wave in terms of range, data rate, and usual applications.
11. What are the different IoT network topologies? Explain the merits and disadvantages of star, mesh, and hybrid topologies, as well as their applications.
12. Analyze the issues of protecting IoT networks and discuss the encryption, authentication, and authorization solutions used to overcome them.
13. Explain the role of RPL in IoT networking. Discuss the structure, components like DAGs and DODAGs, and the significance of rank in packet routing.

C. Short Answer Questions

1. Figure 2.2 depicts IoT devices connected via Wi-Fi; how is Wi-Fi used in IoT applications such as security cameras and smart homes?
2. Explain the concept of publish-subscribe communication as illustrated in figure 2.5 (MQTT Architecture).
3. What are the main advantages of hybrid topology, as illustrated in figure 2.15 (Hybrid Topology)?
4. How does Z-Wave differ from Zigbee in IoT communication?
5. Identify two advantages of mesh architecture in IoT networks.
6. What are the four message types supported by CoAP?
7. Why is encryption necessary in IoT communication?
8. How does WebSocket support real-time communication in IoT?
9. What are the key aspects of the AMQP protocol?
10. Explain the idea of "persistent TCP connections" in XMPP
11. How does figure 2.3 (Bluetooth Low Energy) depict the use of BLE in wearables and smart home devices?
12. How does figure 2.9 (DDS Architecture) depict the interactions between publishers and subscribers in a domain?
13. Discuss the role of endpoints in CoAP communication, as illustrated in figure 2.7 (CoAP Network).

14. What is the function of the central node in figure 2.13 (Star Topology)?
15. How does figure 2.12 (RPL-Based IoT Network) address the challenges of low-power and lossy networks?

Answers for MCQ's

1. d) Application layer
2. b) Compression and fragmentation of IPv6 headers
3. a) MQTT
4. c) Low-power, low-data-rate applications
5. b) Star topology
6. b) Long-range communication
7. a) Persistent sessions
8. a) Bluetooth Low Energy
9. b) High energy consumption for distant nodes
10. b) RPL

REFERENCES

1. M. R. Palattella *et al.*, "Standardized Protocol Stack for the Internet of (Important) Things," in *IEEE Communications Surveys & Tutorials*, vol. 15, no. 3, pp. 1389-1406, Third Quarter 2013.
2. IEEE Standard for Local and Metropolitan Area Networks—Part 15.4: Low-Rate Wireless Personal Area Networks (LR-WPANs), IEEE Std. 802.15.4-2011 (Revision of IEEE Std. 802.15.4-2006), (2011) 1-314, 2011.
3. IEEE Standard for Local and Metropolitan Area Networks—Part 15.4: Low-Rate Wireless Personal Area Networks (LR-WPANs) Amendment 1: MAC Sublayer, IEEE Std. 802.15.4e-2012 (Amendment to IEEE Std. 802.15.4-2011), (2011) 1-225, 2012.
4. N. Kushalnagar, G. Montenegro, and C. Schumacher, "IPv6 over LowPower Wireless Personal Area Networks (6LoWPANs): Overview, Assumptions, Problem Statement", RFC 4919, 2007.
5. G. Montenegro, N. Kushalnagar, J. Hui, and D. Culler, Transmission of IPv6 Packets Over IEEE 802.15.4 Networks, RFC 4944, 2007.
6. J. Hui and P. Thubert, Compression Format for IPv6 Datagrams Over IEEE 802.15.4-Based Networks, RFC 6282, 2011.
7. P. Thubert et al., RPL: IPv6 Routing Protocol for Low-Power and Lossy Networks, RFC 6550, 2012.
8. C. Bormann, A. Castellani, and Z. Shelby, "CoAP: An application protocol for billions of tiny Internet nodes," IEEE Internet Comput., vol. 1, no. 2, pp. 62–67, Mar./Apr. 2012.
9. J. Granjal, E. Monteiro, J. Sá Silva, Security for the internet of things: a survey of existing protocols and open research issues, *IEEE Communication. Surveys Tutorials* 17, 2015.
10. A. Raoof, A. Matrawy and C. -H. Lung, "Routing Attacks and Mitigation Methods for RPL-Based Internet of Things," in *IEEE Communications Surveys & Tutorials*, vol. 21, no. 2, pp. 1582-1606, Second Quarter 2019, doi: 10.1109/COMST.2018.2885894.
11. X. Vilajosana, T. Watteyne, T. Chang, M. Vučinić, S. Duquennoy and P. Thubert, "IETF 6TiSCH: A Tutorial," in *IEEE Communications Surveys & Tutorials*, vol. 22, no. 1, pp. 595-615, First quarter 2020, doi: 10.1109/COMST.2019.2939407.

3 ARDUINO PROGRAMMING

UNIT SPECIFICS

In this unit, the following aspects will be discussed:

- Introduction to Arduino: Understanding the hardware components and functions
- Basic Arduino programming using the C/C++ language
- Arduino is integrated with sensors, actuators, and other electronic components
- Creating and simulating Arduino-based circuits with tools such as Tinkercad.
- Arduino's real-world applications include home automation, robotics, and IoT

Hands-on projects including circuit assembly and Arduino programming are offered to help students learn the material more practically. Some commonly used libraries and functions are introduced to help you understand programming principles. Diagrams are used to demonstrate key design principles and hardware setups.

This section includes exercises with theoretical and practical problems, multiple-choice questions, a reference list, and recommended reading to help students learn via experimentation and experience. QR codes are used to give students additional information and resources, such as tutorials, sample projects, and advanced Arduino subjects.

RATIONALE

This Arduino fundamentals unit covers both the hardware and programming components of the platform. The subject focuses on the integration of sensors, actuators, and other components with Arduino, allowing students to construct and simulate fundamental circuits. Key programming constructs in C/C++ are discussed, as well as typical libraries and functions found in Arduino

projects. Real-world applications, such as home automation and robotics, are investigated to demonstrate Arduino's adaptability in practical situations. The section offers exercises and examples to assist students grasp the procedures involved in circuit design and programming, which promotes hands-on learning. The content given in this lesson lays a solid basis for working with Arduino and piques students' curiosity in embedded systems and IoT applications.

PRE-REQUISITES

No prerequisites are required for studying this unit. .

UNIT OUTCOMES

The list of outcomes of this unit is as follows:

U3-O1: Understand architecture of Arduino, including microcontrollers, sensors, and actuators

U3-O2: Learn programming for Arduino and apply them to develop basic projects

U3-O3: Integrate Arduino with sensors and actuators

U3-O4: Simulate and test Arduino-based circuits

U3-O5: Explore Arduino's role in IoT applications and analyze its scalability and relevance in building innovative solutions

Unit Outcomes	Expected Mapping with Course Outcomes *(1- Weak Correlation; 2- Medium correlation; 3- Strong Correlation)*				
	CO-1	**CO-2**	**CO-3**	**CO-4**	**CO-5**
U3-O1	3	2	1	2	1
U3-O2	3	3	3	3	1
U3-O3	3	3	3	3	2
U3-O4	3	3	3	3	2
U3-O5	3	3	3	3	3

3.1 What is Arduino?

Arduino is an open-source electronic platform for doing hardware and software applications.

3.1.1 History

Hernando Barragán (creator of Wiring), Massimo Banzi and David Cuartielles created **Arduino** in 2005 at the Interaction Design Institute Ivrea, Italy [1]. David Mellis developed the Arduino software. Gianluca Martino and Tom Igoe joined the project, and the five (Massimo Banzi, David Cuartielles, Tom Igoe, Gianluca Martino, and David Mellis) are known as the original founders of Arduino. Figure 3.1 shows a picture of an Arduino UNO board.

Figure 3.1: Arduino UNO

They created a simple inexpensive device for students which is easy to connect and easy to program. For doing this, they selected the AVR family of 8-bit microcontroller (MCU or µC) devices from Atmel and designed a self-contained circuit board. They wrote bootloader firmware for the microcontroller, and packaged it all into a simple **integrated development environment (IDE)** that used programs called "sketches." The result was the easy-to-use programmable device, Arduino. Arduino is used to design different projects. Arduino boards read inputs and produce output.

3.1.2 ATmega168 Microchip

Basic arduino board consists of microprocessors and controllers. There are varieties of Arduino boards found, such as Arduino UNO, Arduino Nano, Arduino Mega, Arduino Due, Arduino Bluetooth etc.. Different arduino boards have different I/O pins and sizes. Initially arduino boards used the FTDI USB-to-UART serial chip and an ATmega168 [2] as shown in Figure 3.2. The Uno board used the ATmega328P microcontroller and an ATmega16U2 (Atmega8U2 up to version R2) programmed as a USB-to-serial converter.

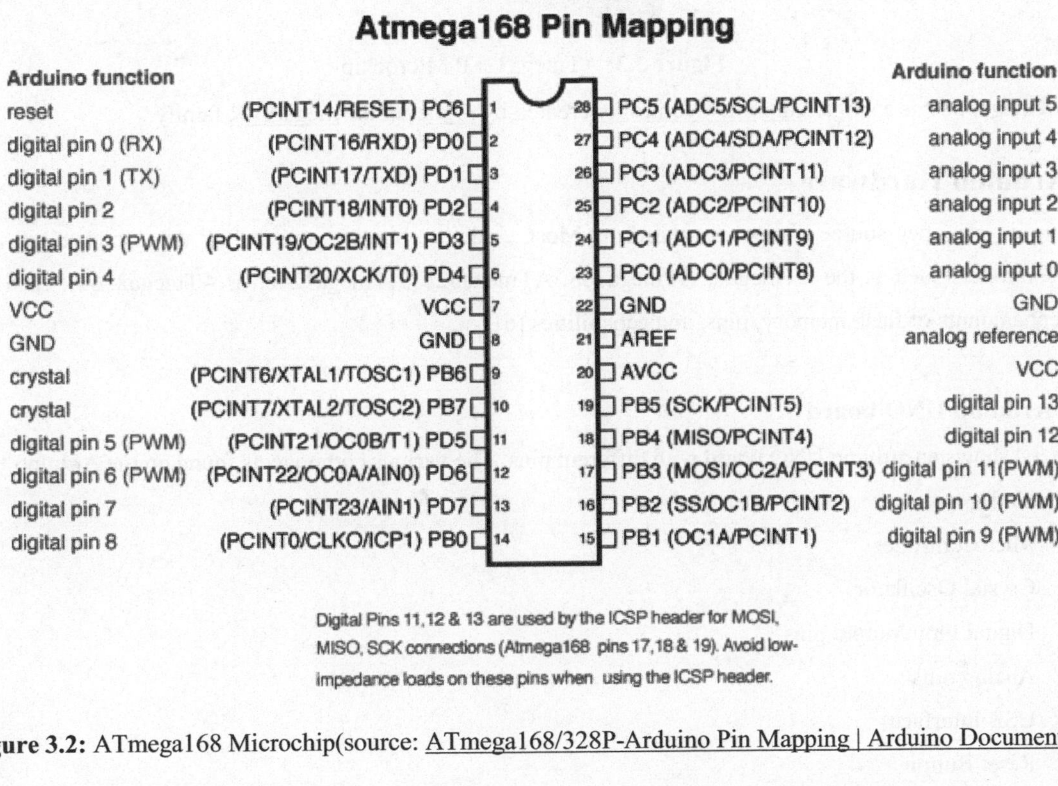

Figure 3.2: ATmega168 Microchip(source: ATmega168/328P-Arduino Pin Mapping | Arduino Documentation)

Arduino boards [2] consist of a printed circuit board (PCB) with an ATmega328 microcontroller, an IDE based on Processing and library functions to easily program the microcontroller [3]. The **ATmega328P** [5] is a high-performance, low-power Microchip picoPower 8-bit AVR® RISC-based microcontroller combines 32 KB ISP

Flash memory with read-while-write capabilities, 1024B EEPROM, 2 KB SRAM, 23 general purpose I/O lines, 32 general purpose working registers, three flexible timer/counters with compare modes, internal and external interrupts, serial programmable USART, a byte-oriented Two-Wire serial interface, SPI serial port, a 6-channel 10-bit A/D converter (8-channels in TQFP and QFN/MLF packages), programmable watchdog timer with internal oscillator, and five software selectable power saving modes. The device operates between 1.8-5.5 volts. Figure 3.3 shows ATmega328P in 32-pin thin quad flat pack.

Figure 3.3: ATmega328P Microchip

The **ATmega328P** is a single-chip microcontroller created by Atmel in the megaAVR family.

3.2 Arduino Hardware

Arduino is an open-source hardware platform. Most Arduino boards consists of an Atmel 8-bit AVR microcontroller (such as the ATmega8, ATmega168, ATmega328, ATmega1280, or ATmega2560), each with different amounts of flash memory, pins, and capabilities [6].

3.2.1 Arduino UNO board

Figure 3.4 shows an arduino UNO board with different pins. The various components found on the Arduino UNO board include:

a. Microcontroller
b. Crystal Oscillator
c. Digital Input/output pins
d. Analog pins
e. USB Interface
f. Reset Button
g. USB connector
h. DC Barrel Jack

i. Power pins
j. AREF pin
k. LED's
l. Voltage Regulator
m. I2C
n. SPI

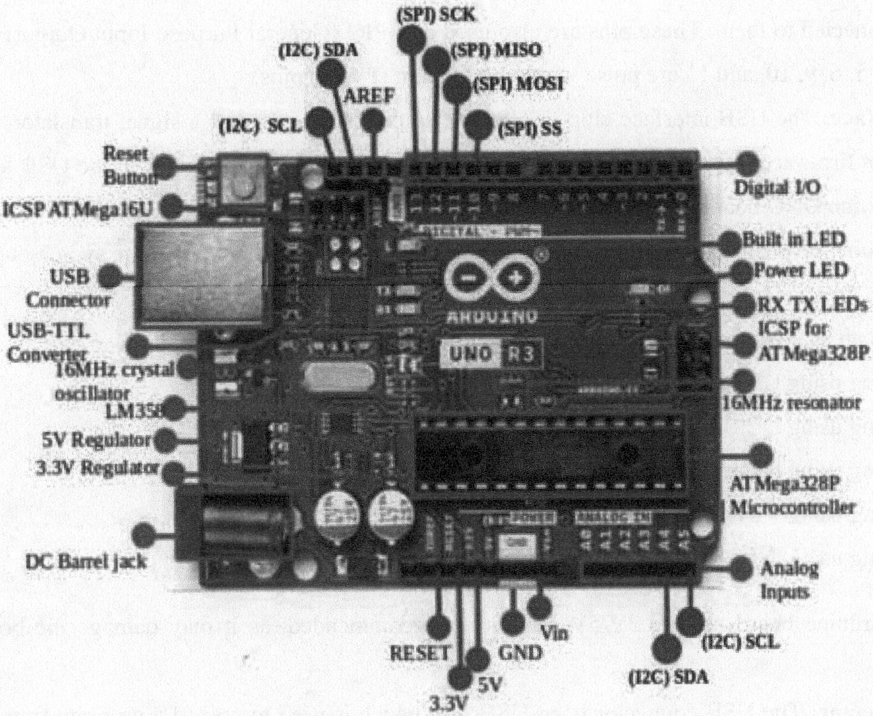

Figure 3.4: Arduino Uno board

a. **Microcontroller:** ATMega328P microcontroller is the heart of the Arduino UNO. The 16MHz resonator provides necessary clock signal to the ATMega328P for operation. The reset button helps to reset the ATMega328P. ATmega328P has 14 Digital I/O Pins. Out of the 14 pins, 6 provide PWM (pulse width modulation) output. The USB connector and DC barrel jack on the left side used to power the Arduino either through the USB port or the barrel jack. On the UNO board, there is another microcontroller, the ATMega16U, which functions as a USB-to-TTL converter. The ICSP ATMega16U port is used to burn the firmware.
b. **Crystal Oscillator:** A microcontroller needs a clock source to operate. The ATMega series microcontroller uses two types of clock sources, internal RC oscillator and external clock generator. The built-in internal oscillator lacks accuracy. Therefore, a 16MHz crystal oscillator is used as an external clock generator for the ATMega16U2 chip, and a 16MHz resonator is used for the ATMega328P microcontroller.

c. **Digital Input/output:** The Arduino UNO has 14 digital I/O pins from D0 to D13 as shown in figure 3.3. The digital I/O pins are 5V logic level with the value HIGH or LOW. We can also use the Analog pins as digital I/O too. The two pins '0' and '1' are used to **receive (RX) and transmit (TX)** serial data. Additionally, on pin 12, the TX pin flashes the in-built LED when data is being sent, while the RX pin flashes when data is being received. Pins 2 and 3 can be configured to act as external interrupts. These can trigger specific functions to run when a change is detected, such as when a button is pressed or released.

d. **Analog pins:** Pins labeled A0 to A5 are analog pins. Their primary function is to read signals from analog sensors connected to them. These pins are also used as GPIO (General Purpose Input/Output) pins. The pin numbers 3, 5, 6, 9, 10, and 11 are pulse width modulation (PWM) pins.

e. **USB Interface:** The USB interface chip or USB-TTL converter is used as a signal translator. ATMega16U with custom firmware is used for the USB-TTL interface chip. It converts signals in the USB level to a level that an Arduino UNO board understands.

f. **Reset Button:** Reset pin is used to reset the ATMega328 microcontroller. When the switch is pressed it sets all values to their default values.

Arduino board can be powered by dedicated connectors or dedicated pins:

- Powering using USB connector
- Powering using DC Barrel jack
- Powering using battery connector (if available on the board)
- Powering using VIN pin
- Powering using 3.3V/5V pin

Powering the arduino board using 3.3V/5V pins is not recommended, as it may damage the board's voltage regulator.

g. **USB Connector:** The USB connector is an USB port which is used to upload a program from the Arduino IDE onto the Arduino board. This port can also be used to power the Arduino board.

h. **DC Barrel Jack:** This is used to supply power to the Arduino UNO. A 12V or 9V DC adapter is used on this Jack to power the Arduino board.

i. **Power pins:** The **Vin, 5V, 3.3V, and GND pins** are Arduino power pins [7]. The **Vin** pin is used for input voltage for regulated external power supplies and recommended without a barrel jack connector. This pin can also work as a voltage output when an external power supply is connected to the barrel jack connector. This pin does not have reverse polarity protection. Therefore, it is not recommended, as it may damage the board's voltage regulator. You cannot power your sensors and modules from the Vin pin. The **5V and 3.3V (3V3)** can work as power outputs since these pins are directly connected to the onboard 3V3 and 5V voltage regulators outputs [7]. Additionally, 5V and 3.3V pins are also used for power inputs if no regulated power supply is connected through the other power inputs, such as USB port, barrel jack connector or VIN pin. 5V and 3.3V pins are not recommended for power inputs. Sometimes, large current may flow into the voltage regulator from its output pin to its input pin. This large current may permanently damage the arduino board's voltage regulator. The **ground (GND) pin** acts as a pin with zero voltage.

j. **AREF:** The analog reference (AREF) pin is used to set an upper limit to the voltage to the Arduino UNO board from the external power supply.

k. **LED's**: The **RX and TX LED's** stand for receive and transmit LEDs. These are indicator LEDs which blink whenever the UNO board transmits or receives data. The **Power LED Indicator** is ON mean the power is activated. When the power is OFF, the LED will not light up. The **built-in LED** is present near pin #13. It is identified by the letter L. In most arduino boards, the *digital pin 13* is connected to an on-board LED in series with a resistor. The constant LED_BUILTIN is the number of the pin to which the on-board LED is connected.

l. **Voltage Regulator:** The voltage regulator converts the input voltage to 5V. The ATMega328 and ATmega16U2 have a maximum input voltage of around 5V. The Arduino can accept 7-12V through the Vin pin or the DC barrel jack and step it down. There are two regulators on board 5V and 3.3V. 5V regulator is used for the microcontrollers and the other one is a 3.3V regulator which is used to provide 3.3V through 3.3V pin.

m. **I2C:** I2C is a 2-wire serial communication protocol (SDA and SCL) ideal for short-range data transfer. It is commonly used to interface sensors, displays, and communication modules. Supporting multiple master and slave devices, the Arduino Uno provides one I2C port located on pins A4 (SDA) and A5 (SCL).

n. **SPI:** SPI is a 4-wire serial communication protocol (MOSI, MISO, SCK, and CS) designed for high-speed data transfer. It is commonly used for peripherals like SD cards, LCD displays, and sensors. The Arduino Uno features one SPI port on pins 10 (SS), 11 (MOSI), 12 (MISO), and 13(SCK).

3.2.2 Types of Arduino Boards

In this section, we will discuss the different types of Arduino boards.

Arduino Nano: The Arduino Nano is a compact, complete, breadboard-compatible board based on the ATmega328 (Arduino Nano 3.x). It provides almost the same capabilities as the Arduino Duemilanove (ATmega328) but in a different package. It only has a DC power jack and operates with a Mini-B USB cable rather than a standard one. Its compact size has made it a popular choice for embedded systems and other projects where space efficiency and flexibility are more important.

MEGA 25560 rev 3: The Arduino Mega 2560 is a fully equipped microcontroller board based on the ATmega2560. You can simply connect it via USB or power it with an adapter or battery to get started. It's compatible with most Uno shields and is ideal for tasks requiring many I/O pins or multitasking, such as data logging or motor control. Its robust features and connectivity make it a top choice for advanced projects.

Arduino pro mini: The Arduino Pro Mini is a compact, low-power microcontroller board based on the ATmega328P. It is ideal for space-limited, semi-permanent installations. Available in 3.3V and 5V versions, it is perfect for permanent setups. Its header-free design offers flexibility for connectors or direct soldering.

Arduino Micro: The Micro is a microcontroller board based on the ATmega32U4, which was developed in collaboration with Adafruit.The Micro board, like the Arduino Leonardo, features the ATmega32U4 with built-in USB communication, removing the need for a secondary processor. This enables the Micro to function as a mouse, keyboard, and virtual (CDC) serial/COM port when connected to a computer.

Uno R4 WiFi: The Arduino UNO R4 WiFi integrates the processing power of the RA4M1 microcontroller with the wireless capabilities of the ESP32-S3. It features a 12x8 LED matrix, a Qwiic connector, VRTC, and OFF pin, making it versatile for any project. This board allows for easy wireless connectivity upgrades, catering to both beginners and experienced makers.

MKR WAN 1300/1310: The Arduino MKR 1310 is an ideal entry point to IoT and LoRa technology, offering quick connectivity to the internet from anywhere with LoRa coverage. It's also suitable for developers and makers aiming to build IoT projects that require dependable, low-power, and long-distance communication, such as for organizations and educational purposes.

Arduino Due: The Arduino Due is the first Arduino board based on a 32-bit ARM core microcontroller. Arduino Due is ideal for large scale Arduino projects as it is based on the Atmel SAM3X8E ARM Cortex-M3 CPU. The Arduino Due board operates at 3.3V which makes it different from other Arduino boards. In fact, the I/O pins have a maximum voltage tolerance of 3.3V. Any I/O pin that receives a voltage higher than 3.3V may damage the board.

Arduino Uno R3: The Arduino Uno R3 is a microcontroller board based on the ATmega328, the third and the latest revision of the Arduino Uno. It supports the microcontroller via USB cable or AC-to-DC adapter. Unlike previous boards, it doesn't use the FTDI driver chip and features an ATmega16U2 USB-to-serial converter with its own USB bootloader for advanced user use.

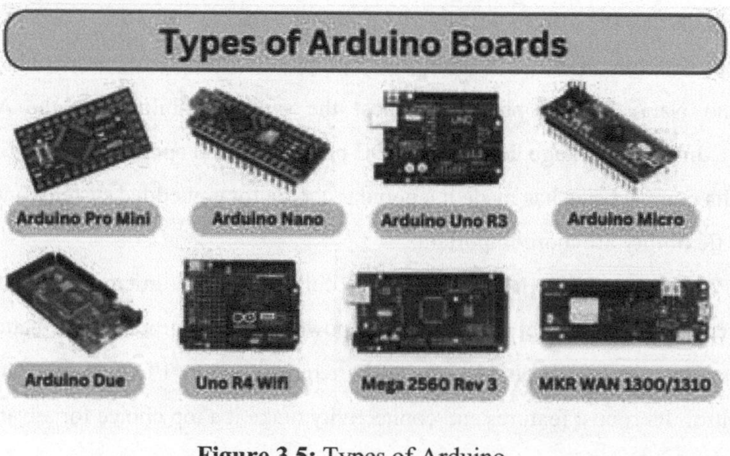

Figure 3.5: Types of Arduino

3.3 Arduino Software (IDE)

Arduino is programmed using a software called Arduino Integrated Development Environment (IDE) as shown in figure 3.6. IDE platform is used for writing, compiling, and uploading code to Arduino-compatible boards. The Arduino IDE is open-source, simple and user-friendly software for beginners and advanced users.

Figure 3.6: Arduino IDE icon (Icon copied from the source)

The Arduino IDE contains a **text editor** for writing code, a message area, a text console, a toolbar with buttons for common functions and a series of menus. The IDE upload program directly to the Arduino board via a USB connection.

3.3.1 Software Download and installation

Download Arduino IDE from this website:
https://www.arduino.cc/en/software as shown in figure 3.7.

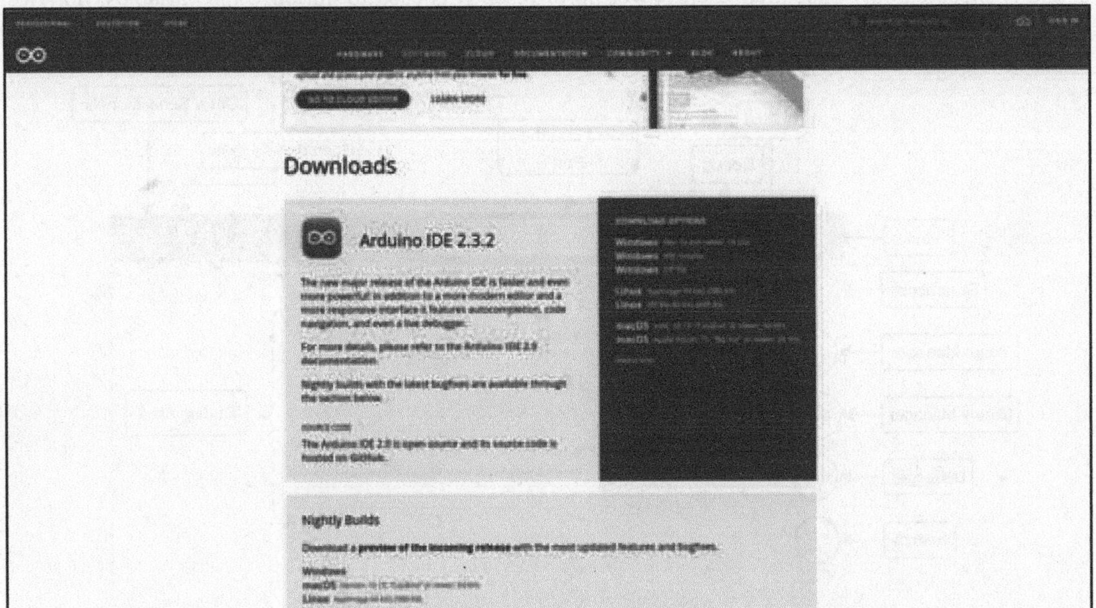

Figure 3.7: Arduino Downloads

There are currently two versions of the Arduino IDE, one is the IDE 1.x.x and the other is IDE 2.x. The IDE 2.x includes a modern editor, interface and advanced features to help users with their coding and debugging. Follow the following steps to download the IDE.

a. Download and install the Arduino Software IDE in different environments by using the given link: https://docs.arduino.cc/software/ide-v2/tutorials/getting-started/ide-v2-downloading-and-installing/

b. Connect your Arduino board to your device.

c. Open the Arduino Software (IDE) by double clicking the Arduino IDE icon.

3.3.2 Basics of Arduino programming

In this section, we will discuss basics of arduino programming and basic syntax, such as variables, data types, operators and control structures.

3.3.2.1 Structure of an Arduino sketch

Sketches: Arduino Software (IDE) - connects to the Arduino boards to upload programs and communicate with them. Programs written using Arduino Software (IDE) are called **sketches** as shown in Figure 3.8. These sketches are written in the text editor and are **saved** with the file extension **.ino**. The Arduino IDE uses a simplified version of C++ programming language. Figure 3.8 shows the editor of Sketch.

The Arduino IDE has two common functions:

- setup()
- loop()

These **two functions** are called automatically in the background. The **setup()** function is called when a sketch starts and is executed only once after each power up or reset. It is used to initialize the variables, libraries, pin modes etc. The **loop()** function runs consecutively until power is lost or a new sketch is loaded.

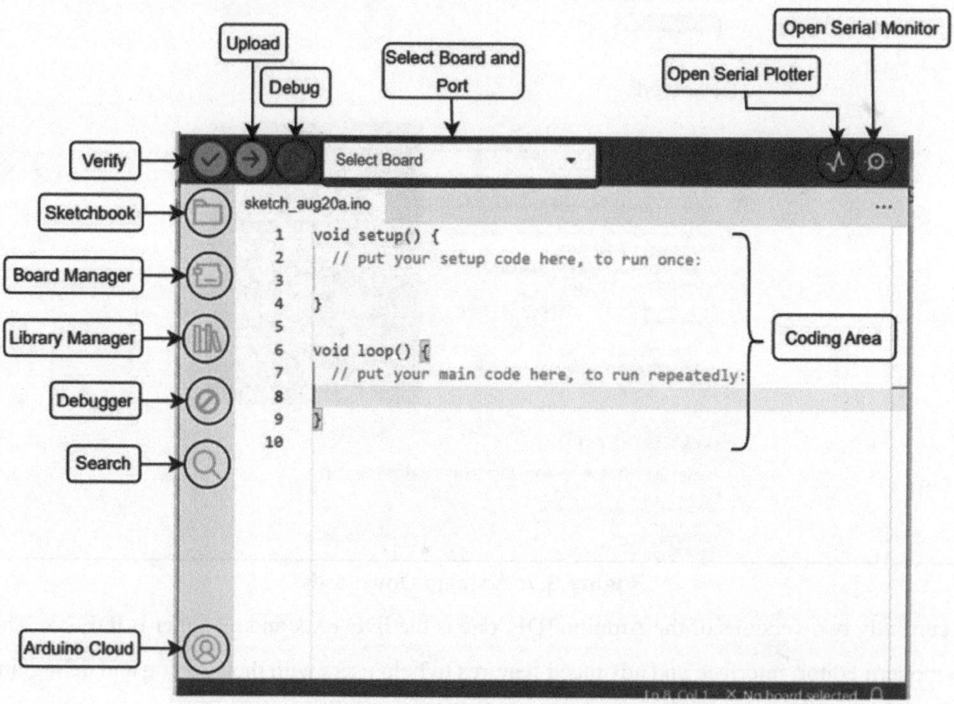

Figure 3.8: Sketch

3.3.2.2 Basic syntax

It generally follows the basics of C programming syntax.

A. Variables

In Arduino programming, understanding variable scope is essential for knowing about the variables used.

i) Variable scope: Variables in Arduino follow the C programming language which has a property called **Scope.** A scope defines a region within a program where variables can be declared, and there are three locations where this can occur.

Within a function or block, variables are declared as **local variables**. When defining function parameters, they are known as **formal parameters**. Variables declared outside of all functions are referred to as **global variables.**

ii) Local Variables: These variables can only be accessed by the statements within that specific function or block of code. Local variables are not accessible to any functions outside their own scope. Below is an example demonstrating the use of local variables:

```
void setup () {
}
void loop () {
    int a , b ;
    int c ; // Local variable declaration
    a = 10;
    b = 20; //actual initialization
    c = 30;
}
```

iii) Global Variables: These are defined outside of the all function, typically at the beginning of the program. They retain their value throughout the entire lifetime of the program.

Any function within the program can access a global variable, making it available for use across the entire program once it has been declared.

```
// Global variable
int globalVar = 10;
void setup() {
    // Iniialize serial communication at 9600 bits per second:
    Serial.begin(9600);
    // Print the global variable
    Serial.print("Global variable value: ");
    Serial.println(globalVar);
}
```

```
void loop() {
        // Local variable
        int localVar = 20;
        // Print the local variable
        Serial.print("Local variable value: ");
        Serial.println(localVar);
        // Add some delay so it doesn't print too fast
        delay(1000);
}
```

Output:

Global variable value: 10

Local variable value: 20

Local variable value: 20

Local variable value: 20

Local variable value: 20

B. Data types

In Arduino programming, data types define the type and size of data that a variable can hold. Table 3.1 listed some of the commonly Arduino data types (with examples):

Table 3.1: Data types

S. No.	Data Types	Uses	Example

1.	void	Indicates that a function does not return a value.	void setup() {
			// Code to initialize the program
			}

2.	Boolean	Represents true or false values	boolean ledOn = true;
3.	char	Stores a single character (1 byte)	char letter = 'B';
4.	unsigned char	Stores a small positive number (0 to 255)	unsigned char smallNumber = 253;
5.	byte	Stores an 8-bit unsigned number (0 to 255)	byte pinNumber = 11;
6.	int	Stores a 16-bit integer (-32,768 to 32,767)	int temperature = 27;
7.	unsigned int	Stores a 16-bit unsigned integer (0 to 65,535)	unsigned int distance = 102;

S. No.	Data Types	Uses	Example
8.	word	Stores a 16-bit unsigned number (same as unsigned int)	word sensorValue = 1024;
9.	long	Stores a 32-bit integer	long largeNumber = 100000L;
10.	unsigned long	Stores a 32-bit unsigned integer	unsigned long timer = millis();
11.	short	Stores a 16-bit integer (same as int but can be used for clarity)	short height = 156;
12.	float	Stores a 32-bit floating-point number	float pi = 3.14;
13.	double	Stores a 32-bit floating-point number (on Arduino, double is the same as float)	double gravity = 9.80;
14.	array	Stores a collection of values of the same data type	int scores[] = {10, 20, 30, 40, 50};
15.	String (char array)	Stores a sequence of characters in a character array	char name[] = "Arduino";
16.	String (object)	Stores a sequence of characters using the String class	String greeting = "Hello, world!";

C. Operators

Operators in Arduino programming are symbols that instruct the compiler to perform specific mathematical, logical, or bitwise operations. Below is the brief overview of the common types of oper1ators in Arduino, (with examples):

i) Arithmetic Operators: These operators are used to perform basic *mathematical operations* as shown in table 3.2 (with examples):

Table 3.2: Arithmetic Operators

Operators	Examples
Addition ('+')	int sum = 5 + 4; // sum is 9
Subtraction ('-')	int difference = 10 - 3; // difference is 7
Multiplication ('*')	int product = 7 * 3; // product is 21
Division ('/')	int quotient = 6 / 2; // quotient is 3
Modulus ('%')	int remainder = 9 % 4; // remainder is 1

ii) Comparison Operators: These operators are used to Compare two values and return *true* or *false* as shown in table 3.3 (with examples):

Table 3.3: Comparison Operators

Operators	Examples
Equal to ('==')	boolean result = (7 == 7); // result is true
Not equal to ('!=')	boolean result = (6 != 3); // result is true
Greater than ('>')	boolean result = (8 > 3); // result is true
Less than ('<')	boolean result = (2 < 5); // result is true
Greater than or equal to ('>=')	boolean result = (5 >= 5); // result is true
Less than or equal to ('<=')	boolean result = (3 <= 4); // result is true

iii) Boolean Operators: These operators are used to perform logical operations on boolean values as shown in table 3.4 (with examples):

Table 3.4: Boolean Operators

<table>
<tr><th>Operators</th><th>Examples</th></tr>
<tr><td>Logical AND ('&&')</td><td>boolean result = (true && false); // result is false</td></tr>
<tr><td>Logical OR ('||')</td><td>boolean result = (true || false); // result is true</td></tr>
<tr><td>Logical NOT ('!')</td><td>boolean result = !true; // result is false</td></tr>
</table>

iv) Bitwise Operators: These operators are used to perform operations on individual bits of integer types as shown in table 3.5 with examples:

Table 3.5: Bitwise Operators

<table>
<tr><th>Operators</th><th>Examples</th></tr>
<tr><td>AND ('&')</td><td>int result = 6 & 3; // result is 2 (binary: 0110 & 0011 = 0010)</td></tr>
<tr><td>OR ('|')</td><td>int result = 6 | 3; // result is 7 (binary: 0110 | 0011 = 0111)</td></tr>
</table>

Operators	Examples
XOR ('^')	int result = 6 ^ 3; // result is 5 (binary: 0110 ^ 0011 = 0101)
NOT ('~')	int result = ~6; // result is -7 (binary: ~0110 = 1001, inverting all bits)
Shift left ('<<')	int result = 3 << 2; // result is 12 (binary: 0011 << 2 = 1100)
Shift right ('>>')	int result = 8 >> 1; // result is 4 (binary: 1000 >> 1 = 0100)

v) Compound Operators: These operators are used to combine arithmetic operations with assignment as shown in table 3.6 with example.

Table 3.6: Compound Operators

Operators	Examples
Addition assignment ('+=')	int a = 5; a += 4; // a is now 9
Subtraction assignment ('-=')	int b = 10; b -= 5; // b is now 5
Multiplication assignment ('*=')	int c = 7; c *= 3; // c is now 21
Division assignment ('/=')	int d = 24; d /= 4; // d is now 6
Modulus assignment ('%=')	int e = 9; e %= 4; // e is now 1

D. Control structures

Decision-making structures in programming involve specifying one or more conditions to be evaluated by the program. Based on whether these conditions are true or false, certain statements or blocks of code are executed as shown in figure 3.9.

The general form of these structures typically includes: -

Condition: The criteria that are evaluated.

Statements for True: The code that runs if the condition is true.

Optional Statements for False: The code that runs if the condition is false.

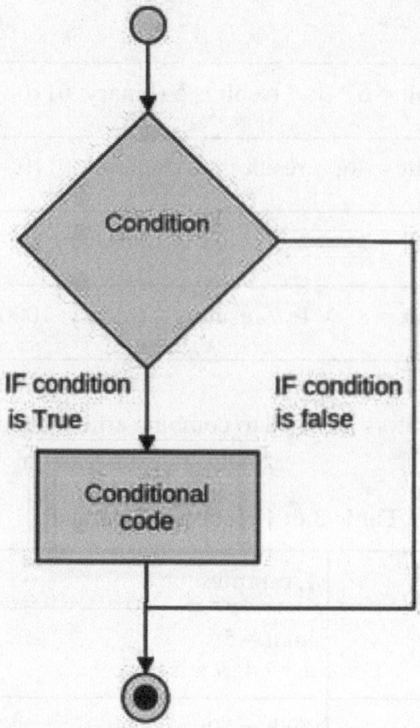

Figure 3.9: Control Structure flowchart

Table 3.7: Control Structures

Statement	Explanation
If Statement	Executes a block of code only if a specific condition is true. If the condition is false, the code inside the block is skipped.
If…else Statement	Provides an alternative action if the initial condition is false. If the condition is true, one block of code is executed; if false, a different block of code is executed.
If…else if…else Statement	Checks multiple conditions in sequence. If the first condition is false, it checks the next one, and so on, until it finds a true condition or reaches the final *'else'* block.
Switch Case Statement	Similar to multiple *'if'* statements, this statement lets you execute different blocks of code depending on the value of a variable. It's useful when you have many conditions to check.
Conditional Operator ('? :')	A shorthand way to write an *'if_else'* statement. It evaluates a condition and returns one value if true, and another if false.

3.3.2.3 Some useful functions

Functions enable you to structure programs into segments of code that perform specific tasks. A common reason for creating a function is when you need to execute the same action multiple times within a program. Table 3.8 shows some useful functions of Arduino.

Syntax:

```
returnType functionName(parameter1 Type parameter Name, parameter2 Type parameter Name, ...)
{
  // Function body: statements to be executed
  return returnValue; // If returnType is not void
}
```

Return Type: The data type of the value that the function returns. Use "void" if the function does not return a value.

Function Name: The name you choose for your function.

Parameter Type Parameter Name: The data type and name of each parameter the function takes.

Return returnValue: The value to be returned by the function (not needed if the return type is void).

Table 3.8: Useful functions of Arduino

Function	Definition
PinMode()	Used to configure a pin as an input or output
digitalWrite()	Used to set a digital pin to either HIGH or LOW
digitalRead()	Used to read the value from a digital pin
analogRead()	Used to read the value from an analog pin
analogWrite()	Used to set the PWM (Pulse Width Modulation) value on a pin
delay()	Used to pauses the program for a specified amount of time
millis()	Returns the number of milliseconds since the Arduino board began running the current program

pinMode(): This function is used to configure a specific pin on the Arduino as either an input or an output. For example, you might set a pin as an input to read data from a sensor, or as an output to control an LED.

digitalWrite(): This function is used to set a digital pin to either a high (5V) or low (0V) state. It is typically used to turn things on or off, such as an LED.

digitalRead(): This function reads the current state of a digital pin, either high or low. It's commonly used to check the status of a button or switch.

analogRead(): This function reads the value from an analog pin, which can range from 0 to 1023 on most Arduino boards. It is commonly used with sensors that provide a range of values rather than a simple on/off signal.

analogWrite(): This function writes an "analog" value (which is actually a PWM value) to a pin. It can be used to control the brightness of an LED or the speed of a motor. The value can range from 0 (off) to 255 (fully on).

delay(): This function pauses the program for a specified amount of time in milliseconds. For example, delay(1000) pauses the program for 1 second.

millis(): This function returns the number of milliseconds that have passed since the Arduino board began running the current program. It's useful for tracking time without pausing the program, allowing you to perform actions at regular intervals.

3.4 Examples of Arduino Programming

3.4.1 Overview of Tinkercad

In this section, we discussed how to use tinkercad software for easy understanding of arduino programming. In chapter 5, we will discuss the features of Tinkercad in detail with IoT case studies. Tinkercad is a free, web-based platform that enables users to design and simulate 3D objects, circuits, and Arduino projects. It is widely utilized for learning and prototyping, particularly in the fields of electronics, programming, and 3D modeling.

Figure 3.10: Tinkercad icon (Copied from the source)

To run a simulation in Tinkercad, follow these steps:

Step 1: Open a web browser and navigate to https://www.tinkercad.com/dashboard.

Step 2: Create an account by signing up with your email.

Step 3: Once signed in, create a new circuit by navigating to your profile and selecting **New Design → Circuit**, as shown in Figure 3.11.

Step 4: In the simulation workspace, drag and place the required components for your experiment.

Step 5: Write the program by clicking on the **Code** button, as shown in the figure 3.12.

Step 6: Start the simulation by pressing the **Start Simulation** button, as depicted in the Figure 3.12.

Figure 3.11: Tinkercad Dashboard

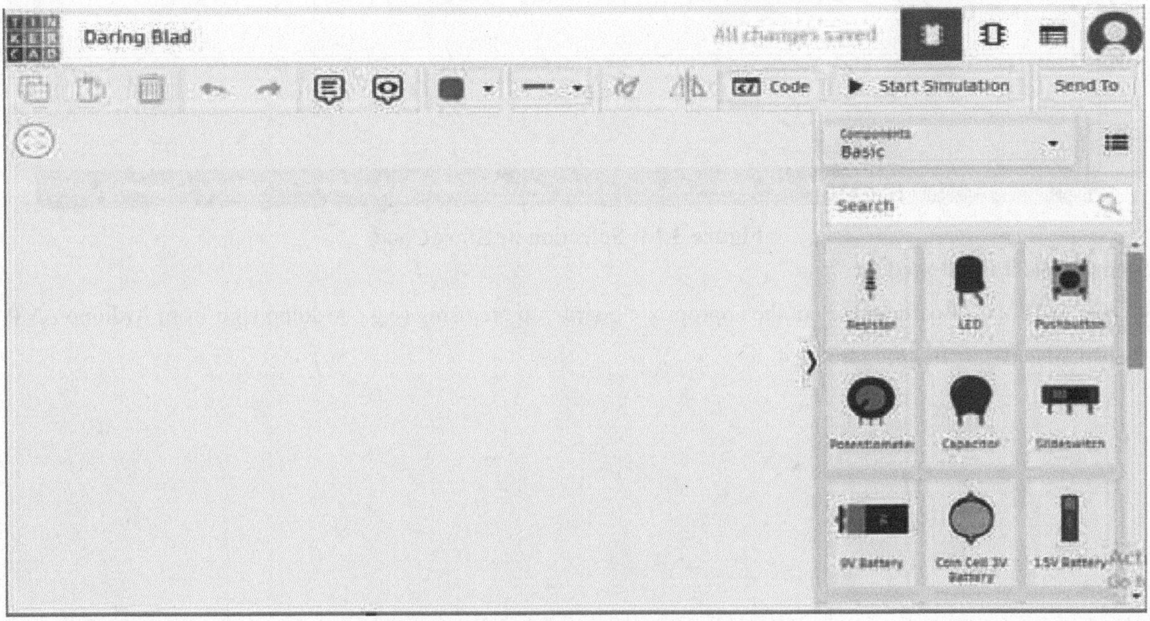

Figure 3.12: Tinkercad simulation setup

3.4.2 Simple code for blinking of LED (inbuilt)

Step-1: Select the Blink code

- Go to File > Examples > 01. Basics as shown in figure 3.13. Select the appropriate code for example ***Blink*** then you will be redirected to a new file with blink inbuilt code.

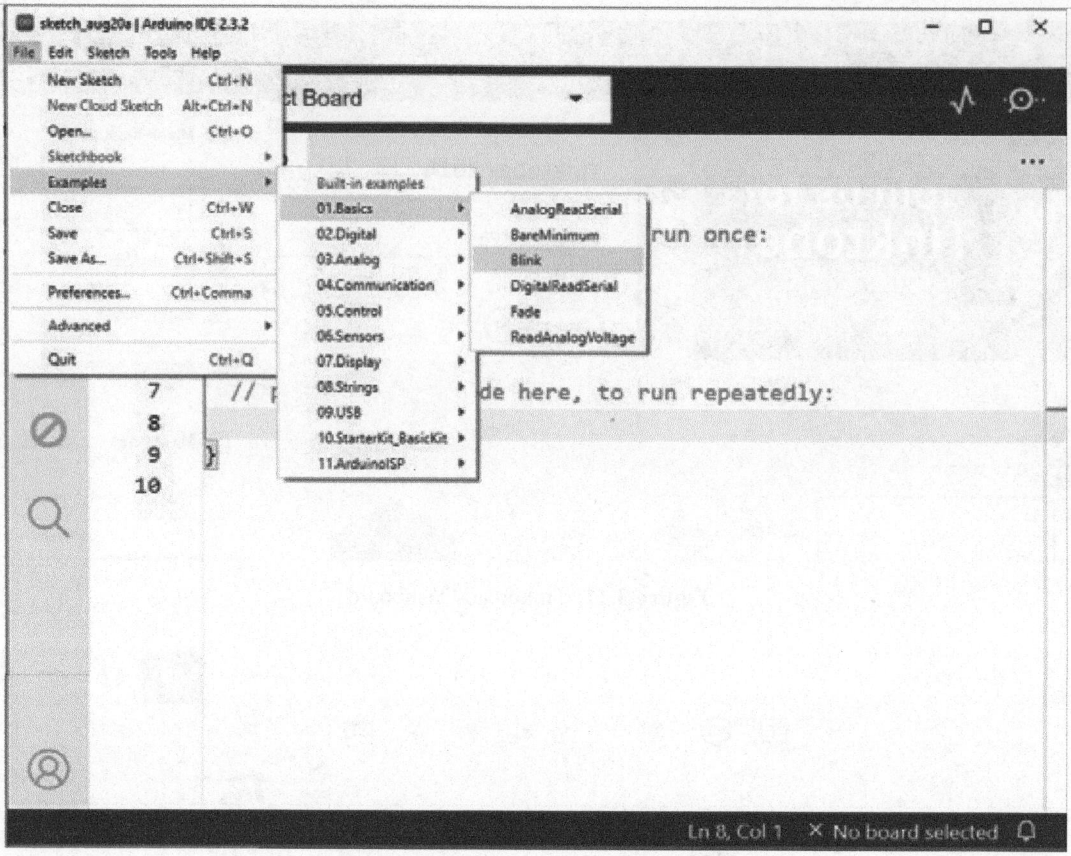

Figure 3.13: Selection of Blink Code

Step-2: Select the Board

- Go to Tools > Board and select the appropriate board you are using (e.g., Arduino Uno from Arduino AVR Boards) as shown in Figure 3.14.

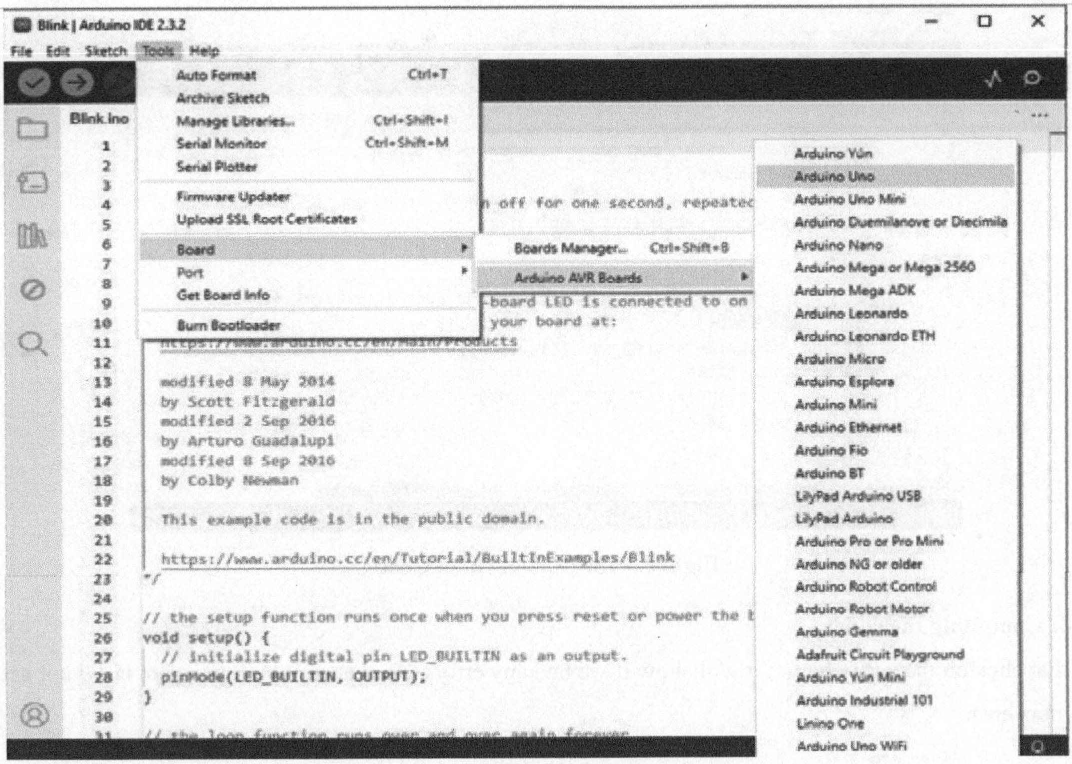

Figure 3.14: Selection of Arduino Uno Board

Step-3: Explanation of Default code

Default code will appear with all the instructions and it contains two functions as we discussed in Section **3.3.2.1.** The line **pinMode(LED_BUILTIN, OUTPUT)** configures the digital pin connected to the onboard LED as an output. **LED_BUILTIN** is a constant that refers to the pin connected to the onboard LED, typically **pin 13** on the Arduino Uno. The command **digitalWrite(LED_BUILTIN, HIGH)** is used to apply a voltage to the **LED_BUILTIN** pin, which corresponds to the built-in LED on the Arduino board. When this pin is set to **HIGH**, the LED lights up.

Following this, the **delay(1000)** function pauses the program for 1000 milliseconds, or 1 second, ensuring the LED stays illuminated during this time.

After the delay, the line **digitalWrite(LED_BUILTIN, LOW)** sets the **LED_BUILTIN** pin to **LOW**, cutting the voltage and turning off the LED. Another **delay(1000)** is called, which pauses the program for an additional second, keeping the LED off for this duration as shown in 3.15.

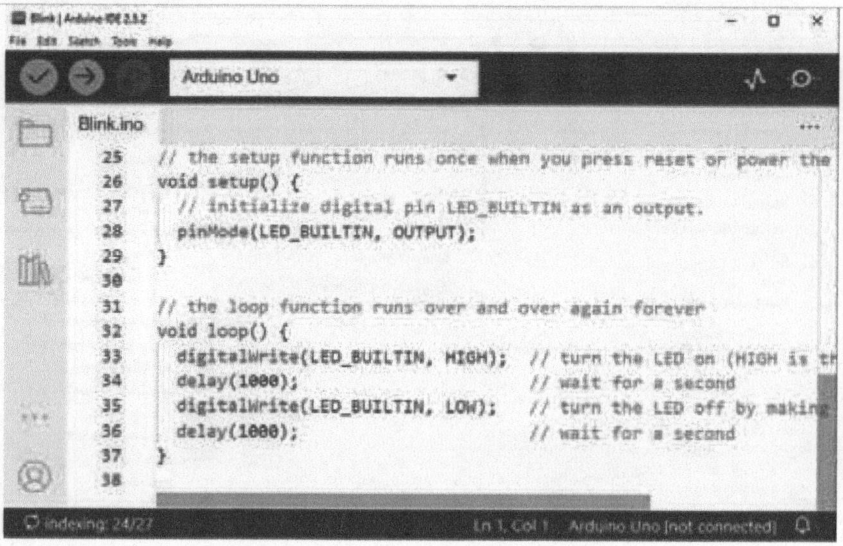

Figure 3.15: Default Blink Code

Step-4: Compiling the code:

After that click on the verify button it will show if we had any errors. As it is an inbuilt program it did not get any syntax error.

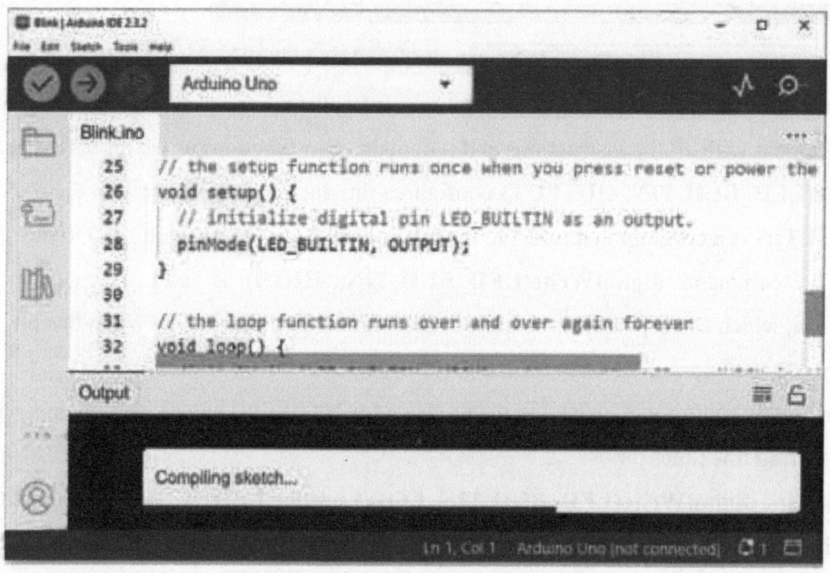

Figure 3.16: Compilation of Code

If done with the compilation without errors, we will see the below message. Before uploading code to the microcontroller, the IDE automatically verifies it. If errors are found, a prominent orange message box will appear above the compiler window, and the code cannot be uploaded until these issues are resolved.

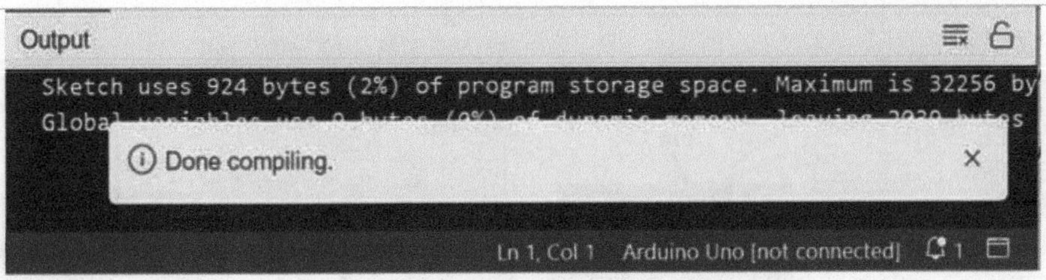

Figure 3.17: Message after Compilation

The other way of compiling is to go to Sketch → Verify/Compile in the Arduino IDE. After verifying, you can upload the code to the Arduino Uno.

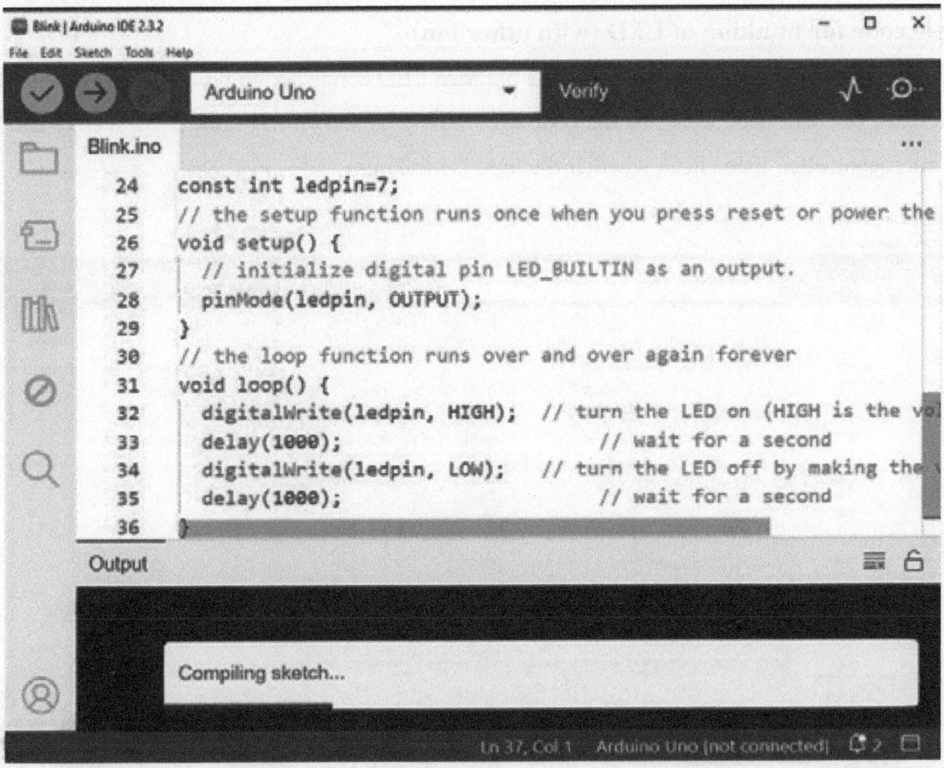

Figure 3.18: Alternate way of Code Compilation

Demonstration of Blinking of LED

For the demonstration of the output, we have included the figures below with the connections. We used Tinkercad to perform the simulation. The first figure shows the connections and the LED blinking. After every 1000 seconds, it will turn off. The second figure shows the LED turned off.

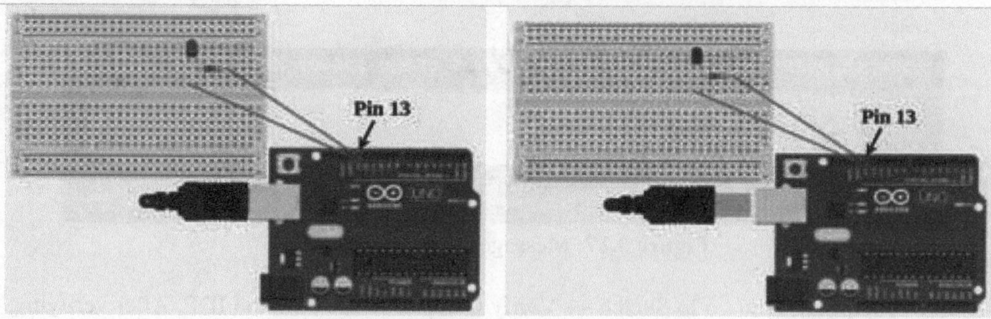

Figure 3.19: Blinking of LED

3.4.3 Simple code for blinking of LED (with other pin)

In the Arduino Uno, the default Blink code uses the onboard LED connected to pin 13. However, if you prefer to use pin 7 instead, you will need to adjust the code accordingly as shown in Figure 3.20. Verify and upload the code to the microcontroller, then check whether the light is blinking.

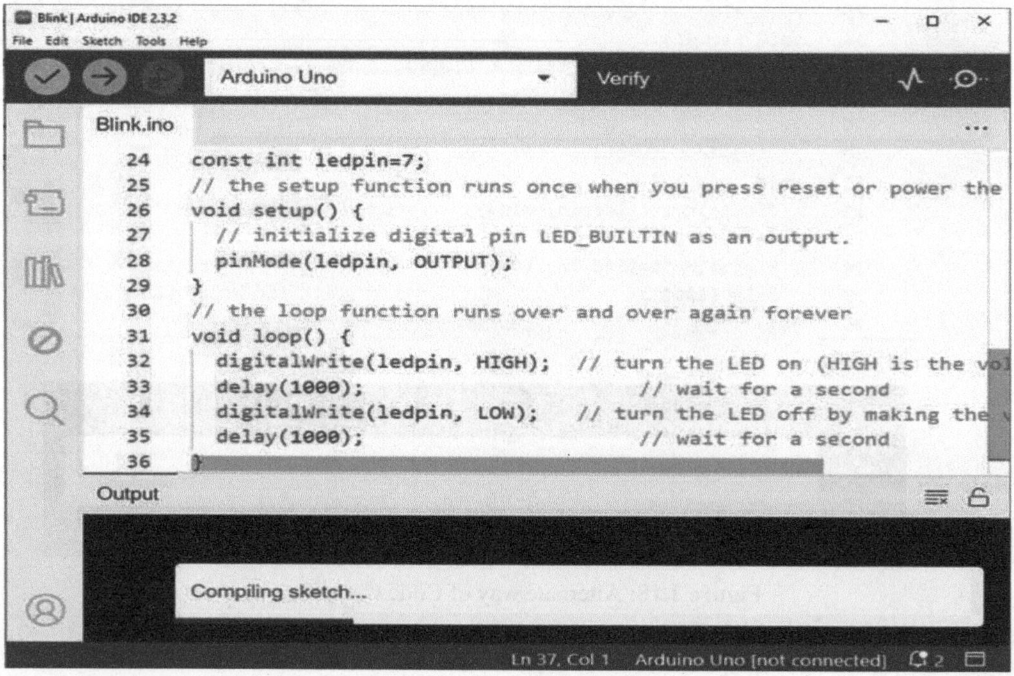

Figure 3.20: LED Blinking Code for Pin 7

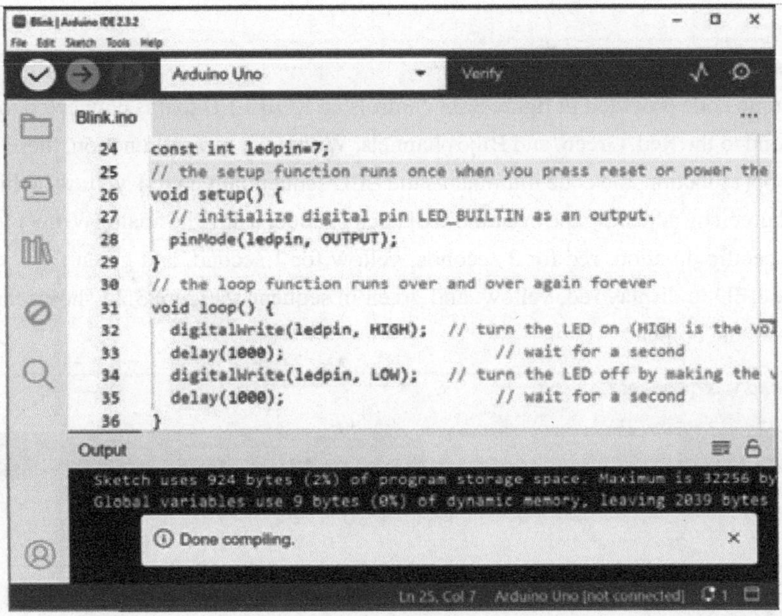

Figure 3.21: Compilation of Code

Figure 3.22 (a) shows the connections of **ledpin 7** with Arduino Uno.

We used Tinkercad to perform the simulation. The figure 3.22 (a) shows the connections and the figure 3.22 (b) shows the LED is blinking after compilation. After every 1000 seconds, it will turn off.

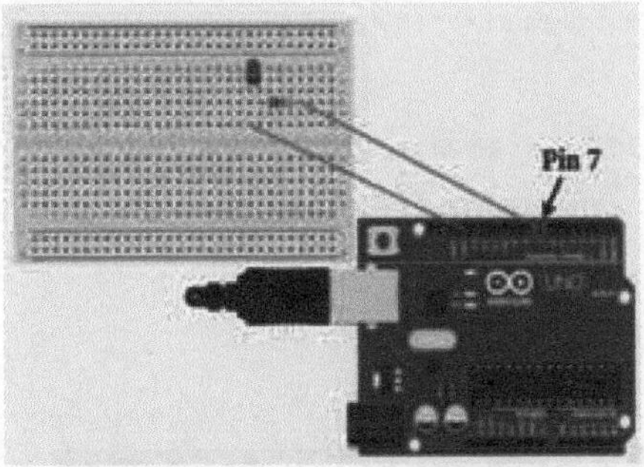

Figure 3.22 (a): Connection for Pin 7

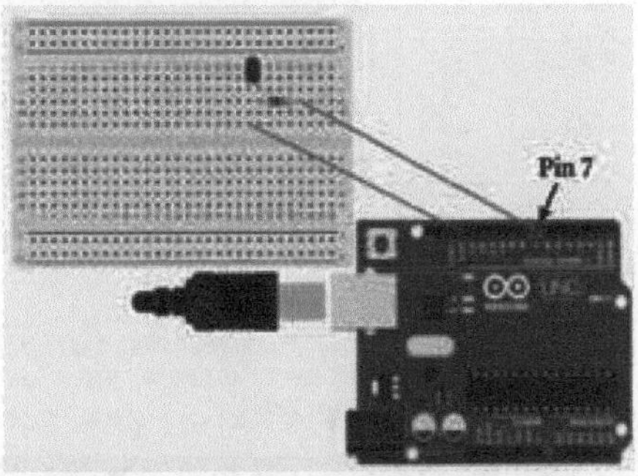

Figure 3.22 (b): LED is glowing

3.4.4 Simple Code for Traffic light using LED

We will discuss the code that controls an RGB LED connected to an Arduino, cycling through red, yellow, and green lights with specific delays.

Components:

- **RGB LED** (Common Cathode)
- **Resistors** (one for each color channel)
- **Arduino Uno**

- **Breadboard**
- **Jumper Wires**

The following Arduino code provided in figure 3.23 controls an RGB LED that is connected to pins 9, 10, and 11. These pins correspond to the Red, Green, and Blue channels. Within the setup() function, these pins are configured as outputs. In the loop() function, the code illuminates the LED sequentially in red, yellow (achieved by combining red and green), and green by adjusting the brightness of each channel using the analogWrite() function. Each color is displayed for a specific duration: red for 3 seconds, yellow for 1 second, and green for 3 seconds. This cycle repeats, causing the LED to display red, yellow, and green in sequence. Figure 3.24 shows the code compilation and figure 3.25 shows the output.

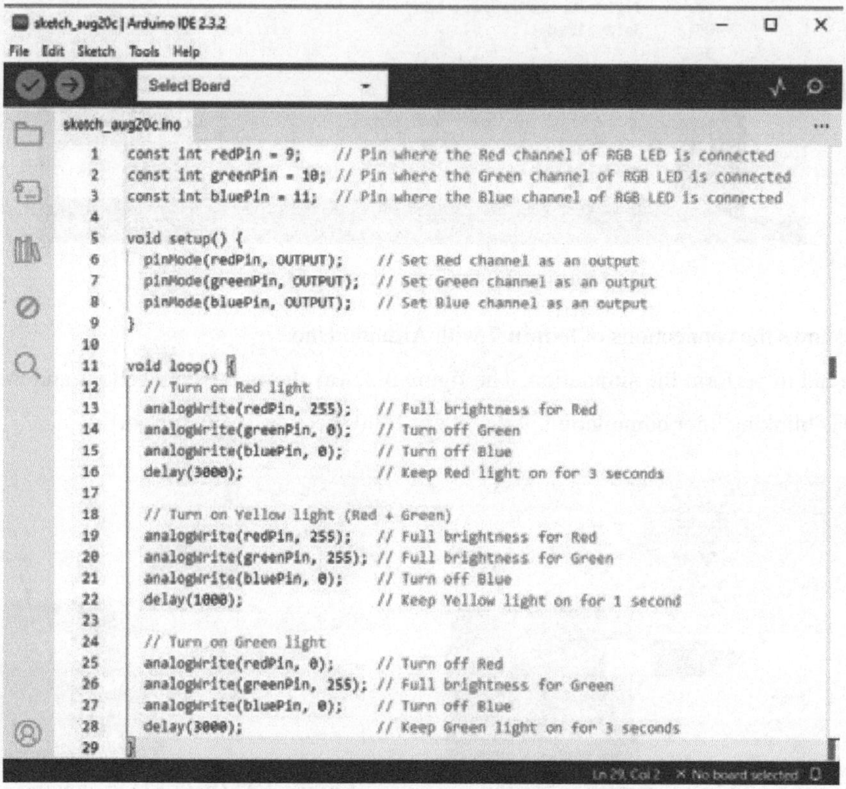


```
const int redPin = 9;     // Pin where the Red channel of RGB LED is connected
const int greenPin = 10; // Pin where the Green channel of RGB LED is connected
const int bluePin = 11;  // Pin where the Blue channel of RGB LED is connected

void setup() {
  pinMode(redPin, OUTPUT);      // Set Red channel as an output
  pinMode(greenPin, OUTPUT);  // Set Green channel as an output
  pinMode(bluePin, OUTPUT);    // Set Blue channel as an output
}

void loop() {
  // Turn on Red light
  analogWrite(redPin, 255);     // Full brightness for Red
  analogWrite(greenPin, 0);     // Turn off Green
  analogWrite(bluePin, 0);      // Turn off Blue
  delay(3000);                  // Keep Red light on for 3 seconds

  // Turn on Yellow light (Red + Green)
  analogWrite(redPin, 255);     // Full brightness for Red
  analogWrite(greenPin, 255); // Full brightness for Green
  analogWrite(bluePin, 0);      // Turn off Blue
  delay(1000);                  // Keep Yellow light on for 1 second

  // Turn on Green light
  analogWrite(redPin, 0);       // Turn off Red
  analogWrite(greenPin, 255); // Full brightness for Green
  analogWrite(bluePin, 0);      // Turn off Blue
  delay(3000);                  // Keep Green light on for 3 seconds
}
```

Figure 3.23: Traffic light code using LED

Scan for more on exmples on Tinckercad

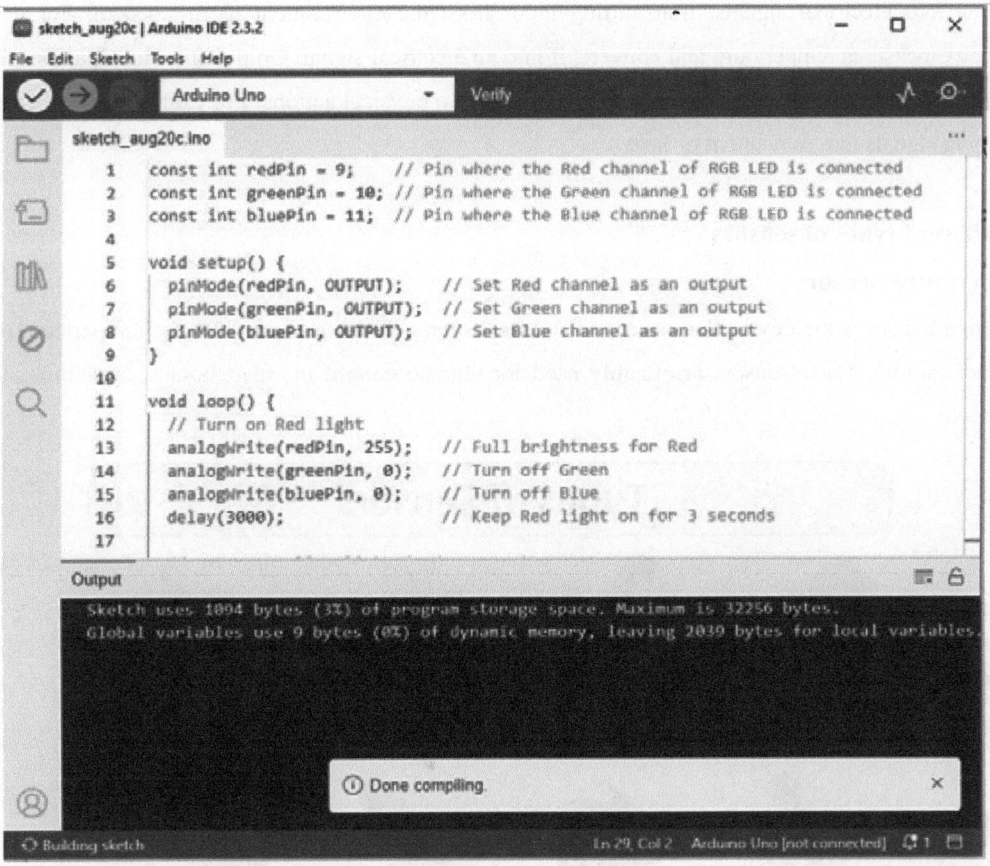

Figure 3.24: Code Compilation

Figure 3.25: Connections with Output

3.5 Introduction to Sensors and Actuators

Sensors and actuators are the basic components in many electrical and mechanical systems. Sensors detect changes in the environment, while actuators perform actions in response to those changes. A **sensor** converts physical phenomena into electrical signals, transmitting input from the environment to the system. For example, a thermometer measures temperature and converts it into an electrical signal. On the other hand, an **actuator** does the reverse. It converts electrical signals from the system into physical actions. For example, motors and heaters transforming signals into movement or heat.

3.5.1 Different types of sensors

i) Temperature Sensor

Temperature Sensor is the device that measures and tracks temperature and provides the temperature reading as an electrical signal. These sensors are mainly used for climate control in smart homes, agriculture, industrial processes etc.

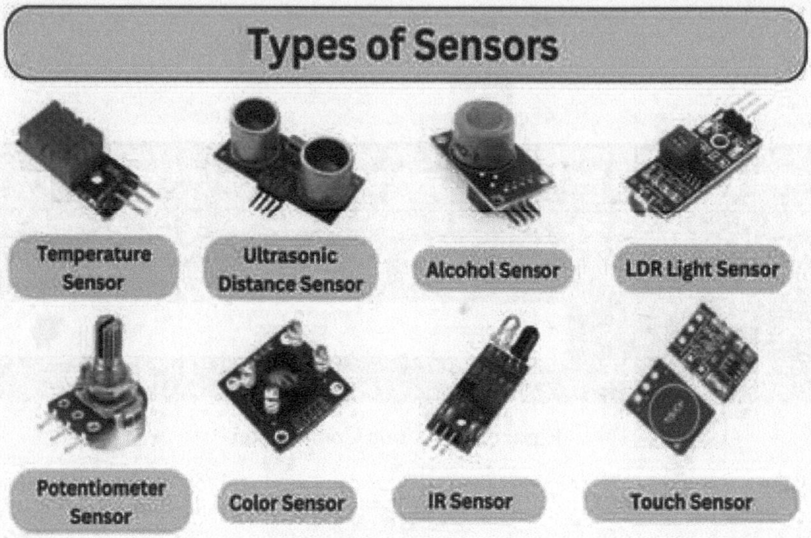

Figure 3.26: Types of Sensors

ii) Ultrasonic Sensor

The ultrasonic sensor is the device that measures the distance to an object using ultrasonic sound waves. The working of an ultrasonic sensor is comparable to that of a SONAR or RADAR. Apart from distance measurement, these sensors are also used for object detection in various applications such as robotics, automotive parking systems, and industrial automation.

iii) Light Sensor

Light sensor is one of the most important sensors, also known as a photo sensor. LDR (Light Dependent Resistor) is the most commonly used light sensor. Other examples include photodiodes, photoresistors, phototransistors, and photovoltaic light sensors. These sensors are mostly used in mobile devices for light sensing, automatic outdoor lighting etc.

iv) Alcohol Sensor

The alcohol sensor, technically referred as MQ3 sensor, detects ethanol in the air. This sensor measures the amount of ethanol in a person's breath when they breathe close to it, and it outputs a reading based on the amount of alcohol in the breath.

v) Color Sensor

A color sensor is a device that detects the color of the material. Usually, this sensor detects color in RGB scale, which means it can categorize the color as red, blue or green. Some of the applications are the light color temperature measurement, RGB LED consistency control, medical diagnosis systems, industrial process control, etc.

vi) IR Sensor

IR or Infrared Sensor is a device that can detect infrared radiation in its surroundings and provide electric signals as an output. This sensor not only measures the heat of an object but also detects its movement. This sensor has a wide range of applications, from industrial robots to home security systems.

vii) Touch Sensor

A touch sensor is a small, simple and low-cost device, also known as a tactile sensor. It is used in detecting and recording physical touch. Similar to a switch, a touch sensor opens an electrical circuit and permits currents to pass through it when it detects contact, touch, or pressure on its surface. The most commonly used applications include smartphones, automotive, industrial applications, robotics etc.

viii) Potentiometer Sensor

A potentiometer is a type of position sensor which is used to measure displacement in any direction. Linear potentiometers linearly measure displacement and rotary potentiometers measure rotational displacement. They are commonly used to control electrical devices like audio volume, fan speed, and serve as position transducers in mechanisms like joysticks.

3.5.2 Different types of actuators

i) Hydraulic actuator

A hydraulic actuator is a device that converts fluid pressure into mechanical motion. It typically consists of a cylinder or a fluid motor that operates using hydraulic power to perform mechanical tasks. The actuator produces motion, which can be rotary, linear, or oscillatory. Since liquids are nearly incompressible, hydraulic actuators are capable of generating significant force.

ii) Pneumatic actuator

A pneumatic actuator converts compressed air into mechanical motion, either linear or rotary. It consists of a piston, cylinder, and valves or ports. Linear actuators are ideal for high-temperature and steam applications, such as angle seat control valves, while rotary actuators are better suited for quarter-turn valves, depending on the application's requirements.

iii) Electric actuator

An electric actuator generates motion or force, such as clamping, using an electric motor. The motor produces rotary motion, which drives a helical screw via a drive shaft. As the screw rotates, a ball screw nut moves along it, creating linear motion through a hollow piston rod attached to the nut. The motor's clockwise or counterclockwise rotation controls the direction of the actuator's movement.

iv) Mechanical actuator

A mechanical actuator uses a power source, such as electric current, pneumatic, or hydraulic energy, to produce physical movement. Commonly found in automated machines, it converts rotary motion into linear motion through gearing. Mechanical actuators include lead screws, ball screws, rack and pinion systems, and belt-driven mechanisms, and can be operated manually or automated.

3.5.3 Connecting and Programming common sensors

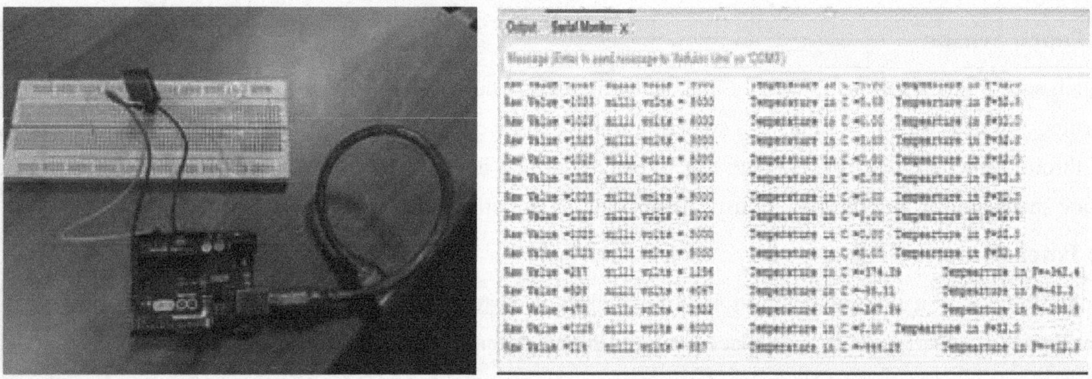

Figure 3.27: Temperature Sensor with Output on Serial Monitor

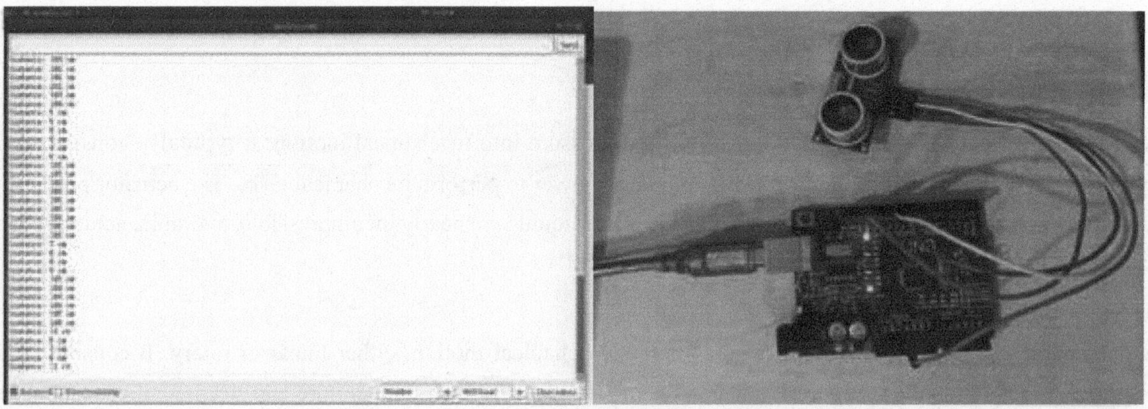

Figure 3.28: Distance Sensor with Output on Serial Monitor

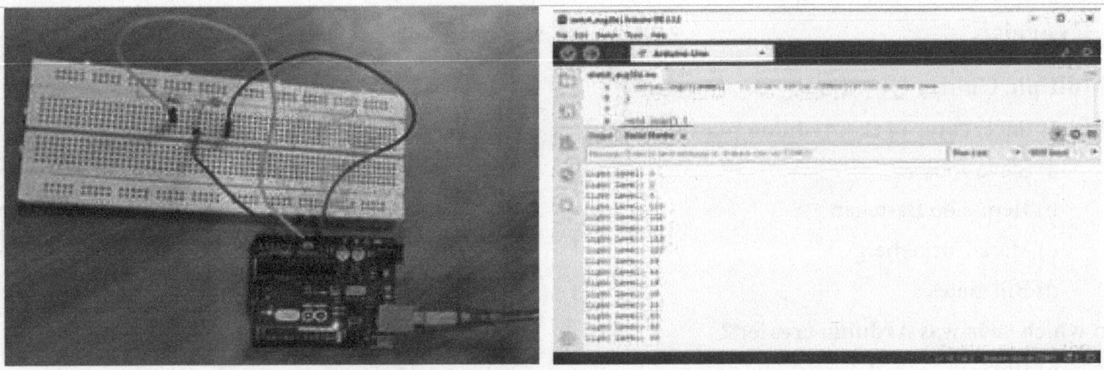

Figure 3.29: Light Sensor with Output on Serial Monitor

3.5.4 Working with analog inputs: using potentiometers and sensors

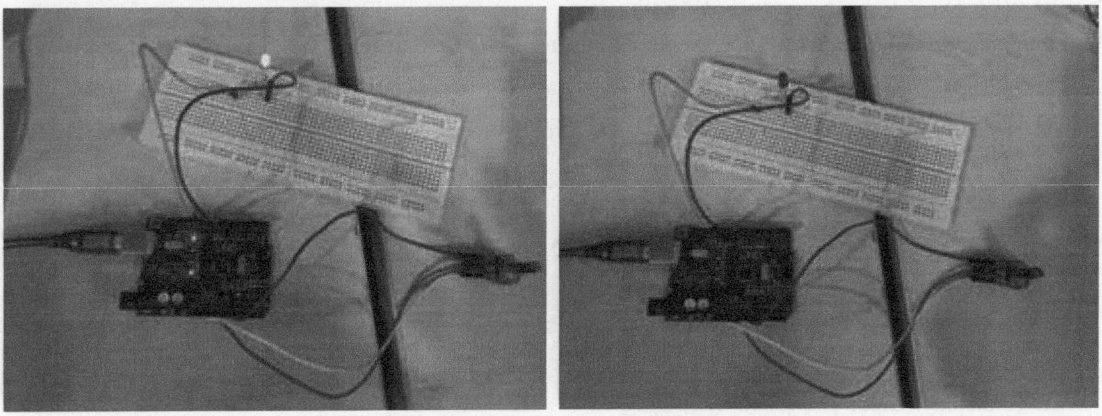

Figure 3.30: Potentiometer and LED Connections

3.6 Summary

This unit exposes students to the essentials of Arduino, including hardware components such as microcontrollers, sensors, and actuators, as well as the fundamentals of programming with the Arduino IDE. It focuses on hands-on learning, allowing students to create and model circuits with tools such as Tinkercad. The unit investigates real-world Arduino applications in fields like homeautomation, robotics, and IoT, with a focus on integrating sensors and actuators into practical projects. By mixing theory and experience, the unit prepares students to create and test working prototypes for a variety of applications.

3.7 Exercise

A. Multiple Choice Questions

1. Who is the creator of the Arduino platform?

a) Steve Jobs

b) Hernando Barragán

c) Mark Zuckerberg

d) Bill Gates

2. In which year was Arduino created?

a) 1995

b) 2000

c) 2005

d) 2010

3. Which microcontroller is commonly used on Arduino UNO boards?

a) ATmega168

b) ATmega328P

c) ATmega2560

d) ATmega32U4

4. What is the 'setup()' function's primary role in an Arduino sketch?

a) To run the code infinitely

b) To initialize variables, libraries, and pin modes

c) To create loops

d) To display output

5. Which pin is connected to the onboard LED on an Arduino UNO?

a) Pin 9

b) Pin 11

c) Pin 13

d) Pin 7

6. Which function is used to read analog signals in Arduino?

a) digitalRead()

b) digitalWrite()

c) analogRead()

d) analogWrite()

7. Which sensor is used to measure temperature?

a) LDR sensor

b) LM35 sensor

c) MQ3 sensor

d) Ultrasonic sensor

8. Which of the following is an output device in Arduino projects?

a) Temperature sensor

b) LDR sensor

c) LED

d) Light sensor

9. Which type of sensor is used for detecting motion?

a) Light sensor

b) Potentiometer

c) PIR sensor

d) Color sensor

10. Which function would you use to pause an Arduino program for a set time?

a) millis()

b) delay()

c) sleep()

d) pinMode()

11. Which function would be used to control the brightness of an LED using PWM?

a) analogRead()

b) analogWrite()

c) digitalRead()

d) digitalWrite()

12. Which of the following microcontrollers is not used in Arduino boards?

a) ATmega168

b) ATmega328P

c) ATmega2560

d) ATmega328U

13. What type of actuator is used for controlling motor speed in an Arduino project?

a) Stepper motor

b) Servo motor

c) Relay

d) Hydraulic actuator

14. What is the purpose of a relay in an Arduino project?

a) To detect light

b) To control high-voltage devices

c) To read temperature

d) To detect sound

15. Which of the following types of Arduino is best suited for IoT projects?

a) Arduino Nano

b) Arduino Uno R4 WiFi

c) Arduino Due

d) Arduino Mega

16. What kind of function is 'millis()'?

a) It pauses the program

b) It returns the number of milliseconds since the Arduino started running the program

c) It controls the brightness of an LED

d) It counts the number of loops

17. Which sensor is used for distance measurement?

a) PIR sensor

b) Ultrasonic sensor

c) Alcohol sensor

d) Touch sensor

18. Which Arduino model uses the ATmega32U4 microcontroller?

a) Arduino Due

b) Arduino Micro

c) Arduino Nano

d) Arduino Uno

19. Which data type in Arduino stores 8-bit unsigned numbers?

a) int

b) unsigned int

c) byte

d) word

20. What type of actuator converts electrical signals into physical actions?

a) Sensor

b) Relay

c) Actuator

d) LCD

B. Short Answer questions

1. In Arduino programming, what does the 'loop()' function accomplish?
2. Identify two typical sensor kinds found in Arduino applications.
3. What is a sensor that is analog? Give an illustration.
4. Describe how digitalRead() and digitalWrite() differ.
5. What role does the Arduino Uno boards' ATmega328P microcontroller play?
6. How does Arduino simulation use the Tinkercad platform?
7. Explain how a potentiometer is used in Arduino projects.
8. Identify the two kinds of actuators that Arduino projects use.

C. Long Answer questions

1. Describe the composition and operation of an Arduino sketch. How are the' setup()' and 'loop()' functions used in a program?
2. Talk about how crucial it is to use sensors and actuators in Arduino projects. Give instances of how they are used.
3. Explain how an ultrasonic sensor calculates distance and how to attach it to an Arduino board.
4. Examine and contrast various Arduino board varieties, including the Uno, Mega, and Nano. What are the main distinctions between their features?
5. Describe how Arduino applications are debugged using the Serial Monitor. Give an example of how it facilitates data communication between a computer and an Arduino.
6. In Arduino programming, what are local and global variables? Give instances of each and describe their scope.
7. Explain how high-voltage devices are controlled by integrating an Arduino board with a relay. Provide a working principle explanation along with a diagram.
8. Talk about how important it is to use various data types when programming an Arduino. What effects does selecting the appropriate data type have on a project's performance?
9. Describe how to set up the Arduino IDE and create a basic program that blinks an LED. Provide instructions on how to upload and compile the code.

Answers for MCQ's

1. b) Hernando Barragán
2. c) 2005
3. b) ATmega328P
4. b) To initialize variables, libraries, and pin modes
5. c) Pin 13
6. c) analogRead()
7. b) LM35 sensor
8. c) LED
9. c) PIR sensor
10. b) delay()
11. b) analogWrite()
12. d) ATmega328U
13. a) Stepper motor

14. b) To control high-voltage devices
15. b) Arduino Uno R4 WiFi
16. b) It returns the number of milliseconds since the Arduino started running the program
17. b) Ultrasonic sensor
18. b) Arduino Micro
19. c) byte
20. c) Actuator

REFERENCES

1. Get *Arduino: A Technical Reference* now with the O'Reilly learning platform, https://www.oreilly.com/library/view/arduino-a-technical/9781491934319/ch01.html
2. Barragán, Hernando (2016-01-01). "The Untold History of Arduino". *arduinohistory.github.io*. Last retrieved 2016-03-06.
3. Arduino- Wikipedia, Retrieved 3rd July 2024. https://en.wikipedia.org/wiki/Arduino
4. ATmega128 Microchip, Retrieved 3rd July 2024. https://www.microchip.com/en-us/product/atmega128
5. ATMEGA328PMicrochip, Retrieved 3rd July 2024. https://www.microchip.com/en-us/product/atmega328p#sampling-options
6. "Arduino - Products". *www.arduino.cc*. Retrieved 3rd July 2024.
7. Arduino Docs. https://docs.arduino.cc/learn/electronics/power-pins/#3v35v-pin-1, Retrieved 3rd July 2024.

4 IMPLEMENTATION OF IOT WITH RASPBERRY PI

UNIT SPECIFICS

In this unit, the following aspects will be discussed:

- Overview of the Raspberry Pi, including models and specification
- Configuring the Raspberry Pi for IoT applications, includes hardware and software settings
- Interfacing sensors and actuators with Raspberry Pi GPIO pins
- Programming IoT systems with Python and packages like RPi, GPIO, and Adafruit
- Data gathering, processing, and visualization with Raspberry Pi and Python

Hands-on exercises with Raspberry Pi are given to help students learn the material more practically. Standardized project formats, such as data acquisition systems and home automation prototypes, are presented. Raspberry Pi model specifications and features are presented in tabular style, and students are guided through implementation via visual demonstrations.

This unit includes practical exercises, long and short-term questions, multiple-choice questions, and project-based assignments. QR codes or links to lessons and further readings are supplied for extended learning.

RATIONALE

This unit focuses on the practical development of IoT systems with the Raspberry Pi and Python programming. It begins with an overview of the Raspberry Pi's architecture, models, and specs, followed by in-depth discussions on how to set up and configure the device for IoT applications.

Students learn how to interface sensors and actuators using Raspberry Pi GPIO pins and create IoT systems in Python. Techniques for data collecting, processing, and visualization are investigated, allowing students to create comprehensive IoT applications. This lesson takes a ands-on approach, allowing students to apply theoretical knowledge to real-world circumstances, developing problem-solving abilities, and increasing their confidence in designing IoT projects.

PRE-REQUISITES

No prerequisites are required for studying this unit.

UNIT OUTCOMES

The list of outcomes of this unit is as follows:

U4-O1: Explain the architecture and models of Raspberry Pi

U4-O2: Utilize GPIO and hardware interfaces for IoT

U4-O3: Develop Python-based IoT systems

U4-O4: Implement data acquisition techniques using Python

U4-O5: Design complete IoT solutions using Raspberry Pi

Unit Outcomes	Expected Mapping with Course Outcomes *(1- Weak Correlation; 2- Medium correlation; 3- Strong Correlation)*				
	CO-1	CO-2	CO-3	CO-4	CO-5
U4-O1	3	3	2	1	3
U4-O2	3	3	3	3	3
U4-O3	3	3	3	3	3
U4-O4	3	3	3	3	3
U4-O5	3	3	3	3	3

4.1 Introduction to Raspberry Pi

The Raspberry Pi is a series of small single-board computers developed by the Raspberry Pi Foundation in collaboration with Broadcom as shown in Figure 4.1. Initially conceived to promote teaching basic computer science in schools, the Raspberry Pi's accessibility and low cost have made it popular among hobbyists, educators, and tech enthusiasts for various projects from gaming devices to weather stations. It can be plugged into a monitor and used as a minicomputer by connecting peripherals like a keyboard and mouse[1].

4.1.1 History and Development of Raspberry Pi

The Raspberry Pi project was initiated by the Raspberry Pi Foundation in the UK. The Foundation aimed to create an affordable computer to stimulate the teaching of basic computer science in schools and developing countries. The first Raspberry Pi model was released in 2012, and since then, several iterations and versions have been developed, each improving on the performance and capabilities of its predecessors.

Figure 4.1: Raspberry Pi Board

The project started in response to a significant decline in the number of students applying for computer science courses. The founders, who were from academic and industry backgrounds, saw that many students lacked the skills and enthusiasm for programming and hardware tinkering that had been prevalent in earlier generations. They decided to create a low-cost, accessible platform to bridge this gap. Since its invention, the Raspberry Pi has grown beyond its educational roots. It has become popular amongst hobbyists, makers, and professionals, finding applications in a wide range of fields such as home automation, robotics, industrial control systems, and more.

4.1.2 Various Models and Their Specifications

Raspberry Pi models are categorized into three main product lines: the standard series, the Zero series, and the Pico series. Each line offers different levels of processing power and size to cater to various project requirements.

Standard Series:

The standard series includes models designed for a broad range of applications, providing a balance of performance, connectivity, and flexibility.

- **Raspberry Pi 1 Model B (2012):** The original model features a 700 MHz single-core ARM1176JZF-S CPU, 256MB RAM (later upgraded to 512MB), 2 USB ports, and 10/100 Ethernet. It set the foundation for future models.
- **Raspberry Pi 1 Model A (2013):** A lower-cost variant with 256MB RAM, 1 USB port, and no Ethernet port, designed for lower-power applications.
- **Raspberry Pi 1 Model B+ (2014):** An enhanced version with 512MB RAM, 4 USB ports, better power management, and a 40-pin GPIO header.
- **Raspberry Pi 2 Model B (2015):** Quad-core 900 MHz ARM Cortex-A7 CPU, 1GB RAM, maintaining the form factor of the B+ model. This model significantly improved the performance.
- **Raspberry Pi 3 Model B (2016):** Integrated Wi-Fi and Bluetooth, 1.2 GHz quad-core ARM Cortex-A53 CPU, 1GB RAM, maintaining compatibility with earlier models.
- **Raspberry Pi 3 Model B+ (2018):** Enhanced with a 1.4 GHz CPU, improved thermal management, and faster Ethernet.
- **Raspberry Pi 4 Model B (2019-2020):** Major upgrades with a 1.5 GHz quad-core ARM Cortex-A72 CPU, up to 8GB RAM, dual HDMI outputs, USB 3.0 ports, and Gigabit Ethernet. This model introduced significant performance improvements and more connectivity options.

Zero Series:

The Zero series is designed for ultra-compact projects, offering a smaller form factor and lower power consumption.

- **Raspberry Pi Zero (2015):** Ultra-compact model with a 1GHz single-core ARM11 CPU, 512MB RAM, mini HDMI port, and 40-pin GPIO header. Designed for low-cost, space-constrained applications.
- **Raspberry Pi Zero W (2017):** Adds integrated Wi-Fi and Bluetooth to the original Zero model, making it more versatile for wireless projects.
- **Raspberry Pi Zero WH (2017):** Pre-soldered GPIO headers for easier prototyping and connectivity.

Pico Series:

The Pico series is based on a microcontroller rather than a full-fledged CPU, designed for lightweight, embedded applications.

- **Raspberry Pi Pico (2021):** Based on the RP2040 microcontroller, featuring a dual-core ARM Cortex-M0+ processor running at 133 MHz, 264KB RAM, 2MB flash memory, and 26 multi-function GPIO pins. It supports 802.11n wireless LAN and USB connectivity, and it is suitable for microcontroller-based projects.

4.1.3 Connectivity and Expansion

Raspberry Pi boards offer various connectivity and expansion options to interface with peripherals and external devices.

- **USB Ports:** The number of USB ports varies by model. The Raspberry Pi 4 has two USB 3.0 ports and two USB 2.0 ports, while older models typically have only USB 2.0 ports.
- **HDMI Ports:** Models like the Raspberry Pi 4 have dual micro HDMI ports, supporting up to 4K resolution, while older models have a single full-sized HDMI port.
- **Ethernet:** Available on models from Raspberry Pi 1 Model B onwards, with the Raspberry Pi 4 offering Gigabit Ethernet. Older models like the Raspberry Pi 3 have 10/100 Ethernet.
- **Wi-Fi and Bluetooth:** Integrated on models from the Raspberry Pi 3 onwards. The Raspberry Pi 4 supports dual-band 802.11ac Wi-Fi and Bluetooth 5.0.
- **GPIO Headers:** All models feature a 40-pin GPIO header for interfacing with external electronics. The header includes pins for power, ground, and general-purpose input/output, as well as dedicated interfaces for I2C, SPI, and UART.
- **Camera and Display Interfaces:** The Camera Serial Interface (CSI) and Display Serial Interface (DSI) ports are present on most models, allowing the connection of camera modules and LCD displays.

4.1.4 Power Requirements

Raspberry Pi boards have specific power requirements to ensure stable operation. The power supply should match the model's needs to avoid issues such as random reboots or peripheral failures.

- **Raspberry Pi 4 Model B:** Requires a 5V/3A USB-C power supply.
- **Raspberry Pi 3 Model B+:** Requires a 5V/2.5A micro USB power supply.
- **Raspberry Pi Zero W:** Requires a 5V/1.2A micro USB power supply.

4.1.5 Storage

Raspberry Pi uses a microSD card for storage, which holds the operating system and user data. It is recommended to use high-quality, high-speed SD cards to ensure reliable performance.

4.1.6 Setting Up Raspberry Pi

Setting up a Raspberry Pi involves several steps, from assembling the physical hardware to installing and configuring the software.

Required Components

- **Raspberry Pi Board:** Select a model based on your needs.
- **MicroSD Card:** A minimum of 8 GB recommended, used to load the operating system and store data.
- **Power Supply:** Typically a 5V USB-C or micro USB charger with at least 2.5A for adequate power.
- **Peripherals:** A USB keyboard, USB mouse, and HDMI monitor are essential for setting up.
- **Case:** Optional but recommended to protect the board from physical damage.

Installing the Operating System

- **Download:** The official Raspberry Pi OS (formerly Raspbian) is available on the Raspberry Pi Foundation's website.
- **Writing Software:** Use software like BalenaEtcher to write the Raspberry Pi OS image to the MicroSD card.
- **Installation:** Insert the MicroSD card into the Raspberry Pi, connect all peripherals, and power up the device. The Raspberry Pi will boot into the installer, where you can configure the OS installation.

Initial Configuration

- **Network Setup:** Configure either a Wi-Fi connection or a wired Ethernet connection.
- **SSH Configuration:** Enable SSH to allow remote access to the Raspberry Pi.
- **Update and Upgrade:** Use the commands sudo apt update and sudo apt upgrade to update the system to the latest software packages.

Establishing Network Connectivity

To get the most out of a Raspberry Pi, network connectivity is crucial:

- **Wired Ethernet:** Simply connect an Ethernet cable from your router to the Raspberry Pi for a stable connection.
- **Wi-Fi Setup:** Through the Raspberry Pi OS graphical interface or the command line (raspi-config), you can set up Wi-Fi by entering the network details.

4.1.7 Architecture of Raspberry Pi

The components that play an important role in defining the Raspberry Pi's functionality and versatility as a computing platform are described below and as shown in Figure 4.2:

Figure 4.2: Architecture of Raspberry Pi

Processor:

The heart of the Raspberry Pi is its processor, typically a Broadcom system-on-chip (SoC), which integrates both a central processing unit (CPU) and a graphics processing unit (GPU). In many models, such as the Raspberry Pi 1 through 3, the Broadcom BCM2835 SoC is used. This SoC features an ARM CPU, which is renowned for its energy efficiency and cost-effectiveness, making it ideal for the compact and affordable design of the Raspberry Pi. The VideoCore IV GPU embedded within the BCM2835 is capable of handling multimedia processing, such as video playback and 3D graphics, which are essential for creating interactive user experiences.

HDMI:

High-Definition Multimedia Interface (HDMI) is a standard for transmitting digital video and audio data. The Raspberry Pi features an HDMI port that allows it to connect to modern monitors, televisions, and other digital display devices. This connection supports high-resolution output, making it possible to use the Raspberry Pi for media centers, gaming, digital signage, and other visual applications. The versatility of the HDMI port also means that users can set up their Raspberry Pi as a full desktop computer or a media streaming device.

GPIO Ports:

General Purpose Input/Output (GPIO) ports are crucial for the Raspberry Pi's functionality as an embedded device controller. These pins allow the Raspberry Pi to interact with and control a wide range of external devices, from simple sensors and LEDs to more complex systems like motors and other electronic components. The GPIO pins can be programmed to serve either input or output functions, providing a flexible interface for a variety of DIY projects and commercial products.

Audio Output:

The audio output port on the Raspberry Pi allows it to connect to external audio devices such as headphones, speakers, and sound systems. This feature is particularly useful when the Raspberry Pi is used as a media center or for sound processing projects. The audio jack typically outputs analog audio, but digital audio can also be transmitted through the HDMI port, providing flexibility depending on the user's audio setup requirements.

USB Ports:

USB ports on the Raspberry Pi are used to connect a variety of peripherals, enhancing the functionality of the Raspberry Pi. Common peripherals include keyboards, mice, USB storage devices, network adapters, and more. These ports are essential for expanding the capabilities of the Raspberry Pi, allowing it to function as a computer or to interface with other systems in a larger project.

SD Card Slot:

The SD card slot is an essential component of the Raspberry Pi as it holds the device's operating system and user data. When the Raspberry Pi is powered on, it boots from the operating system installed on the SD card. This setup allows for easy updating and swapping of operating systems, making the Raspberry Pi a highly versatile development platform. Users can use different SD cards for different projects or purposes, simplifying development and deployment processes.

Ethernet:

The Ethernet port, available on many Raspberry Pi models, provides a reliable wired network connection. This is crucial for applications where stable internet connectivity is necessary, such as in server applications or where wireless connectivity is not available or reliable. The Ethernet connection can be used for internet access, local network interactions, and network-based file transfers, making it a vital feature for many professional and hobbyist projects.

Power Supply:

The power supply for the Raspberry Pi is typically delivered through a micro USB or USB-C port, depending on the model. The device requires a stable 5V power source, and the current requirements can vary depending on the model and the peripherals connected to the Raspberry Pi. Proper power management is crucial to maintain the stability and reliability of the Raspberry Pi, especially in complex projects or when multiple peripherals are connected.

Camera Module:

The Camera Serial Interface (CSI) on the Raspberry Pi allows for the connection of a dedicated camera module designed specifically for the Raspberry Pi. This feature is particularly useful in projects involving image processing, video recording, or surveillance systems. The CSI connection provides a high-speed method to transmit image data directly to the processor for real-time processing.

Display Interface:

The Display Serial Interface (DSI) is used to connect LCD panels directly to the Raspberry Pi. This interface supports high-resolution displays and is typically used for embedded projects that require a built-in display with compact wiring. The DSI is particularly useful for projects like custom tablets, digital dashboards, or any application that requires a graphical interface directly controlled by the Raspberry Pi.

Scan for more knowldge on Raspberry Pi

4.2 Introduction to Python Programming

Python is an ideal programming language for Raspberry Pi users due to its simplicity and readability, making it accessible for beginners and powerful enough for experienced developers. It supports various libraries that simplify tasks in web development, data analysis, artificial intelligence, and more. For Raspberry Pi, Python is particularly valuable because it supports hardware interfaces, allowing users to easily control GPIO pins and communicate with peripherals.

Python is an interpreted language, meaning that scripts are run line-by-line, which can simplify debugging and iterative testing. The language's syntax is clean and its command structure is intuitive, which helps new programmers to pick it up quickly. Furthermore, Python has a vast community and a wealth of libraries and tutorials, making it easy to find help and resources.

Python comes pre-installed on the Raspberry Pi OS, but you can update it to the latest version using the following commands:

1. *sudo apt update*
2. *sudo apt upgrade*
3. *sudo apt install python3*

To write a Python program, you can use any text editor, such as Nano or Thonny, which is specifically designed for beginners and comes pre-installed on the Raspberry Pi.

1. Open Thonny from the Programming menu.
2. Write your first program: *print("Hello, World!").*
3. Save the file with a .py extension and run it.

The key Python Libraries for IoT are:

1. ***RPi.GPIO***: Directly control the GPIO pins for basic digital input and output.
2. ***gpiozero***: A higher-level library built on top of RPi.GPIO, which simplifies the code for controlling devices connected to the GPIO pins.
3. ***Adafruit_Blinka***: Provides a compatibility layer that allows code written for Adafruit hardware to run on Raspberry Pi.

4.2.1 Using GPIO (General Purpose Input/Output) Pins

The GPIO pins on the Raspberry Pi allow it to interact with the external world. These digital pins can be programmed to read digital inputs (like switches) or output digital signals (like controlling an LED). Some pins also have specialized functions like PWM (Pulse Width Modulation) for controlling motors or servos, SPI (Serial Peripheral Interface) for serial communication, and I2C (Inter-Integrated Circuit) for connecting multiple integrated circuits using just two wires.

To use GPIO pins with Python, you can use the RPi.GPIO library (now succeeded by the GPIO Zero library for simpler projects). These libraries provide a straightforward API to control the pins. For example, setting up a pin as an output and turning it on or off can be done in just a few lines of code.

To interact with GPIO pins, you'll need to install the RPi.GPIO library:

```
sudo apt install python3-rpi.gpio
```

4.2.2 Example Projects

Blinking LED:

1. **Connect an LED:** Connect the positive leg of an LED to GPIO pin 18 and the negative leg to a resistor, which is then connected to the ground (GND).
2. **Write the Code:**

```
import RPi.GPIO as GPIO
import time
GPIO.setmode(GPIO.BCM)
GPIO.setup(18, GPIO.OUT)
try:
    while True:
        GPIO.output(18, GPIO.HIGH)
        time.sleep(1)
        GPIO.output(18, GPIO.LOW)
        time.sleep(1)
except KeyboardInterrupt:
    GPIO.cleanup()
```

3. Run the Script: The LED should blink on and off every second.

Sound Alarm with Buzzer:

1. Connect the positive lead of the buzzer to GPIO 18.
2. Connect the negative lead to the GND pin.
3. Write the Code:

```
import RPi.GPIO as GPIO
```

```
import time
BUZZER_PIN = 18
GPIO.setmode(GPIO.BCM)
GPIO.setup(BUZZER_PIN, GPIO.OUT)
try:
  while True:
     GPIO.output(BUZZER_PIN, GPIO.HIGH)  # Turn buzzer on
     time.sleep(1)                       # Wait for one second
     GPIO.output(BUZZER_PIN, GPIO.LOW)   # Turn buzzer off
     time.sleep(1)                       # Wait for one second
except KeyboardInterrupt:
  GPIO.cleanup()
```

4. Run the Script: The buzzer should make a simple sound alarm.

Example 4.1: Temperature Monitoring System

A simple IoT project using Raspberry Pi is building a temperature monitoring system. You might use a digital temperature sensor like a DHT22 sensor. Once you set it up, you can periodically read the temperature and even send it over the internet to a remote server or a cloud service like AWS, Azure, or Google Cloud for storage and further analysis.

Components Required:

Raspberry Pi

DHT11 or DHT22 temperature and humidity sensor

Breadboard and jumper wires

Setting Up the Sensor:

Connect the sensor's VCC pin to the 3.3V pin on the Raspberry Pi.

Connect the GND pin to a ground pin on the Raspberry Pi.

Connect the data pin to GPIO pin 4.

Python Code:

Install the Required Libraries:

```
sudo pip3 install Adafruit_DHT
```

Write the Code:

```
import Adafruit_DHT
import time
DHT_SENSOR = Adafruit_DHT.DHT22
DHT_PIN = 4
```

```
while True:
    humidity, temperature = Adafruit_DHT.read_retry(DHT_SENSOR, DHT_PIN)
    if humidity is not None and temperature is not None:
        print(f"Temp: {temperature:.1f}C  Humidity: {humidity:.1f}%")
    else:
        print("Failed to retrieve data from humidity sensor")
    time.sleep(2)
```

Run the Script: The temperature and humidity values will be printed to the console every 2 seconds.

Example 4.2: Home Automation System

Another popular project is a home automation system where you control various home appliances using your Raspberry Pi. This might involve using relays to turn devices like lamps, fans, or heaters on and off. The Raspberry Pi acts as the central controller that sends commands to the relays which, in turn, control the power to these devices.

Components Required:

Raspberry Pi

Relay module

Lamp or any appliance

Jumper wires

Setting Up the Relay:

Connect the relay module's VCC to the 5V pin on the Raspberry Pi.

Connect the GND to the ground pin.

Connect the IN pin to GPIO pin 17.

Connect the lamp to the relay.

Python Code:

```
import RPi.GPIO as GPIO
import time
RELAY_PIN = 17
GPIO.setmode(GPIO.BCM)
GPIO.setup(RELAY_PIN, GPIO.OUT)
try:
    while True:
        GPIO.output(RELAY_PIN, GPIO.HIGH)  # Turn on the relay
        print("Lamp ON")
        time.sleep(5)
```

```
        GPIO.output(RELAY_PIN, GPIO.LOW)  # Turn off the relay
        print("Lamp OFF")
        time.sleep(5)
except KeyboardInterrupt:
    GPIO.cleanup()
```

Run the Script: The lamp should turn on for 5 seconds and then turn off for 5 seconds in a loop.

4.3 Data Collection and Storage

While implementing IoT projects using the Raspberry Pi, one of the important aspect is the effective collection and storage of data. This involves not only capturing data from various sensors but also determining the most appropriate ways to store this data for further analysis or real-time actions.

4.3.1 Data Acquisition

Data acquisition with the Raspberry Pi typically involves interfacing with a variety of sensors to monitor environmental parameters such as temperature, humidity, motion, and more. This can be achieved through several methods:

1. **Direct GPIO Manipulation:** Using Python libraries like RPi.GPIO or GPIO Zero, developers can directly control the GPIO pins on the Raspberry Pi. This method is ideal for simple binary sensors or outputs, such as switches, buttons, or LEDs.
2. **Serial Communication Protocols:** For more complex sensors that require continuous data transmission or have higher data bandwidth requirements, serial communication protocols like SPI, I2C, and UART are used. Python provides support for these protocols through libraries such as pyserial for UART, which enables data transmission over serial ports, and smbus for I2C, which is used for connecting multiple sensors with fewer GPIO pins.
3. **Utilizing External Libraries and Frameworks:** For ease of use, especially for those new to electronics and programming, high-level libraries and frameworks such as those provided by Adafruit can be incredibly beneficial. Adafruit, for instance, offers tailored libraries that support a vast array of sensors and make coding more intuitive. GPIO Zero is another high-level library that simplifies coding by abstracting much of the lower-level GPIO interactions.

4.3.2 Data Storage Solutions

Once data is collected, determining where and how to store it is crucial. The Raspberry Pi offers several storage options:

1. **Local Storage:** Local storage solutions for data collected by a Raspberry Pi primarily involve using the SD card (as shown in Figure 4.3) or USB storage devices. The SD card is the default storage device for the Raspberry Pi, where the operating system is installed and data can be stored. While easy to use and directly accessible through the OS, SD cards have a limited lifespan under heavy write operations and are slower compared to other storage options.

Figure 4.3: Location of SD Card in Raspberry Pi

Alternatively, USB storage devices such as external hard drives or USB flash drives offer more storage capacity and durability. They are particularly useful for projects requiring extensive data logging over extended periods. However, they may require additional configuration and can consume more power, which is an important consideration for power-sensitive applications.

2. **Cloud Storage:** Storing data in the cloud provides significant advantages in terms of accessibility, scalability, and redundancy. Major cloud service providers such as Google Cloud, Amazon Web Services (AWS), and Microsoft Azure offer various services tailored for IoT data storage and management.

   Google Cloud provides services like BigQuery for big data analytics and Cloud Storage for file storage, both of which can be accessed directly from a Python script running on a Raspberry Pi. AWS offers a comprehensive suite of services for IoT applications, including AWS S3 for file storage, AWS IoT Core for managing IoT devices, and DynamoDB for NoSQL database services.

   Integration with AWS can be achieved using the Boto3 SDK for Python, enabling seamless data transfer and device management. Microsoft Azure offers similar capabilities with Azure Blob Storage for data storage and Azure IoT Hub for managing IoT communications, which can be integrated using the Azure IoT SDK for Python.

3. **Databases:** Choosing the right database depends on the specific requirements of the project, such as data complexity, size, and access patterns. For lightweight, local storage, SQLite is an excellent choice due to its simplicity and ability to store data in a single file without requiring a separate server process. However, SQLite may not be suitable for applications with high concurrency or extremely large datasets.

   For more robust and feature-rich database needs, MySQL is a popular choice. It supports large databases and multiple concurrent users but requires running a separate database server, which adds complexity to setup and maintenance. NoSQL options like MongoDB and Cassandra offer scalable and flexible data models, making them efficient for handling large volumes of unstructured data. These databases, however, can be complex to deploy and manage, often requiring additional infrastructure.

4.4 Data Processing and Analytics

After collecting and storing data, the next step is to process this data and extract meaningful insights, which can then inform decisions or trigger actions. Data processing on the Raspberry Pi involves taking raw data collected from various sources, such as sensors or online interactions, and transforming it into a format that is easier to analyze and understand. This step is needed because raw data often contains inaccuracies, is incomplete, or may be in an unstructured format that is difficult to interpret directly. Raw data often contains noise, missing values, and inconsistencies that can skew analysis results. Preprocessing helps in:

- **Improving Data Quality:** By handling missing values, correcting errors, and removing duplicates, preprocessing ensures the data is accurate and reliable.
- **Enhancing Model Performance:** Clean and well-structured data enables machine learning models to train more effectively, leading to better performance.
- **Reducing Complexity:** Transforming data into a suitable format can simplify the analysis process and make it more efficient.

The quality and precision of insights derived from data analysis depend significantly on the quality of the preprocessing steps. These steps typically include:

1. Cleaning Data involves the crucial task of removing or correcting malformed, corrupt, or inaccurate entries from a dataset. In IoT applications, where data is collected from various sensors, ensuring data integrity is essential. This process often begins with the identification and removal of outliers, which can significantly skew results if left unaddressed. Outliers can be detected using statistical techniques such as the Interquartile Range (IQR) method or Z-scores. Additionally, handling missing values is a significant aspect of data cleaning. Methods for addressing missing data include imputation, where missing values are replaced with the mean, median, or mode of the column, and interpolation, which estimates missing values based on surrounding data points. Correcting data types and formats ensures that all entries conform to expected standards, such as converting string representations of dates into datetime objects or ensuring numerical data is in the correct format.
2. Transforming Data is the next vital step in preprocessing, which involves modifying the data to make it more suitable for analysis. Normalization and scaling are fundamental techniques in this phase, where data values are adjusted to a common scale. Normalization typically scales data to a range between 0 and 1, while standardization adjusts data to have a mean of 0 and a standard deviation of 1. These transformations are especially important for machine learning algorithms that are sensitive to the scale of input data. Another critical aspect of data transformation is feature extraction. This process involves deriving new, more informative features from raw data, enhancing the analytical power of the dataset. Techniques like Principal Component Analysis (PCA) reduce the dimensionality of data by transforming it into a set of orthogonal components that capture the most variance. Fourier Transforms, on the other hand, are used to convert time-series data into the frequency domain, which is particularly useful in signal-processing applications.
3. Data Integration in IoT projects is often necessary due to the diverse range of sensors and devices that generate data. Integrating these various data sources into a unified dataset provides a comprehensive view necessary for thorough analysis. Resolving data conflicts is a key part of this process, involving standardizing units, formats, and removing duplicates. Data fusion is another technique, combining data from multiple sensors to

create a more accurate and complete dataset. For example, temperature readings from different locations within a facility can be combined to provide a holistic view of the environmental conditions. Temporal and spatial alignment is also crucial, ensuring that data from different sources is synchronized in time and space. This might involve normalizing timestamps to a common time zone or aligning spatial data points to a consistent coordinate system.

4.4.1 Data Analytics Tools and Techniques

Data analytics on the Raspberry Pi can range from simple statistical analysis to more complex machine learning models. Given the resource constraints of the Raspberry Pi, it is essential to select tools and techniques that balance computational demand with analytical capabilities. Basic statistical methods are used to summarize data, identify patterns, and test hypotheses. Tools like Python's NumPy library are integral for conducting such analyses, which include computing means, medians, variances, and correlations.

Although training complex models directly on the Raspberry Pi may be challenging due to hardware limitations, simpler models or pre-trained models can be effectively utilized for tasks such as classification, regression, and clustering. Scikit-learn is a robust Python library that provides a wide array of tools for machine learning. It includes algorithms for classification, regression, clustering, and dimensionality reduction, making it a versatile choice for data analysis. On the Raspberry Pi, while the computational constraints may limit the complexity of the models you can train directly, there are effective ways to utilize this library:

- **Simpler Models:** Algorithms that are less computationally intensive, such as linear regression, logistic regression, and k-means clustering, can be effectively executed on the Raspberry Pi. These models provide valuable insights and are suitable for many applications where real-time decision-making or fast analysis is not critical.

```
from sklearn.model_selection import train_test_split
from sklearn.linear_model import LogisticRegression
from sklearn.datasets import load_iris

# Load dataset
data = load_iris()
X_train, X_test, y_train, y_test = train_test_split(data.data, data.target, test_size=0.3, random_state=42)

# Train model
model = LogisticRegression()
model.fit(X_train, y_train)
```

```
# Evaluate model
accuracy = model.score(X_test, y_test)
print(f'Accuracy: {accuracy}')
```

- **Pre-trained Models:** For more complex tasks, consider using models that have been pre-trained on more powerful systems. The Raspberry Pi can then be used to run predictions using these pre-trained models, significantly reducing the computational load. This is particularly effective for applications like image recognition or complex pattern detection, where training deep learning models from scratch would be impractical on the Pi.

```
from sklearn.externals import joblib

# Load pre-trained model
model = joblib.load('pretrained_model.pkl')

# Make predictions
predictions = model.predict(X_test)
```

- **Incremental Learning:** Some machine learning algorithms support incremental learning, which means they can update the learned model incrementally as new data arrives. This approach is particularly useful on devices with limited memory and computational power, like the Raspberry Pi.

Performing data analysis directly on the Raspberry Pi involves leveraging the strengths of the device while mitigating its limitations. Techniques include:

1. **Edge Analytics:** Edge analytics refers to processing data at the edge of the network, close to the data source, rather than sending it to a centralized data center. This approach reduces latency, conserves bandwidth, and allows for immediate action, which is critical in applications like alerting systems or real-time monitoring.
    - **Latency Reduction:** By processing data on the Raspberry Pi, decisions can be made instantaneously without the delay associated with data transmission to and from a central server.
    - **Bandwidth Conservation:** Edge analytics reduces the need to transmit large volumes of raw data over the network, thus saving bandwidth and reducing communication costs.
    - **Immediate Action:** Real-time insights enable immediate responses, such as triggering alarms or adjusting control systems in response to sensor data.
2. **Resource Management:** Given the limited computational resources of the Raspberry Pi, optimizing code for efficiency and selecting suitable algorithms are crucial. Techniques include:
    - **Algorithm Selection:** Choose algorithms that are less computationally intensive. For instance, k-means clustering or decision trees are simpler and faster to execute compared to deep learning models.

- **Code Optimization:** Write efficient code by avoiding unnecessary computations, using efficient data structures, and leveraging optimized libraries like NumPy and Pandas.
- **Offloading Tasks:** For heavy computation, consider offloading complex tasks to more powerful machines and using the Raspberry Pi for lighter, real-time processing.

4.4.2 Real-time Data Processing

Real-time data processing is needed for applications where data needs to be analyzed and acted upon instantly. It involves two primary methods:

1. **Stream Processing:** Data is processed in real-time as it is generated, ideal for applications requiring immediate responses.

   Example: A real-time heart rate monitoring system that alerts medical personnel if the patient's heart rate crosses a threshold.

2. **Batch Processing:** Data is collected over a period of time and processed in large batches. This method is suitable for less time-sensitive applications, like daily sales reports or monthly data summaries.

Example: Analyzing daily sensor readings from a network of weather stations to generate a comprehensive weather report.

Tools for Real-time Analytics:

- **Apache Kafka:** Facilitates building real-time streaming data pipelines that reliably transfer data between systems. It is a distributed streaming platform that can handle high-throughput, real-time data streams.
  Use Case: In an IoT setup, sensors stream data to Kafka topics. Consumers can then process and analyze this data in real-time.

```
from kafka import KafkaProducer, KafkaConsumer
import json

# Producer
producer = KafkaProducer(bootstrap_servers='localhost:9092', value_serializer=lambda v:
json.dumps(v).encode('utf-8'))
data = {'temperature': 22.5, 'humidity': 60}
producer.send('sensor_data', value=data)

# Consumer
consumer = KafkaConsumer('sensor_data', bootstrap_servers='localhost:9092',
value_deserializer=lambda v: json.loads(v.decode('utf-8')))
for message in consumer:
    print(message.value)
```

- **Spark Streaming:** Part of Apache Spark, this tool allows for powerful real-time data processing, enabling complex operations like sliding window algorithms and machine learning in real time. It enables scalable, high-throughput, fault-tolerant stream processing of live data streams.
  Use Case: Spark Streaming can process data from Kafka, perform real-time analytics, and output results to various data stores or dashboards.

```
from pyspark.sql import SparkSession
from pyspark.streaming import StreamingContext
from pyspark.streaming.kafka import KafkaUtils

# Initialize Spark session and streaming context
spark = SparkSession.builder.appName("RealTimeAnalytics").getOrCreate()
ssc = StreamingContext(spark.sparkContext, 1)

# Create Kafka stream
kafkaStream = KafkaUtils.createStream(ssc, 'localhost:2181', 'spark-streaming', {'sensor_data': 1})

# Process stream data
parsed = kafkaStream.map(lambda v: json.loads(v[1]))
parsed.pprint()

# Start streaming
ssc.start()
ssc.awaitTermination()
```

Example 4.3: Temperature Monitoring with Data Processing

Objective: Collect temperature data from a sensor, preprocess the data, and perform real-time analytics to detect anomalies.

Components:

Raspberry Pi

Temperature sensor (e.g., DHT22)

Python with Pandas, NumPy, and Scikit-learn

Steps:

1. Data Collection:

```
import Adafruit_DHT
```

```
import time
import pandas as pd

sensor = Adafruit_DHT.DHT22
pin = 4
data = []

for _ in range(100):
    humidity, temperature = Adafruit_DHT.read_retry(sensor, pin)
    data.append({'Temperature': temperature, 'Humidity': humidity, 'Timestamp': time.time()})
    time.sleep(1)

df = pd.DataFrame(data)
```

2. Data Preprocessing:

```
df.dropna(inplace=True)  # Remove rows with missing values
df['Temperature'] = df['Temperature'].astype(float)
df['Humidity'] = df['Humidity'].astype(float)
```

3. Statistical Analysis:

```
mean_temp = df['Temperature'].mean()
std_temp = df['Temperature'].std()
```

4. Anomaly Detection with Scikit-learn:

```
from sklearn.ensemble import IsolationForest

model = IsolationForest(contamination=0.1)
df['Anomaly'] = model.fit_predict(df[['Temperature']])

anomalies = df[df['Anomaly'] == -1]
print(anomalies)
```

Example 4.4: Real-time Data Processing with Apache Kafka

Objective: Set up a real-time data processing pipeline using Apache Kafka to monitor and analyze sensor data.

Components:

Raspberry Pi

Temperature sensor (e.g., DHT22)

Apache Kafka

Python

Steps:

1. Install and Configure Kafka: Follow Kafka's official documentation to set up Kafka on a server or your Raspberry Pi.

2. Kafka Producer (Raspberry Pi):

```
from kafka import KafkaProducer
import Adafruit_DHT
import json
import time

producer = KafkaProducer(bootstrap_servers='localhost:9092', value_serializer=lambda v:
json.dumps(v).encode('utf-8'))
sensor = Adafruit_DHT.DHT22
pin = 4

while True:
    humidity, temperature = Adafruit_DHT.read_retry(sensor, pin)
    data = {'temperature': temperature, 'humidity': humidity, 'timestamp': time.time()}
    producer.send('sensor_data', value=data)
    time.sleep(1)
```

3. Kafka Consumer and Real-time Analysis:

```
from kafka import KafkaConsumer
import json
import pandas as pd
from sklearn.ensemble import IsolationForest
```

```
consumer = KafkaConsumer('sensor_data', bootstrap_servers='localhost:9092', value_deserializer=lambda v:
json.loads(v.decode('utf-8')))

data = []

for message in consumer:
    data.append(message.value)
    if len(data) > 100:
        df = pd.DataFrame(data)
        df.dropna(inplace=True)
        df['Temperature'] = df['Temperature'].astype(float)
        model = IsolationForest(contamination=0.1)
        df['Anomaly'] = model.fit_predict(df[['Temperature']])
        anomalies = df[df['Anomaly'] == -1]
        print(anomalies)
        data = [] # Reset data for the next batch
```

4.5 Visualization and Reporting

In IoT projects, especially those utilizing the Raspberry Pi, data visualization and reporting are essential components that transform raw data into actionable insights. Effective visualization helps stakeholders understand complex data patterns, trends, and anomalies, facilitating informed decision-making. Data visualization is an important aspect of data analysis in IoT projects as it provides a graphical representation of data, making it easier to interpret large volumes of information quickly. Visualization aids in identifying trends, patterns, and outliers that might not be evident in raw data. It enhances the ability to communicate findings effectively, bridging the gap between complex data analytics and actionable insights for stakeholders.

Understanding the types of data you're working with is fundamental to effective data analysis and visualization. Data can generally be categorized into two primary types: numerical and categorical. Each type has distinct characteristics and requires different approaches for processing and visualization.

Numerical Data, also known as quantitative data, represents measurable quantities and is expressed in numerical form. This type of data is pivotal for performing arithmetic operations and quantitative assessments. Numerical data can be further divided into two subcategories: discrete and continuous data.

Discrete data comprises countable values that represent distinct units, such as the number of students in a classroom or the number of cars in a parking lot. These values are often whole numbers and are best visualized using bar charts, pie charts, or histograms, which effectively illustrate comparisons between categories or frequency distributions.

On the other hand, continuous data includes values that can take any number within a specified range and are typically measurements, such as height, weight, temperature, or time. Continuous data can be subdivided into finer increments, offering a more granular view of the measurements. Visualizations for continuous data include line charts, which show trends over time, and scatter plots, which can highlight relationships between two continuous variables. These types of visualizations help in identifying patterns, trends, and correlations that might not be immediately apparent from raw data.

Categorical Data, or qualitative data, describes attributes or characteristics that can be divided into distinct categories. This type of data is not inherently numerical and often involves labels or names, such as types of fruits, colors, or brands. Categorical data can be further split into nominal and ordinal data. Nominal data represents categories without any inherent order, like types of animals or genres of music, and is best visualized using bar charts or pie charts, which show the frequency or proportion of each category. Ordinal data, while also categorical, includes a meaningful order or ranking, such as survey ratings (e.g., poor, fair, good, excellent) or class grades (A, B, C, D, F). This type of data can also be visualized with bar charts, but additional visualization methods, like heatmaps, can be used to show the intensity or prevalence of categories within a ranked order.

4.5.1 Benefits of visualizing data

Visualizing data in the data analysis process, especially in IoT projects that involve collecting large amounts of data from various sensors and devices has several benefits:

1. **Enhanced Comprehension and Quicker Analysis:** Data visualization facilitates the rapid interpretation of data by leveraging the human brain's ability to process visual information faster than textual data. Visual representations help users see large amounts of data in clear, cohesive ways, and gain insights more quickly and effectively. For instance, trends that might go unnoticed in text-based data can be immediately apparent when data is presented in a graph or trend line over time.
2. **Improved Decision Making:** One of the primary advantages of data visualization is its ability to help decision-makers to make better-informed decisions. By presenting data in a graphical format, complex concepts and relationships between operating conditions and business performance are easier to understand. This clarity leads to more informed decision making, with a deeper understanding of the factors that affect these decisions. Visual tools can also help uncover cause-and-effect relationships and predict sales volumes, enabling organizations to time their decisions more effectively.
3. **Identifying Patterns and Relationships:** Visualizations make it possible to identify patterns, trends, and correlations that might not be evident in text-based data alone. For example, scatter plots can help identify relationships between variables, bar charts provide insights into data distribution across categories, and line charts show changes over time. Recognizing these patterns can lead to new insights and discoveries, driving innovative strategies and solutions.
4. **Revealing Hidden Insights:** Data visualizations can uncover hidden insights by making use of colors, shapes, and dimensions that bring out patterns or anomalies. For example, heat maps can illustrate how individuals interact with websites, while cluster analyses can reveal natural groupings within the data that were previously

undetectable. This ability to highlight what might otherwise remain hidden is a significant strength of data visualization.

5. **Streamlining Communication:** Visualizations convey information in a universal manner that can be understood by everyone, from data scientists to non-technical stakeholders, without the need for extensive explanation. This universality makes it an effective tool for communicating complex data findings to a broad audience. Whether it's stakeholders needing to understand the impact of market trends, or teams that need to work through operational performance data, visualization provides a common ground for discussion.
6. **Enhanced Data Interaction and Accessibility:** Interactive visualizations allow users to drill down into charts and graphs for more detail, interactively changing what data they see and how it's processed. This interactivity enables users to engage with data more directly, exploring what interests them the most and making personalized discoveries that are relevant to their specific needs or tasks.
7. **Saving Time:** In environments where time is of the essence, such as monitoring network traffic in an IT department or tracking performance metrics during a marketing campaign, data visualizations allow for quick, at-a-glance recognition of the current state and any recent changes. This immediate insight is invaluable and can drastically reduce the time spent analyzing raw data.
8. **Facilitating Storytelling:** Data storytelling is a methodology where data visualization plays a pivotal role. A good data visualization tells a story, removing noise from data and highlighting useful information. Effective stories can influence decisions, stir emotions, and lead to action, which is why visualization is so powerful when it comes to corporate presentations or any scenario where you're trying to persuade or inform an audience.

4.5.2 Common types of visualizations

Effective data visualization relies on selecting the appropriate type of chart or graph to represent the data accurately. Each type of visualization serves a specific purpose and is suited to particular kinds of data and analysis goals. Some common types of visualizations used in IoT projects and data analysis are outlined below:

1. **Line Charts:** Line charts are ideal for visualizing data trends over time as shown in Figure 4.4. They display data points connected by straight lines, making it easy to observe changes and trends. In IoT projects, line charts can be used to track sensor readings such as temperature, humidity, or pressure over a specific period. This type of visualization helps in identifying patterns, trends, and cyclical behavior, which are essential for predictive maintenance and forecasting.

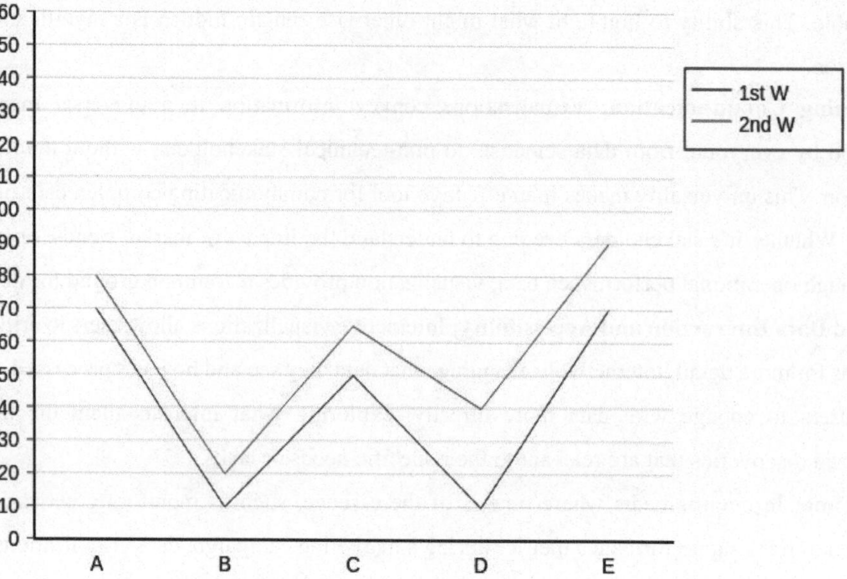

Figure 4.4: Line Chart

2. **Bar Charts:** Bar charts are used to compare different categories or groups as shown in Figure 4.5. Each bar represents a category, and its height corresponds to the value of the category. Bar charts are useful in IoT applications to compare the performance of different sensors, devices, or locations. For instance, a bar chart can display the energy consumption of various devices in a smart home, helping users identify which devices consume the most energy and take appropriate actions to reduce consumption.

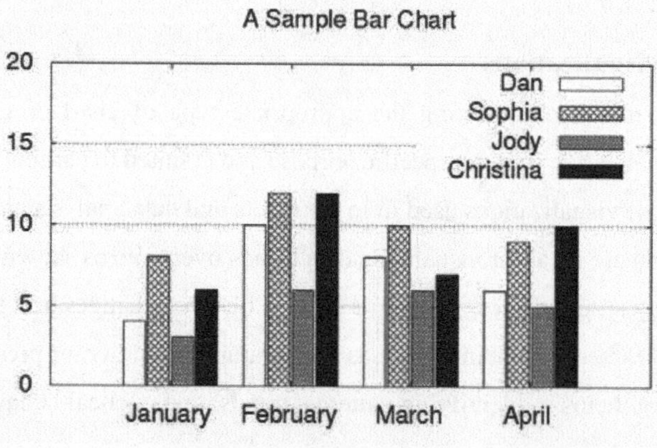

Figure 4.5: Bar Chart

3. **Pie Charts:** Pie charts represent data as slices of a circle, with each slice proportional to the category's value relative to the total as shown in Figure 4.6. They are effective for showing proportions and percentages. In IoT projects, pie charts can illustrate the distribution of various sensor types in a network or the proportion of time different devices spend in various states (e.g., active, idle, maintenance). This helps in understanding the overall composition and allocation of resources.

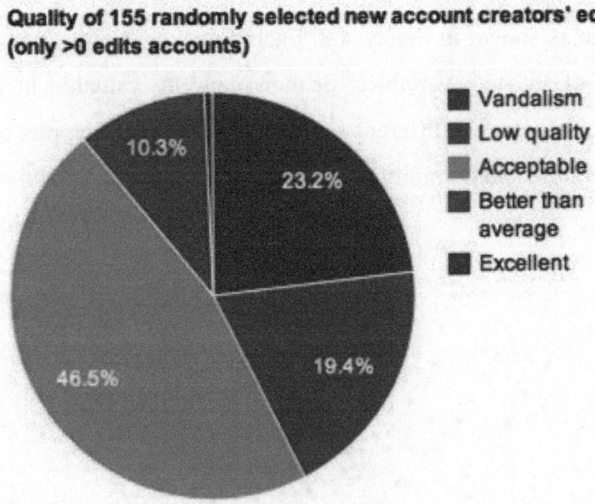

Figure 4.6: Pi Chart

4. **Histograms:** Histograms display the distribution of a dataset by grouping data points into bins and showing the frequency of data points in each bin as shown in Figure 4.7. This type of visualization is particularly useful for understanding the distribution and variability of continuous data, such as temperature readings from a sensor. Histograms can help identify the central tendency, spread, and skewness of the data, providing insights into the sensor's performance and environmental conditions.

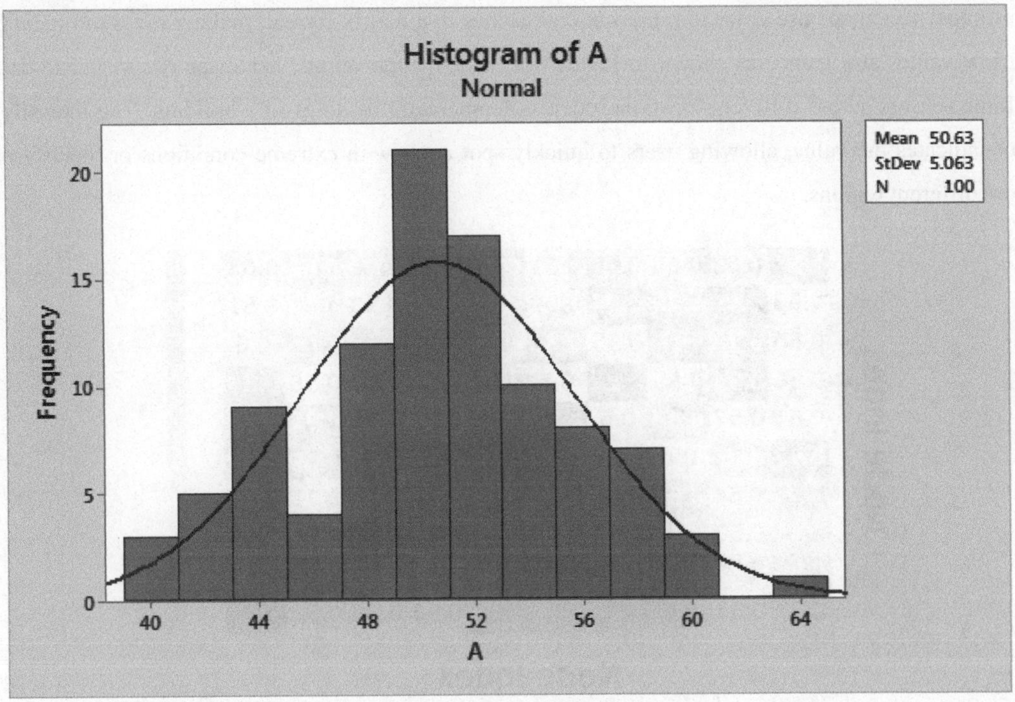

Figure 4.7: Histogram

5. **Scatter Plots:** Scatter plots show the relationship between two continuous variables by displaying data points on a two-dimensional plane as shown in Figure 4.8. Each point represents an observation, with its position determined by the values of the two variables. Scatter plots are valuable in IoT projects for analyzing correlations and dependencies between different sensor readings. For example, a scatter plot can reveal the relationship between temperature and humidity levels, helping to understand how one variable might influence the other.

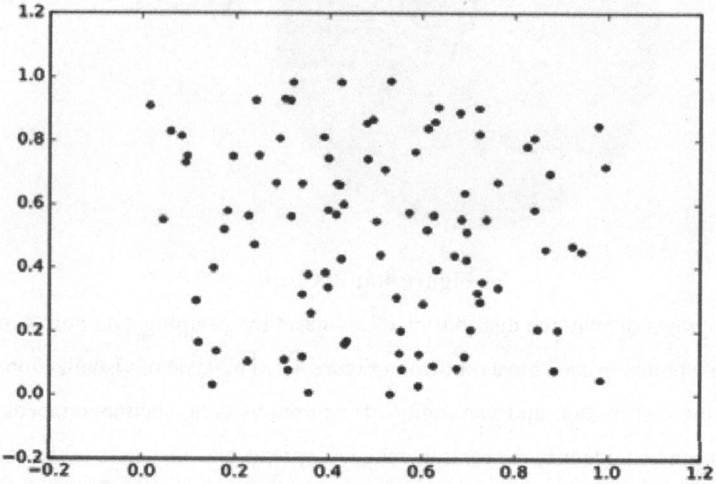

Figure 4.8: Scatter plot

6. **Heatmaps:** Heatmaps use color to represent data values in a matrix format, making it easy to identify high and low values at a glance as shown in Figure 4.9. In IoT applications, heatmaps can visualize data from multiple sensors across different locations, such as temperature readings in a building. The intensity of the color indicates the value, allowing users to quickly spot areas with extreme conditions or identify patterns across different regions.

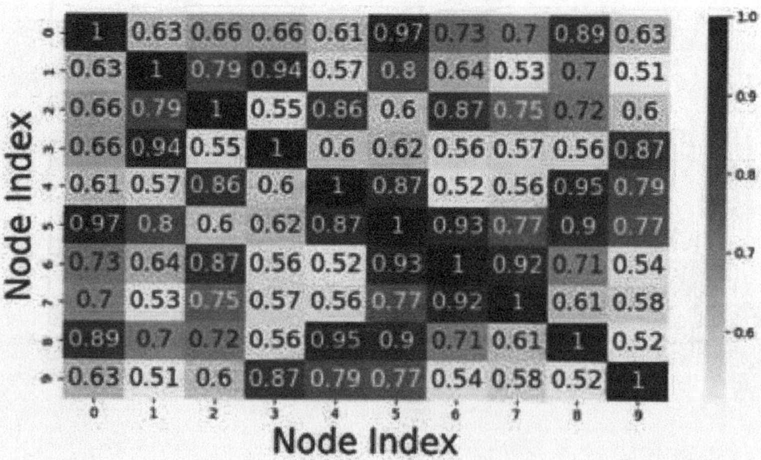

Figure 4.9: Heatmap

7. **Box Plots:** Box plots, also known as box-and-whisker plots, are a standardized way of displaying the distribution of data based on a five-number summary: minimum, first quartile (Q1), median (second quartile, Q2), third quartile (Q3), and maximum as shown in Figure 4.10. They are particularly useful for indicating whether a distribution is skewed and whether there are potential unusual observations (outliers) in the data set. This makes them ideal for monitoring device performance, predictive maintenance, and optimizing system operations in IoT environments.

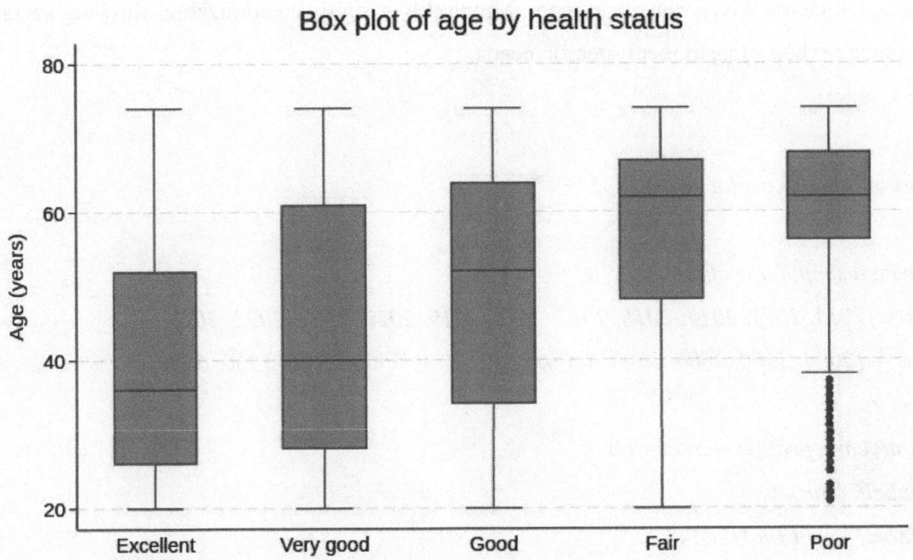

Figure 4.10: Box Plot

Scan for more knowledge on data plotting

4.5.3 Visualization Tools

Visualization tools are essential for transforming raw data into intuitive visual formats that can be easily interpreted and analyzed. These tools range from simple libraries for creating basic plots to advanced platforms for building interactive dashboards and real-time monitoring systems. In the context of IoT projects, especially those utilizing the Raspberry Pi, selecting the right visualization tools can significantly enhance the ability to derive insights and make data-driven decisions.

Python Libraries for Visualization

Python is a preferred programming language for data analysis due to its simplicity and the vast array of libraries available for data manipulation and visualization. Two of the most widely used Python libraries for data visualization are Matplotlib and Seaborn.

1. **Matplotlib:** Matplotlib is a comprehensive library for creating static, animated, and interactive visualizations in Python. It provides a flexible platform for producing a wide range of plots and charts, including line plots, scatter plots, bar charts, histograms, and more. Matplotlib is highly customizable, allowing users to fine-tune the appearance of their plots to meet specific needs.

   Example Usage:

```
import matplotlib.pyplot as plt

# Create a simple line chart
years = [2013, 2014, 2015, 2016, 2017, 2018, 2019, 2020, 2021, 2022, 2023]
profits = [2000, 2500, 3000, 3500, 4000, 3700, 4500, 5000, 5200, 5300, 6000]

plt.plot(years, profits, marker='o')
plt.xlabel('Year')
plt.ylabel('Profit (in USD)')
plt.title('Company Profits from 2013 to 2023')
plt.grid(True)
plt.show()
```

2. **Seaborn:** Seaborn is built on top of Matplotlib and provides a high-level interface for drawing attractive and informative statistical graphics. It simplifies the process of creating complex visualizations and integrates well with pandas data structures. Seaborn is particularly useful for visualizing statistical relationships and distributions.

   Example Usage:

```
import seaborn as sns
import matplotlib.pyplot as plt
import pandas as pd

# Load dataset
data = sns.load_dataset('tips')
# Create a bar plot
```

```
sns.barplot(x='day', y='total_bill', data=data)
plt.title('Total Bill by Day')
plt.show()
```

Dashboard Tools

Dashboards provide a comprehensive view of data through interactive visualizations, allowing users to monitor and analyze key metrics in real time. They are particularly useful in IoT applications where continuous monitoring and quick decision-making are required. Two popular dashboard tools are Grafana and Kibana.

1. **Grafana:** Grafana is an open-source platform for monitoring and observability that allows users to create, explore, and share dashboards. It supports a wide range of data sources, including databases, cloud services, and IoT platforms. Grafana's real-time data visualization capabilities make it ideal for monitoring sensor data, system performance, and other critical metrics.

   Example Usage:

```
import requests

data = {'temperature': 25.3, 'humidity': 60}
response = requests.post('http://your-grafana-instance/api/push-data', json=data)
```

2. **Kibana:** Kibana is a data visualization and exploration tool used primarily with Elasticsearch. It provides powerful features for creating interactive dashboards and visualizing real-time data. Kibana is well-suited for log and event data analysis, making it a valuable tool for monitoring and troubleshooting in IoT systems.

   Example Usage:

```
from elasticsearch import Elasticsearch
es = Elasticsearch(['http://localhost:9200'])
doc = {'temperature': 25.3, 'humidity': 60}
es.index(index='iot-sensors', doc_type='_doc', body=doc)
```

4.5.4 Creating Reports

Creating effective reports in data analysis is a process that transforms raw data into actionable insights for decision-making and strategic planning. Effective reports communicate findings clearly and concisely, influencing decisions and guiding future actions. To achieve this, it is essential to understand the purpose of the report, refine its content and style, and utilize the best tools available.

1. **Data Collection and Verification:** Before beginning the analysis, it is necessary to ensure that the data is accurate, reliable, and comprehensive. This involves verifying the credibility and relevance of data sources,

ensuring data completeness to avoid biases caused by missing information, and performing initial data explorations to identify anomalies or outliers that could skew results. Proper data collection and verification lay the foundation for accurate and meaningful analysis.

2. **Structured Analysis Framework:** Developing a structured framework for analyzing data is essential for systematic and thorough examination. This framework should include defining clear objectives, formulating hypotheses, selecting appropriate analytical methods, and systematically applying these methods to the data. A well-defined framework helps in maintaining focus and consistency throughout the analysis process, ensuring that all relevant aspects are considered.
3. **Report Structure and Content:** A well-structured report enhances readability and comprehension. It should start with an executive summary that provides a concise overview of key findings, recommendations, and the report's purpose. The introduction should outline the objectives, scope, and methodology used for analysis. The main body of the report should present detailed insights, trends, and visualizations derived from the data, using charts, graphs, and tables where applicable. Recommendations should be based on the analysis findings, providing actionable suggestions supported by data-driven insights. The conclusion should summarize the main points discussed in the report, emphasizing key takeaways. Including appendices with supplementary materials such as raw data and technical details can provide additional context and support for the report's findings.
4. **Visualizations and Graphics:** Effective use of visual elements enhances the report's impact by making complex data more accessible and understandable. Charts and graphs, such as bar charts, line graphs, pie charts, scatter plots, and heat maps, illustrate trends, comparisons, and distributions within the data. Incorporating interactive dashboards or dynamic visualizations from tools like Tableau, Power BI, or custom-built solutions can further enhance data exploration and understanding, allowing stakeholders to interact with the data and gain deeper insights.
5. **Writing Style and Clarity:** Clear, concise language is essential for conveying complex concepts and technical details effectively. The report should be organized logically with headings, subheadings, and bullet points to improve readability and navigation. Avoiding unnecessary technical jargon or acronyms ensures that the report is understandable to the intended audience, regardless of their technical expertise.
6. **Automation and Updates:** Implementing tools or scripts to automate report generation for recurring analyses ensures consistency and efficiency. Automated reporting systems can update data and regenerate reports on a scheduled basis, keeping stakeholders informed of evolving trends and performance metrics without manual intervention.

Various tools can help in creating professional and effective reports. Microsoft Word and Excel are widely used for creating structured reports with text, tables, and charts, suitable for non-technical audiences. Google Docs and Sheets offer collaborative features for creating and sharing reports online, integrating with Google's data analysis tools. LaTeX is preferred for technical reports requiring mathematical equations, formulas, and precise formatting. Business intelligence platforms like Tableau, Power BI, and QlikView provide advanced capabilities for creating interactive dashboards and detailed reports with real-time data integration, enhancing the depth and accessibility of the analysis.

Automating Report Generation

Automation of report generation and strategic communication of insights are central to modern data-driven decision-making processes. This detailed discussion explores the methods and tools for automating the creation of reports and effectively sharing those insights with stakeholders. The automation of report generation streamlines the process of turning data into actionable insights. It ensures that reports are produced consistently, without manual intervention, and that they reflect the most current data. This is particularly beneficial in environments where data is continuously updated, such as in monitoring IoT systems or dynamic market conditions.

Using Python for Report Automation:

Libraries like ReportLab for PDF generation and Jinja2 for HTML templates allow for the creation of customized and dynamic reports.

- **ReportLab:** This library is robust for generating PDF documents from Python. You can embed charts, images, or text that is formatted to suit specific reporting needs. As shown in the example provided, ReportLab can be used to create a straightforward report including key metrics such as temperature and humidity, making it invaluable for sectors like manufacturing, agriculture, or environmental monitoring where such factors are crucial.
- **Jinja2:** For HTML-based reports, Jinja2 is an excellent tool. It works by populating HTML templates with data, allowing for the creation of visually appealing and interactive reports that can be viewed in any web browser. This flexibility is particularly useful for creating reports that need to be accessible on various devices or shared online.

Example Code:

```
# Example of using Jinja2 to generate an HTML report
from jinja2 import Environment, FileSystemLoader

env = Environment(loader=FileSystemLoader('templates'))
template = env.get_template('report_template.html')

data = {'temperature': 25.3, 'humidity': 60}
report_html = template.render(data=data)

with open('report.html', 'w') as f:
    f.write(report_html)
```

This script loads an HTML template, injects data, and saves the output as an HTML file. Such reports can include interactive elements like hyperlinks, embedded videos, or animations.

Sharing Insights with Stakeholders

Once reports are generated, the goal is to make the insights accessible and actionable for all stakeholders, regardless of their technical expertise.

- **Emailing Reports:** Automatically sending reports via email is a straightforward and effective method to ensure stakeholders receive the latest data insights directly. The use of Python's smtplib along with email.mime libraries facilitates not only the sending of the textual content but also the attachment of reports in various formats like PDFs or links to interactive dashboards.
- **Web-Based Dashboards:** For a more dynamic and interactive approach, web-based dashboards like Grafana or Kibana can be utilized. These tools allow stakeholders to explore data in real-time, with the ability to drill down into metrics or time periods of interest. They support user interaction, such as selecting specific data points, zooming in on data, or querying for more detailed information, which enhances the user's ability to understand and act on the data presented.

4.6 Summary

This presents an in-depth introduction to Raspberry Pi and its use in IoT systems, including its architecture, multiple models, and specs. It investigates hardware connection via GPIO pins, which enables the integration of sensors and actuators into IoT projects. The section focuses on Python programming, describing major libraries such as RPi.GPIO, gpiozero, and Adafruit for controlling hardware and creating data collecting and processing functions. Real-world IoT projects, such as blinking LEDs, sound alarms, and temperature monitoring systems, are utilized to show practical applications. The unit also discusses data storage alternatives such as local storage with SD cards and cloud integration, as well as the role of Raspberry Pi in the development of end-to-end IoT solutions.

4.7 Exercise

A. Multiple Choice Questions (MCQs)

1. Which of the following is the primary function of Raspberry Pi?

a) Web browsing

b) Teaching basic computer science

c) Video Editing

d) Gaming

2. When was the first Raspberry Pi model released?

a) 2009

b) 2011

c) 2012

d) 2013

3. Which model of Raspberry Pi introduced the quad-core ARM Cortex-A72 CPU?

a) Raspberry Pi 2 Model B

b) Raspberry Pi 3 Model B

c) Raspberry Pi 4 Model B

d) Raspberry Pi Pico

4. What kind of storage does Raspberry Pi use for its operating system?

a) USB Drive

b) Hard Disk

c) microSD Card

d) SSD

5. Which components are necessary for setting up Raspberry Pi?

a) Hard Disk

b) Ethernet Cable

c) Monitor

d) SSD

6. Which interface allows Raspberry Pi to connect to a camera module?

a) USB

b) CSI (Camera Serial Interface)

c) Ethernet

d) HDMI

7. What is the primary power supply requirement for Raspberry Pi 4 Model B?

a) 5V/2A

b) 5V/3A

c) 12V/2A

d) 9V/3A

8. What programming language is recommended for working with Raspberry Pi?

a) Java

b) C++

c) Python

d) Ruby

9. What is the purpose of GPIO pins on Raspberry Pi?

a) Connect to USB devices

b) Power the Raspberry Pi

c) Interact with external electronics

d) Provide network connectivity

10. Which protocol transfers data over the network in IoT systems with low bandwidth?

a) HTTP

b) MQTT

c) SMTP

d) FTP

11. Which Python library controls the GPIO pins on Raspberry Pi?

a) RPi.GPIO

b) GPIO Plus

c) PyBoard

d) Thonny

12. Which Raspberry Pi model is known for its ultra-compact size and low power consumption?

a) Raspberry Pi 1 Model A

b) Raspberry Pi Zero

c) Raspberry Pi 3 Model B

d) Raspberry Pi Pico

13. How many GPIO pins are available on most Raspberry Pi models?

a) 20

b) 30

c) 40

d) 50

14. Which tools are used for installing the Raspberry Pi OS onto a microSD card?

a) Thonny

b) Visual Studio Code

c) BalenaEtcher

d) Notepad++

15. Which communication protocol is commonly used for sensor data acquisition in Raspberry Pi projects?

a) UART

b) I2C

c) SPI

d) All of the above

16. Which Raspberry Pi model first introduced dual HDMI ports?

a) Raspberry Pi Zero

b) Raspberry Pi 2 Model B

c) Raspberry Pi 3 Model B

d) Raspberry Pi 4 Model B

17. What is the use of the Ethernet port on Raspberry Pi?

a) For audio output

b) To power the device

c) To connect to a network

d) To connect a camera

18. Which Raspberry Pi series is based on a microcontroller rather than a CPU?

a) Standard Series

b) Zero Series

c) Pico Series

d) None of the above

19. What is the recommended tool for writing and running Python scripts on Raspberry Pi?

a) Nano

b) Thonny

c) Eclipse

d) Notepad

20. Which data storage option is best for long-term, scalable storage in IoT systems?

a) Local microSD storage

b) Cloud storage

c) USB flash drive

d) RAM

B. Short Questions Answers

1) Explain the steps involved in setting up a Raspberry Pi.
2) Describe the purpose of GPIO pins on a Raspberry Pi.
3) Highlight the key differences between the Raspberry Pi standard and Zero the series.
4) How does the Raspberry Pi 4 Model B improve over its predecessors?
5) What are the main power requirements for different Raspberry Pi models?
6) Name two Python libraries that are used to operate the Raspberry Pi's GPIO pins.
7) What distinguishes the Raspberry Pi Zero from the Standard series?
8) What is the purpose of the Raspberry Pi's Camera Serial Interface (CSI)?
9) Enumerate the three parts needed to configure a Raspberry Pi system.
10) How can a Raspberry Pi be updated to the most recent version of Python?
11) Describe the main function of the Raspberry Pi models' Ethernet port.
12) What role does cloud storage play in Raspberry Pi Internet of Things projects?
13) How may Raspberry Pi-based IoT systems benefit from edge analytics?
14) List two visualization tools that are appropriate for Internet of Things projects with Raspberry Pi.

C. Long Questions Answer

1) **Situation:** Constructing a System for Home Automation

   Question: Suppose you are assigned to use a Raspberry Pi to automate household equipment like fans and lamps. Which Raspberry Pi features would you employ, and how would you configure the system? Provide the necessary processes, parts, and Python code to illustrate automation.

2) **Situation:** Monitoring Temperature in Real Time

   Question: You are utilizing a Raspberry Pi to construct a real-time temperature monitoring system for a greenhouse. Talk about how sensors are connected, data is gathered, and real-time data processing and alarms are configured. Describe the function of the system's Python libraries and code snippets.

3) **Situation:** IoT Project Data Analytics

   Question: To increase operational efficiency, a company want to evaluate sensor data from several Raspberry Pi devices. Explain how you would use local databases or cloud storage to preprocess, store, and analyze this data. How would you present the results to interested parties?

4) **Question:** Improving a Weather Station Project Scenario Temperature, humidity, and pressure readings are recorded using a Raspberry Pi-built weather station. The team intends to examine trends over time and incorporate a real-time dashboard. Describe how you would put this into practice, emphasizing the methods and resources for gathering data, visualizing it, and doing predictive analysis.

Answers for MCQ's

1. b) Teaching basic computer science
2. c) 2012
3. c) Raspberry Pi 4 Model B
4. c) microSD Card
5. c) Monitor
6. b) CSI (Camera Serial Interface)
7. b) 5V/3A
8. c) Python
9. c) Interact with external electronics
10. b) MQTT
11. a) RPi.GPIO
12. b) Raspberry Pi Zero
13. c) 40
14. c) BalenaEtcher
15. d) All of the above
16. d) Raspberry Pi 4 Model B

17. c) To connect to a network

18. c) Pico Series

19. b) Thonny

20. b) Cloud storage

REFERENCES

1. Raspberry Pi official website https://www.raspberrypi.com/books-magazines/

5 IOT APPLICATIONS WITH CASE STUDIES

UNIT SPECIFICS

In this unit, the following aspects will be discussed:

- IoT applications are used in critical fields such as agriculture, healthcare, smart cities, and industrial systems.
- Case studies help to understand practical IoT installations and associated issues.
- Designing IoT systems utilizing tools like Tinkercad to mimic and evaluate real-world scenarios.
- IoT solutions are evaluated using efficiency, scalability, and sustainability criteria.
- Integration of IoT components, such as sensors, actuators, and controllers, into real-world projects.

To improve students' practical comprehension, real-world case studies are presented in depth, as well as step-by-step simulations of IoT systems. Important information is presented in tabular format to facilitate understanding of the topics.

This lesson includes exercises with theoretical and practical problems, multiple-choice questions, a reference list, and suggested readings to encourage active learning. QR codes are also offered to access extra resources such as tutorials, project examples, and advanced IoT subjects, giving students more chances for discovery and skill development.

RATIONALE

This unit on Case Studies and Practical IoT Applications delves deeply into real-world IoT implementations in a variety of areas, including agriculture, healthcare, smart cities, and industrial systems. The subject introduces students to the actual uses of IoT technology, allowing them to better grasp how these systems solve real-world problems and increase efficiency. Students learn to examine the problems and benefits of IoT solutions in a variety of domains using extensive case studies. The use of tools such as Tinkercad to create and simulate IoT systems improves practical understanding. The class also covers the evaluation of IoT systems in terms of scalability, efficiency, and sustainability, which will help students make educated decisions when creating IoT-based solutions. This content is structured to build a solid foundation in applying IoT principles, encouraging students to explore innovative solutions in various industries.

PRE-REQUISITES

No prerequisites are required for studying this unit.

UNIT OUTCOMES

The list of outcomes of this unit is as follows:

U5-O1: Analyze IoT applications in key domains like agriculture, healthcare, smart cities, and industrial systems

U5-O2: Understand the role of IoT in solving practical challenges through case studies

U5-O3: Design and simulate IoT systems using Tinkercad, focusing on smart applications like irrigation and patient monitoring

U5-O4: Evaluate the efficiency, scalability, and sustainability of IoT implementations

U5-O5: Explore the integration of IoT components like sensors, actuators, and microcontrollers in practical projects

Unit Outcomes	Expected Mapping with Course Outcomes *(1- Weak Correlation; 2- Medium correlation; 3- Strong Correlation)*				
	CO-1	CO-2	CO-3	CO-4	CO-5
U5-O1	3	3	3	2	3
U5-O2	3	3	2	2	3
U5-O3	3	3	3	3	2
U5-O4	3	3	3	3	3
U5-O5	3	3	3	3	3

5.1 Discussion of Tinkercad

As discussed in Chapter 3, Tinkercad is an online 3D modeling and circuit simulation tool designed to be user-friendly and accessible to beginners and professionals alike as shown in figure 5.1. It is widely used for creating digital prototypes of physical devices and systems, making it an excellent platform for educational purposes, especially in fields like electronics, IoT, and STEM education. One of the primary reasons Tinkercad is popular in IoT projects is its ability to simulate electronic circuits. Users can create and test virtual circuits using components like Arduino boards, sensors, LEDs, motors, and more. The platform supports drag-and-drop functionality, making it easy to assemble circuits and connect components. Additionally, Tinkercad provides a code editor that allows users to write and simulate Arduino code, integrating programming with circuit design seamlessly. Tinkercad's accessibility and ease of use make it an excellent choice for students and educators. It provides a safe environment to experiment with circuits and code, reducing the risk of damaging actual components. This makes it a valuable resource for teaching and learning about IoT, electronics, and programming.

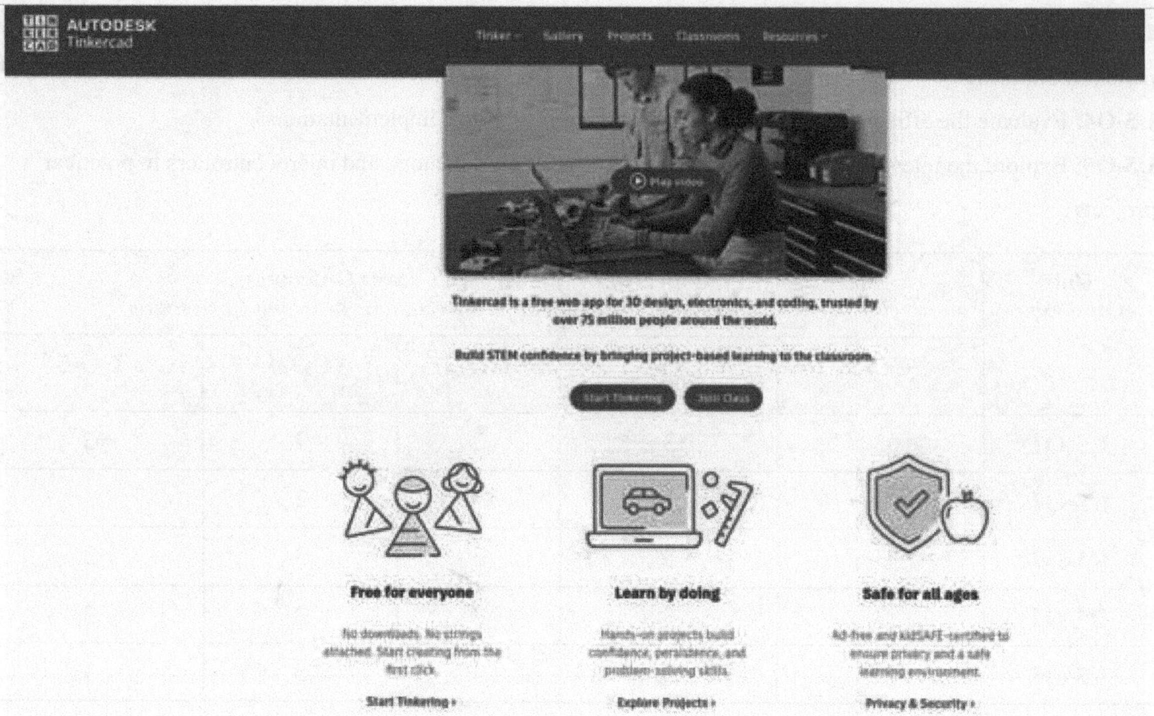

Figure 5.1: A screenshot of Tinkercad opening window.

5.1.1 Electronics

- **Circuit Design:** Tinkercad's circuit design interface is a robust simulation tool that allows users to conceptualize, build, and test electronic circuits virtually. This environment can be beneficial for IoT development where each component's behavior and interaction can be experimented with without the immediate need for physical prototypes. The tool provides a real-time, interactive circuit simulation that mimics the actual response of electronic components. This means that any changes made in the circuit layout or component values are immediately reflected in the simulation, providing instant feedback. Users can design complex circuits that involve multiple layers of connectivity. For instance, integrating multiple sensors with a single microcontroller, setting up parallel and series configurations, and even creating circuits that respond to environmental changes detected by sensors.
- **Component Library:** Tinkercad's extensive component library is a key resource, providing a wide variety of electronic components that are essential for building IoT systems. From basic resistors, capacitors, and LEDs to more complex sensors and actuators, the library allows for extensive experimentation. Users can explore different configurations and combinations of components to best suit their project needs. The ease of dragging and dropping components onto a breadboard and wiring them together with virtual wires simplifies the learning curve for beginners and enhances productivity for advanced users.

- **Simulation:** The simulation feature in Tinkercad goes beyond just visualizing connections and interactions within the circuit. It allows users to input real-time parameters, observe outputs, and tweak settings to see immediate effects, which is crucial for developing reactive IoT systems. By integrating with the Arduino programming environment within Tinkercad, simulations can include not just hardware layouts but also the software that controls them, providing a high-level view of how the entire system operates.

5.1.2 Code Blocks

- **Visual Programming:** Tinkercad supports block-based programming, which is a valuable tool for beginners and educators in the realm of electronics and IoT. By providing a drag-and-drop interface for programming, Tinkercad helps users understand programming logic and structure without getting bogged down by syntax. This method is especially effective in educational settings, helping students and newcomers visualize how code translates into physical actions within an electronic circuit.
- **Text-based Coding:** For users who are more comfortable with traditional programming, Tinkercad offers the capability to write and debug code in a text-based environment. Users can write Arduino sketches directly in the platform, which can then be immediately tested in the virtual circuit environment. It allows for more complex and nuanced programming tasks, such as handling multiple sensor inputs, executing conditional logic, and controlling actuators based on algorithmic decisions.

5.1.3 Components and Tools

- **Arduino and Microcontrollers:** The ability to simulate Arduino boards and other microcontrollers is another feature for IoT projects in Tinkercad. Users can simulate the entire microcontroller ecosystem, including digital and analog I/O, connectivity options like Bluetooth or WiFi, and integration with external devices. Before ever uploading a single line of code to a physical device, users can verify their logic, ensuring that their programs run as expected.
- **Sensors and Actuators:** Sensors and actuators are the hands and eyes of IoT systems, and Tinkercad's library includes a broad spectrum of these components. Temperature, humidity, motion, and other sensors can be tested under various simulated conditions to observe how they would behave in real-world applications. Motors, servos, and relays can be controlled via virtual circuits to mimic real-world mechanical actions based on sensor inputs or programmed conditions.
- **Power Supplies and Measuring Tools:** Proper power management and measurement are crucial in IoT devices, and Tinkercad equips users with tools to simulate and measure these aspects. Users can simulate different power supply scenarios to see how their circuits perform under various voltage and current conditions. Virtual multimeters and oscilloscopes help in diagnosing issues and ensuring that the circuit functions as intended.

5.2 Case Studies in IoT

The evolution of IoT is evident in diverse applications ranging from agriculture and healthcare to smart cities and industrial automation as shown in figure 5.2. This chapter explores detailed case studies that illustrate the utilization of IoT in different domains.

Figure 5.2: An illustration of various IoT applications.

5.2.1 Agricultural Efficiency through IoT

In agriculture, IoT is enhancing productivity and sustainability through precision farming techniques. IoT devices collect real-time data on various parameters such as soil moisture, temperature, and crop health, allowing farmers to make data-driven decisions.

Case Study: Vineyard Management in California

- **Problem:** Traditional farming methods were inefficient in water usage and crop monitoring, leading to lower yields and higher costs.
- **Solution:** IoT sensors were deployed to monitor soil moisture and environmental conditions. Drones equipped with multispectral cameras provided aerial imagery for crop health analysis.

Traditional farming methods in the vineyard were inefficient, particularly in terms of water usage and crop monitoring, leading to lower yields and higher operational costs. The implementation of IoT technology offered a solution to these challenges by providing precise, real-time data and analytics. The vineyard deployed IoT sensors to monitor soil moisture and environmental conditions. Additionally, drones equipped with multispectral cameras were used to provide aerial imagery for crop health analysis.

The implementation began with the strategic placement of soil moisture sensors throughout the vineyard. These sensors were designed to measure the volumetric water content in the soil at different depths and locations, offering a detailed understanding of the vineyard's irrigation needs. Environmental sensors, including temperature and humidity sensors, were also installed to monitor microclimate conditions within the vineyard. These sensors provided continuous data on the environmental factors affecting vine growth and health. The drones played a crucial role in the data collection process. Equipped with multispectral cameras, the drones flew over the vineyard capturing high-resolution images. These images were then processed to assess plant health by analyzing the reflectance of different wavelengths of light. Healthy vines reflect light differently compared to stressed or diseased vines, allowing the vineyard managers to identify and address issues early.

All the data collected by the sensors and drones was transmitted to a central system where it was analyzed. Machine learning algorithms processed the data to predict irrigation needs and optimize water distribution. This data-driven approach ensured that each section of the vineyard received the right amount of water at the right time, significantly improving water use efficiency. The results of implementing IoT technology in the vineyard were impressive. Water usage was reduced by 20%, which was a significant saving considering the scale of the vineyard. Moreover, crop yields increased by 15% due to the precise and timely interventions enabled by real-time monitoring. The vineyard's overall management improved as well, with managers able to make informed decisions based on accurate data rather than relying on estimates or manual checks. Despite the clear benefits, the vineyard faced several challenges during the implementation of IoT technology. One major issue was connectivity, as remote areas often lack reliable internet access. To overcome this, the vineyard employed a mesh network of sensors that relayed data to a central hub with a stronger connection. This ensured continuous data flow even in areas with weak connectivity. Another challenge was the cost of implementation. The initial investment in IoT devices and infrastructure was high. However, the vineyard was able to offset some of these costs by leveraging government grants and subsidies aimed at promoting sustainable farming practices. The long-term benefits of reduced water usage and increased yields also justified the initial expenditure, making the investment worthwhile.

5.2.2 Healthcare with IoT Remote Monitoring

IoT in healthcare is improving patient outcomes and reducing costs by enabling remote monitoring and telemedicine. Wearable devices and home sensors collect health data, which is then analyzed to provide insights and alerts to healthcare providers.

Case Study: Chronic Disease Management

- **Problem:** Managing chronic diseases like diabetes and heart conditions requires constant monitoring, which can be challenging for patients and healthcare providers.
- **Solution:** Patients were equipped with wearable devices that monitored vital signs such as blood glucose levels, heart rate, and physical activity.

Managing chronic diseases traditionally faced significant challenges for both patients and healthcare providers. Frequent visits to healthcare facilities for routine check-ups were inconvenient for patients and placed a heavy burden on healthcare systems. Missed appointments and lack of real-time data often resulted in delayed treatments and suboptimal management of the diseases. The introduction of IoT-based remote monitoring systems aimed to address these issues by providing continuous, real-time health monitoring outside of clinical settings.

In this case study, patients were equipped with wearable devices designed to monitor vital signs such as blood glucose levels, heart rate, blood pressure, and physical activity. These wearables, including smartwatches and specialized health monitors, continuously tracked the patients' health metrics and transmitted the data to a secure, cloud-based platform. This platform was accessible to healthcare providers, enabling them to monitor their patients' health in real time. The implementation of this system involved several critical components. First, the wearable devices needed to be user-friendly and comfortable for continuous use. They also had to be accurate in their measurements and reliable in data transmission. The secure cloud platform served as the central repository for all collected data, offering robust data analytics tools to process and analyze the information. Machine learning algorithms played a vital role in this system by identifying patterns and anomalies in the health data, which could indicate potential health issues.

When abnormal readings were detected, the system generated automated alerts that were sent to healthcare providers via the cloud platform. These alerts enabled timely interventions, such as medication adjustments or emergency care, thereby preventing complications that could arise from delayed treatment. Additionally, the system provided regular summaries and insights into patients' health trends, which helped doctors make informed decisions during routine consultations. The impact of IoT-based remote monitoring on chronic disease management was substantial. One of the most significant outcomes was a 25% reduction in hospital readmissions among patients using the system. The ability to monitor patients continuously and intervene early when issues were detected played a crucial role in achieving this reduction. Furthermore, patient compliance with treatment plans improved markedly. The convenience of wearable devices and the ability to manage their health from home encouraged patients to adhere more strictly to their prescribed regimens.

Data privacy and security were critical considerations in the implementation of this system. Protecting sensitive health data from breaches and unauthorized access was paramount. The system incorporated end-to-end encryption and adhered to stringent healthcare regulations such as the Health Insurance Portability and Accountability Act (HIPAA) to ensure data security and patient confidentiality. Despite its successes, the project faced challenges, particularly in ensuring consistent use of the wearable devices by patients. To address this, comprehensive educational programs were developed to teach patients how to use the devices effectively. The interfaces of the wearable devices and the accompanying apps were designed to be intuitive and user-friendly, reducing the learning curve and increasing patient engagement.

5.2.3 Smart City Solutions

In the case of smart cities, IoT enhances infrastructure management, improves public services, and increases quality of life. One significant application is intelligent traffic management.

Case Study: Traffic Congestion in Singapore

- **Problem:** Traffic congestion was a major issue, causing delays and contributing to pollution.
- **Solution:** An IoT-based traffic management system was implemented, using sensors and cameras to monitor traffic flow and congestion levels in real time.

In the city-state of Singapore, traffic congestion has long been a pressing issue, contributing to delays, increased pollution, and overall inefficiency in transportation. To address these challenges, Singapore implemented an IoT-based traffic management system that leverages real-time data to optimize traffic flow and reduce congestion. This case study illustrates the transformative power of IoT in creating smarter, more efficient urban environments. Rapid urbanization and population growth had led to a significant increase in the number of vehicles on the roads. The existing traffic management infrastructure was not equipped to handle this surge, resulting in frequent traffic jams, long travel times, and higher emissions from idling vehicles. The need for a more dynamic and responsive traffic management system was evident.

The solution involved deploying an IoT-based traffic management system that used a network of sensors, cameras, and advanced data analytics to monitor and manage traffic in real-time. The system's core components included traffic sensors, which were installed at key intersections and along major roads. These sensors measured various parameters, such as vehicle count, speed, and congestion levels. Cameras provided visual data, enabling the system to analyze traffic patterns and detect incidents such as accidents or illegal parking. Data collected from these sensors and cameras was transmitted to a central traffic management center, where it was processed and analyzed using machine learning algorithms. These algorithms were designed to predict traffic patterns based on historical data and real-time inputs, allowing for proactive adjustments to traffic control measures. For example, the system could dynamically adjust the timing of traffic signals to alleviate congestion in areas experiencing heavy traffic.

A significant innovation of the system was its integration with a mobile app that provided real-time traffic updates to drivers. The app offered information on current traffic conditions, estimated travel times, and suggested alternative routes to avoid congested areas. This feature empowered drivers to make informed decisions and plan their journeys more efficiently, reducing the overall load on congested roads. The implementation of the IoT-based traffic management system in Singapore yielded remarkable results. Traffic congestion was reduced by 30%, significantly improving travel times across the city. This reduction in congestion also led to a decrease in vehicle emissions, contributing to improved air quality. The system's ability to adapt to real-time conditions ensured smoother traffic flow, minimizing delays and enhancing the overall efficiency of the transportation network.

The success of the system hinged on several technical and operational factors. First, the accuracy and reliability of the data collected by the sensors and cameras were crucial. Advanced data processing techniques, including redundancy checks and data validation algorithms, were employed to ensure the integrity of the data. Second, the machine learning models used for traffic prediction were continually refined and updated with new data to maintain their accuracy and relevance. Public acceptance and cooperation were also vital to the system's success. The introduction of the new traffic management measures required a shift in driver behavior and public perception. The city conducted extensive awareness campaigns to educate the public about the benefits of the system and how to use the mobile app effectively. Incentives, such as discounts on toll fees for app users, were offered to encourage adoption. Despite the numerous benefits, the project faced challenges, particularly in integrating data from various types of sensors and ensuring seamless communication between different components of the system. To address these challenges, standardized protocols and interfaces were developed, enabling interoperability and data exchange between devices from different manufacturers.

5.2.4 Industrial IoT with Predictive Maintenance

In the industrial sector, IoT is transforming operations through predictive maintenance. By continuously monitoring equipment, IoT devices can predict failures before they occur, thus minimizing downtime and maintenance costs.

Case Study: Manufacturing Plant Efficiency

- **Problem:** Unplanned equipment downtime led to significant production losses and maintenance costs.
- **Solution:** IoT sensors were installed on critical machinery to monitor parameters like vibration, temperature, and operational performance.

In the case of industrial operations, unplanned equipment downtime poses significant challenges, often leading to substantial production losses and increased maintenance costs. This case study explores how IoT technology was harnessed to transform a manufacturing plant's operations through predictive maintenance, thereby enhancing efficiency and reliability. The manufacturing plant in question faced recurring issues with unplanned equipment failures. These unexpected breakdowns not only disrupted production schedules but also incurred high repair costs and led to extended periods of inactivity. Traditional maintenance practices, which relied on periodic inspections and reactive repairs, were insufficient to prevent these issues. There was a clear need for a more proactive and efficient approach to equipment maintenance. To address these challenges, the plant implemented an IoT-based predictive maintenance system. The core of this system involved installing IoT sensors on critical machinery to continuously monitor various operational parameters such as vibration, temperature, and pressure. These sensors collected real-time data on the equipment's health and performance, providing a detailed overview of its operational status.

The collected data was transmitted to a central monitoring system where it was processed and analyzed using advanced predictive analytics algorithms. These algorithms were designed to detect early signs of wear and tear or potential failures by identifying patterns and anomalies in the data. For example, an increase in vibration or temperature could indicate a misalignment or a component that was beginning to fail. By predicting these issues before they escalated into major problems, the system enabled maintenance teams to schedule repairs proactively. The implementation of predictive maintenance required several key steps. First, the selection and installation of appropriate sensors were crucial. These sensors needed to be highly sensitive and capable of operating in the harsh industrial environment. Once installed, the sensors continuously transmitted data to the central system, where it was stored and analyzed. The predictive maintenance algorithms, trained on historical data, were then applied to identify potential issues and generate maintenance alerts.

The impact of the IoT-based predictive maintenance system on the manufacturing plant was profound. One of the most significant outcomes was the reduction in unplanned downtime. By identifying and addressing potential issues before they resulted in equipment failure, the plant minimize disruptions to production. This led to a 40% decrease in unplanned downtime, significantly improving operational efficiency. Moreover, the system optimized maintenance schedules, ensuring that maintenance activities were performed only when necessary. This approach, known as condition-based maintenance, reduced unnecessary maintenance tasks and extended the lifespan of machinery components. As a result, maintenance costs dropped by 25%, contributing to substantial cost savings for the plant. Another benefit was the improved reliability and performance of the equipment. With continuous monitoring and timely maintenance, machinery operated more smoothly and efficiently, reducing the risk of catastrophic failures. This reliability translated into higher productivity and consistent production quality, enhancing the plant's overall competitiveness. Implementing predictive maintenance also required addressing several challenges. Ensuring the accuracy and reliability of sensor data was paramount. Regular calibration and maintenance of sensors were necessary to maintain data integrity. Additionally, integrating the IoT system with the plant's existing infrastructure posed challenges, particularly in terms of data compatibility and communication protocols. To overcome these issues, middleware solutions were utilized to facilitate seamless data flow between old and new systems.

Data security was another crucial consideration. Protecting sensitive operational data from potential breaches and ensuring secure communication between sensors and the central system were essential. The plant implemented robust cybersecurity measures, including encryption and secure data transmission protocols, to safeguard its data. The success of the predictive maintenance system also hinged on the expertise and collaboration of the maintenance and IT teams. Training programs were conducted to equip maintenance personnel with the skills needed to interpret data and respond to predictive maintenance alerts effectively. The IT team played a crucial role in managing the data infrastructure and ensuring the smooth operation of the system.

In the previous section, we have discussed some of the applications of IoT with its approach to the real world problems. In the following section, we discuss the demonstartion of these case studies through programming and simulation in tinkercad.

5.3 Smart Agriculture

5.3.1 Smart Irrigation System in Tinkercad

A smart irrigation system uses sensors to monitor soil conditions and automatically activates a water pump when the soil requires water. In this project, we use Tinkercad to simulate such a system, demonstrating the use of various electronic components and Arduino programming to automate irrigation based on soil temperature as shown in figure 5.3.

Components Required:

- Arduino Uno
- Soil temperature sensor (simulated with a potentiometer)
- DC motor (to simulate the water pump)
- LEDs (Red and Green)
- Buzzer
- Liquid Crystal Display (LCD)
- Breadboard and connecting wires

Arduino Connections:

1. **Temperature Sensor:** Connect the potentiometer to simulate the soil temperature sensor. The middle pin of the potentiometer goes to A1, and the other two pins go to 5V and GND.
2. **LCD:** Connect the LCD to pins 2, 3, 4, 5, 6, and 7 of the Arduino.
3. **Motor:** Connect the DC motor terminals to pins 10 and 11.
4. **LEDs:** Connect the Red LED to pin 12 and the Green LED to pin 9.
5. **Buzzer:** Connect the buzzer to pin 8.

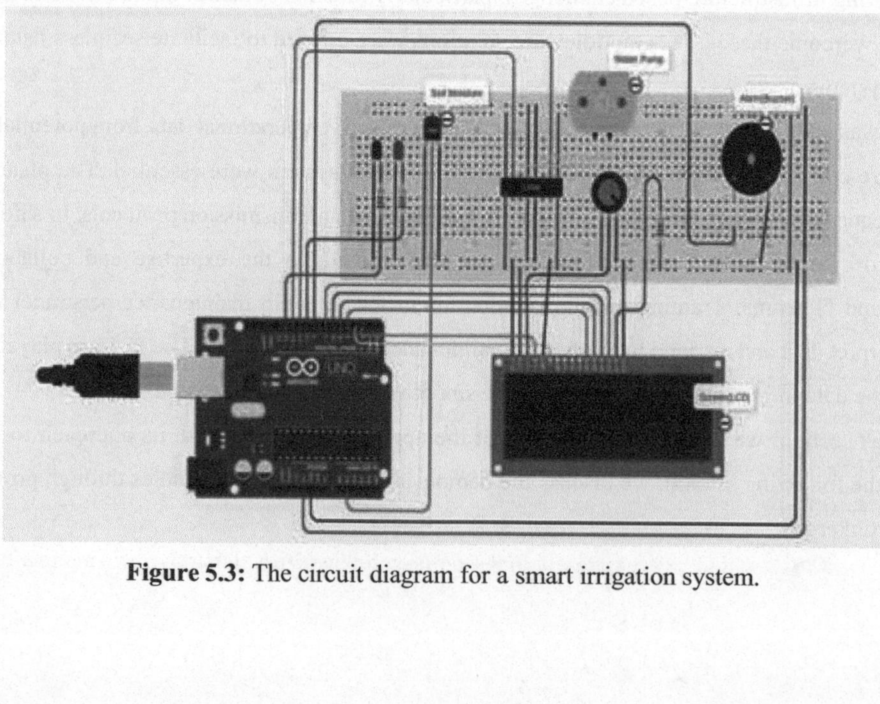

Figure 5.3: The circuit diagram for a smart irrigation system.

Explanation:

1. **Libraries and Constants:**
   - #include <LiquidCrystal.h>: Includes the library for controlling the LCD.
   - Constants define pin connections for the temperature sensor, motor, LEDs, and buzzer.
2. **Setup Function:**
   - Initializes the serial communication for debugging.
   - Sets up the LCD with the initial message.
   - Defines the pin modes for the buzzer, LEDs, and motor terminals.
3. **Loop Function:**
   - Reads the analog value from the temperature sensor.
   - Displays the temperature on the LCD and the serial monitor.
   - If the temperature exceeds 50 (threshold value), it activates the water pump, lights the red LED, and sounds the buzzer.
   - If the temperature is below the threshold, it turns off the pump, sounds no buzzer, and lights the green LED.

Simulation in Tinkercad:

To simulate this project in Tinkercad:

1. **Setup the Components:** Place the Arduino, potentiometer (as the temperature sensor), DC motor, LEDs, buzzer, and LCD on the Tinkercad workspace. Connect them as per the pin configurations mentioned above as shown in figure 5.5.
2. **Upload the Code:** Copy and paste the provided code into the Tinkercad code editor as shown in figure 5.4. Start the simulation.
3. **Adjust the Potentiometer:** By adjusting the potentiometer, you simulate different soil temperatures. When the simulated temperature exceeds the threshold (value of 50), the motor (representing the water pump) will turn on, the red LED will light up, and the buzzer will sound, indicating that the soil needs watering. When the temperature is below the threshold, the motor will turn off, the green LED will light up, and the buzzer will be silent.

Code Operation:

- The system starts by initializing the serial monitor and LCD display, indicating the system has started.
- It continually reads the temperature from the sensor.
- If the temperature exceeds 50 degrees, it indicates high soil temperature:
  - Turn on the red LED.
  - Activates the water pump.
  - Sounds a buzzer.
  - Displays a warning on both the LCD and serial monitor.
- If the temperature is below 50 degrees:

- Turn on the green LED.
- Turn off the water pump and buzzer.
- Updates the LCD and serial monitor with the status.

```

#include <LiquidCrystal.h>

const int temp = A1;
const int motor_terminal1 = 10;
const int motor_terminal2 = 11;
const int LedRed = 12;
const int LedGreen = 9;
const int Buzzer = 8;


LiquidCrystal lcd(2, 3, 4, 5, 6, 7);

void setup() {
  Serial.begin(9600);
  Serial.print("Smart irrigation system");
  Serial.print("\n");
  Serial.print("\n");
  lcd.begin(16, 2);
  lcd.print("Smart Irrigation");
  lcd.setCursor(4,1);
  lcd.print("System!!");
  pinMode(Buzzer, OUTPUT);
  pinMode(LedRed, OUTPUT);
  pinMode(LedGreen, OUTPUT);
  pinMode(motor_terminal1, OUTPUT);
  pinMode(motor_terminal2, OUTPUT);
  delay(2000);
  lcd.clear();
  lcd.print("Temp = ");
  lcd.setCursor(0,1);
  lcd.print("WaterPump= ");
}

void loop() {

  int value = analogRead(temp);
  float Temperature = value;
  Serial.print("Soil Temperature = ");
  Serial.print(Temperature);
  Serial.print("\n");Serial.print("\n");
  lcd.setCursor(6,0);
  lcd.print(Temperature);
  lcd.setCursor(11,1);


  if (Temperature > 50){
    digitalWrite(motor_terminal2, HIGH);
    digitalWrite(motor_terminal1, LOW);
    digitalWrite(LedRed, HIGH);
    digitalWrite(LedGreen, LOW);
    tone(Buzzer,220,100);
    lcd.print("ON ");
    Serial.print("Warning...!!!! Soil temperature is high");
    Serial.print("\n");Serial.print("\n");
    Serial.print("Need water!! Switch on water pump");
    Serial.print("\n");Serial.print("\n");
  }
  else {
    digitalWrite(motor_terminal2, LOW);
    noTone(Buzzer);
    digitalWrite(LedRed, LOW);
    digitalWrite(LedGreen, HIGH);
    lcd.print("OFF");
    Serial.print("Soil Temperature is fine...!!!");
    Serial.print("\n");Serial.print("\n");
  }

   delay(1000);
}

```

Figure 5.4: Code for smart irrigation system.

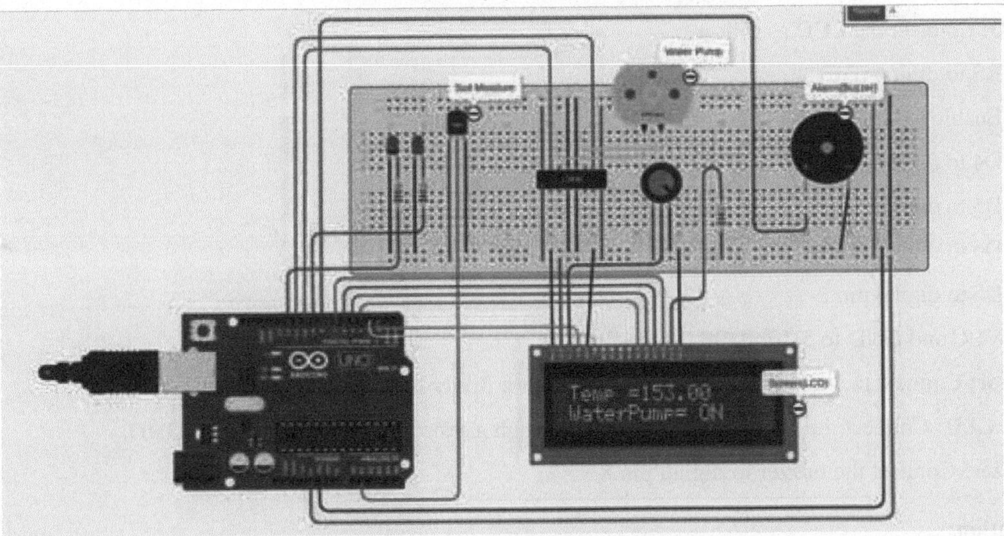

Figure 5.5: Working of the circuit.

5.3.2 Irrigation Control System in Tinkercad

Using an Arduino Uno, this automated irrigation control system monitors soil temperature, moisture, and humidity levels through simulated sensors. When the temperature or moisture readings exceed the set thresholds, corresponding LEDs light up to alert the user. The system also displays real-time sensor data on an LCD, ensuring optimal water usage and plant health.

Components Required:

- Arduino Uno
- Potentiometers (3) to simulate soil temperature, moisture, and humidity sensors
- LED (Red)
- Buzzer
- Liquid Crystal Display (LCD)
- L293D Motor Driver IC (to control the DC motor simulating the water pump)
- Breadboard and connecting wires

Arduino Connections:

1. **Temperature Sensor:** Connect the potentiometer to simulate the soil temperature sensor. The middle pin of the potentiometer goes to A0, and the other two pins go to 5V and GND as shown in figure 5.6.
2. **Soil Moisture Sensor:** Connect the potentiometer to simulate the soil moisture sensor. The middle pin of the potentiometer goes to A1, and the other two pins go to 5V and GND.
3. **Humidity Sensor:** Connect the potentiometer to simulate the humidity sensor. The middle pin of the potentiometer goes to A2, and the other two pins go to 5V and GND.

4. **LCD:** Connect the LCD as follows:
   - RS to digital pin 12
   - Enable to digital pin 11
   - D4 to digital pin 5
   - D5 to digital pin 4
   - D6 to digital pin 3
   - D7 to digital pin 2
   - VCC and GND to 5V and GND respectively
5. **Motor:** Connect the motor through the L293D motor driver IC to pins 10 and 11.
6. **Red LED:** Connect the anode to digital pin 9 through a resistor, and the cathode to GND.
7. **Buzzer:** Connect the buzzer to digital pin 8.

Explanation:

1. **Libraries and Constants:**
   - #include <LiquidCrystal.h>: This library is included to control the LCD.
   - Constants define the pin connections for the sensors and LEDs.
2. **Setup Function:**
   - Initializes the serial communication for debugging purposes.
   - Set up the LCD with the initial message.
   - Defines the pin modes for the LED.
3. **Loop Function:**
   - Reads the analog values from the temperature, soil moisture, and humidity sensors.
   - Displays each sensor's reading on the LCD and the serial monitor.

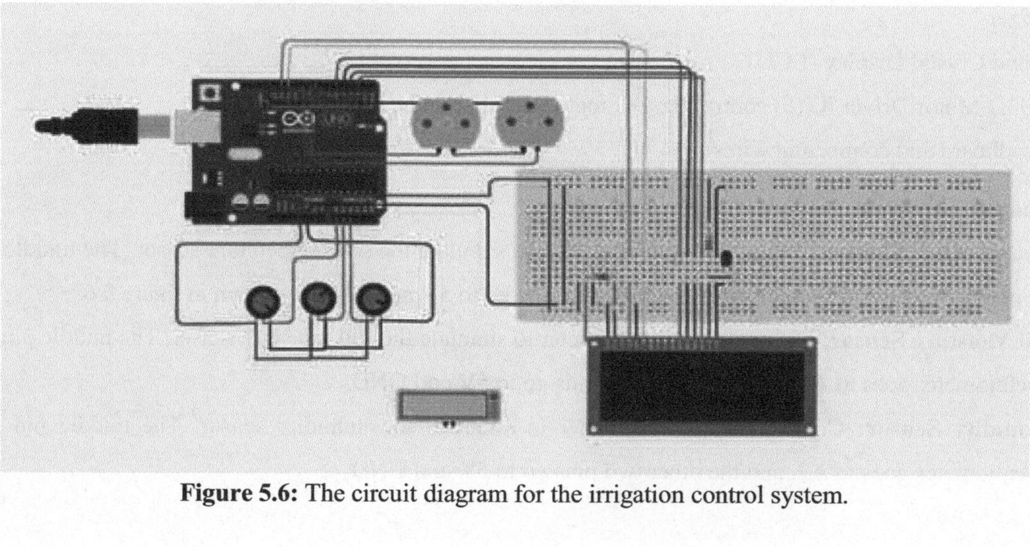

Figure 5.6: The circuit diagram for the irrigation control system.

Simulation in Tinkercad:

To simulate this project in Tinkercad:

1. **Setup the Components:** Place the Arduino, three potentiometers (for temperature, moisture, and humidity sensors), LCD, LED, buzzer, and the motor driver IC with the motor on the Tinkercad workspace. Connect them according to the specified pin configurations.
2. **Upload the Code:** Copy and paste the provided Arduino code into Tinkercad's code editor. Start the simulation.
3. **Adjust the Potentiometers:** By adjusting the potentiometers, you simulate different sensor readings. When the simulated temperature exceeds the threshold (value of 300), the motor (representing the water pump) will turn on, the LED will light up, and the buzzer will sound, indicating that the soil needs watering. When the readings are below the threshold, the motor will turn off, the LED will switch off, and the buzzer will be silent.

Code Operation:

- **Initialization:** The system initializes the serial monitor and LCD display to indicate the system startup. It also sets up the pin modes for the sensors and LED.
- **Reading Sensors:** Continuously reads the analog values from the temperature, soil moisture, and humidity sensors.
- **Displaying Values:** The sensor readings are displayed on the LCD and printed to the serial monitor.
- **Threshold Checks:**
  - If the temperature reading exceeds 300, it turns on the red LED, activates the water pump, and sounds the buzzer.
  - The soil moisture and humidity sensor readings are displayed but do not control any outputs in this code as shown in figure 5.7.

```
#include<LiquidCrystal.h>
LiquidCrystal lcd(12, 11, 5, 4, 3, 2);

void setup() {
  pinMode(A0, INPUT);
  pinMode(A1, INPUT);
  pinMode(A2, INPUT);
  pinMode(10, OUTPUT);
  pinMode(11, OUTPUT);
  pinMode(10, OUTPUT);
  Serial.begin(9600);
  // set up the LCD's number of columns and rows:
  lcd.begin(16, 2);
}

void loop() {
  analogRead(A0);

  analogRead(A1);

  analogRead(A2);
  delay(100);

  Serial.print( "Temp Reading = ");
  Serial.println( analogRead(A0));
  lcd.setCursor(0, 0);
  lcd.print("Temperature");
  lcd.setCursor(0, 1);
  lcd.print(analogRead(A0));
  delay(1000);
  lcd.clear();
  if( analogRead(A0)>300)
 {

   digitalWrite(9,1);
   delay(1000);
 }
 digitalWrite(9,0);
  delay(1000);

Serial.print( "Moisture Reading = ");
Serial.println( analogRead(A1));
lcd.setCursor(0, 0);
  lcd.print("Moisture");
  lcd.setCursor(0, 1);
  lcd.print(analogRead(A1));
  delay(1000);
  lcd.clear();
if( analogRead(A1)>300)
 {

   digitalWrite(8,1);
   delay(1000);
 }
digitalWrite(8,0);
  delay(1000);

Serial.print( "Humidity Reading = ");
Serial.println( analogRead(A2));
lcd.setCursor(0, 0);
  lcd.print("Humidity");
  lcd.setCursor(0, 1);
  lcd.print(analogRead(A2));
  delay(1000);
  lcd.clear();
  delay(1000);
}
```

Figure 5.7: Code for irrigation control system.

5.4 Smart Healthcare

5.4.1 BMI Measurement System in Tinkercad

This system measures the height and weight of a person using an ultrasonic sensor and a force sensor, respectively. The height is calculated based on the time taken for an ultrasonic pulse to bounce back from the ground, and the weight is read from a force sensor (simulated with a potentiometer). The system then calculates the Body Mass Index (BMI) using the formula: BMI = weight (kg) / height^2 (m^2). Based on the calculated BMI, the system categorizes the person's weight status (e.g., underweight, normal, overweight) and lights up the corresponding LED as shown in figure 5.8.

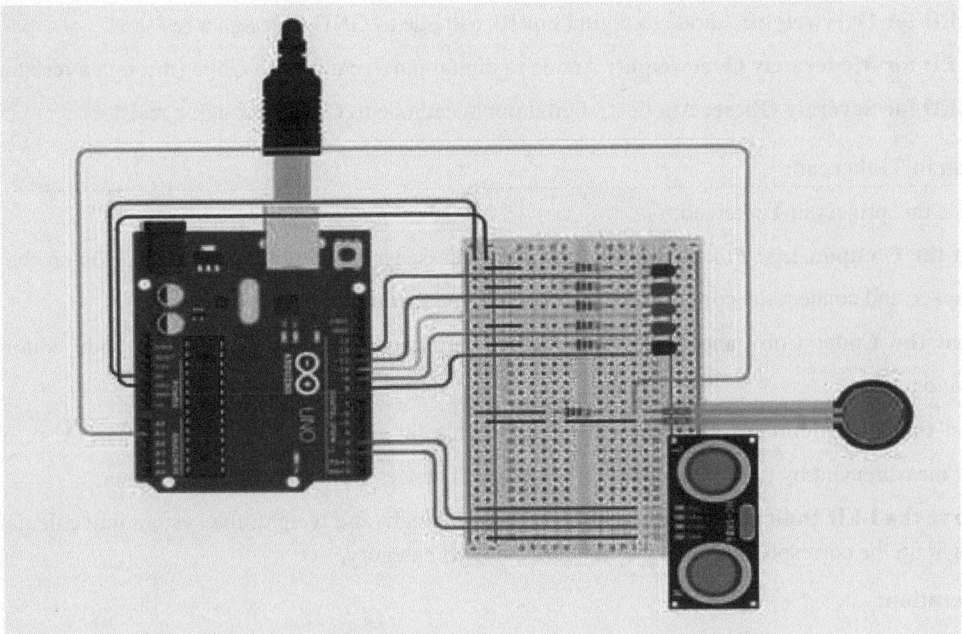

Figure 5.8: The circuit diagram for the BMI measurement system.

Components Required:

- Arduino Uno
- Ultrasonic sensor (HC-SR04) for height measurement
- Force sensor (simulated with a potentiometer) for weight measurement
- LEDs (5) to indicate different BMI categories
- Breadboard and connecting wires

Arduino Connections:

1. **Ultrasonic Sensor (HC-SR04):**
    - **Trig Pin:** Connect to digital pin 3

- **Echo Pin:** Connect to digital pin 2
- **VCC:** Connect to 5V
- **GND:** Connect to GND

2. **Force Sensor (Potentiometer):**
   - **Middle Pin:** Connect to analog pin A1
   - **Other Pins:** Connect to 5V and GND
3. **LEDs:**
   - **LED for Underweight:** Anode to digital pin 12, cathode to GND (through a resistor)
   - **LED for Normal:** Anode to digital pin 11, cathode to GND (through a resistor)
   - **LED for Overweight:** Anode to digital pin 10, cathode to GND (through a resistor)
   - **LED for Moderately Overweight:** Anode to digital pin 9, cathode to GND (through a resistor)
   - **LED for Severely Obese:** Anode to digital pin 8, cathode to GND (through a resistor)

Simulation in Tinkercad:

To simulate this project in Tinkercad:

1. **Setup the Components:** Place the Arduino, ultrasonic sensor, potentiometer, and LEDs on the Tinkercad workspace and connect the components according to the specified pin configurations.
2. **Upload the Code:** Copy and paste the provided Arduino code into Tinkercad's code editor. Start the simulation.
3. **Adjust the Potentiometer:** Simulate different weights by adjusting the potentiometer. Also, observe the height measurement by placing an object at different distances from the ultrasonic sensor.
4. **Observe the LED Indicators:** Based on the simulated height and weight, the system will calculate the BMI and light up the corresponding LED to indicate the BMI category.

Code Operation:

- **Initialization:** The system initializes the serial communication for debugging. It also sets up the pin modes for the ultrasonic sensor, force sensor, and LEDs as shown in figure 5.9.
- **Reading Height:** The ultrasonic sensor measures the time taken for an ultrasonic pulse to travel to the ground and back. It calculates the height based on the time measured.
- **Reading Weight:** It reads the analog value from the force sensor. It then converts the analog reading to weight in kilograms using a formula that extends the sensor's range.
- **Calculating BMI:** Calculates the BMI using the formula: BMI = weight (kg) / height^2 (m^2).
- **Displaying Values:** Prints the height, weight, and BMI values on the serial monitor.
- **Categorizing BMI and Lighting LEDs:** Based on the BMI value, the system lights up the corresponding LED to indicate the weight category. The categories are underweight, normal, overweight, moderately overweight, and severely obese.

```
long duration;
double Forcesensor=A1;
double height1;
double height2;
double weightNewton=0;//Force sensor measures in Newtons
double weightKG=0;
double BMI1;
double BMI2;

void setup()
{
  pinMode (Forcesensor, INPUT);
  pinMode(12, OUTPUT);
  pinMode(11, OUTPUT);
  pinMode(10, OUTPUT);
  pinMode(9, OUTPUT);
  pinMode(8, OUTPUT);
  pinMode(3, OUTPUT);
  pinMode(2, INPUT);
  Serial.begin (9600);
}

void loop()
{
 //Distance Formulas
 digitalWrite (3,LOW);
 delayMicroseconds(2);

 digitalWrite (3,HIGH);
 delayMicroseconds(10);
 digitalWrite (3,LOW);

 duration = pulseIn (2,HIGH);

 height1 = duration*0.034/2;
 height2 = height1/100; //Convert CM to M

 //Weight Formulas
 weightNewton= analogRead(Forcesensor);
 //The forcesensor has a limited range for KG, So this formula ass
 weightKG= weightNewton*weightNewton*weightNewton*weightNewton*wei


 //Print the Values on Serial Monitor
 Serial.print ("Height: ");
 Serial.print (height2);
 Serial.println ("m");

 Serial.print ("Weight: ");
 Serial.print (weightKG);
 Serial.println ("kg");

 BMI1= height2*height2;
 BMI2= weightKG/BMI1;

 Serial.print ("BMI: ");
 Serial.println (BMI2);

//Categorizing BMI and turning on corresponding LEDs
  if (BMI2<18.5){
  Serial.println ("UNDERWEIGHT");
  digitalWrite (12,HIGH);
  delay(200);
  digitalWrite (12,LOW);
  }
  else if (BMI2>18.5&&BMI2<25){
  Serial.println ("NORMAL");
  digitalWrite (11,HIGH);
  delay(200);
  digitalWrite (11,LOW);
  }
  else if (BMI2>=25&&BMI2<30){
  Serial.println ("OVERWEIGHT");
  digitalWrite (10,HIGH);
  delay(200);
  digitalWrite (10,LOW);
  }
  else if (BMI2>=30&&BMI2<35){
  Serial.println ("MODERATELY OVERWEIGHT");
  digitalWrite (9,HIGH);
  delay(200);
  digitalWrite (9,LOW);
  }
  else if (BMI2>=35){
  Serial.println ("SEVERELY OBESE");
  digitalWrite (8,HIGH);
  delay(200);
  digitalWrite (8,LOW);
  }
}
```

Figure 5.9: Code for BMI measurement system.

5.4.2 Patient Monitoring System in Tinkercad

This patient monitoring system measures body temperature and body position using a temperature sensor and a flex sensor, respectively. The system displays real-time data on an LCD and alerts if the patient's temperature exceeds 37.2°C or if their body position changes significantly, indicating the need for medical attention. The LED indicates when the patient needs attention.

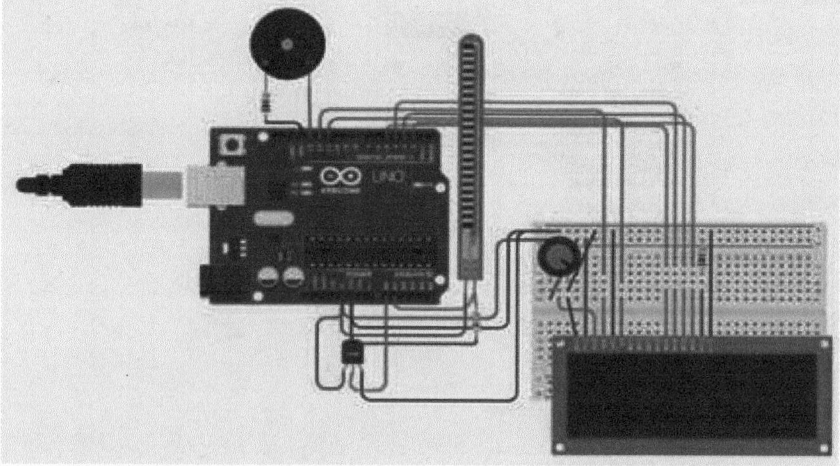

Figure 5.10: The circuit diagram for the patient monitoring system.

Components Required:

- Arduino Uno
- Temperature sensor (simulated with a potentiometer)
- Flex sensor
- LCD Display (16x2)
- LED
- Resistor (for voltage divider)
- Breadboard and connecting wires

Arduino Connections:

1. **Temperature Sensor (Potentiometer):**
   - **Middle Pin:** Connect to analog pin A0
   - **Other Pins:** Connect to 5V and GND
2. **Flex Sensor:**
   - Connect one end of the flex sensor to analog pin A1.
   - Connect the other end of the flex sensor to a voltage divider circuit using a 47kΩ resistor, with the junction connected to GND.
3. **LCD Display:**
   - RS: Connect to digital pin 12
   - Enable: Connect to digital pin 11
   - D4: Connect to digital pin 5
   - D5: Connect to digital pin 4
   - D6: Connect to digital pin 3
   - D7: Connect to digital pin 2

- VCC: Connect to 5V
- GND: Connect to GND

4. **LED:**
   - Connect the anode to digital pin 13 through a resistor, and the cathode to GND.

Simulation in Tinkercad:

To simulate this project in Tinkercad:

1. **Setup the Components:** Place the Arduino, potentiometer (for temperature sensor), flex sensor, LCD, and LED on the Tinkercad workspace. Connect the components according to the specified pin configurations as shown in figure 5.10.
2. **Upload the Code:** Copy and paste the provided Arduino code into Tinkercad's code editor. Start the simulation.
3. **Adjust the Potentiometer:** Simulate different temperatures by adjusting the potentiometer. Also, observe the body position by manipulating the flex sensor.
4. **Observe the LED and LCD Display:** The LCD will show the temperature and body position. The LED will light up when the temperature is above 37.2°C or when there is a significant change in body position as shown in figure 5.11.

Code Operation:

- **Initialization:** The system initializes the serial communication and LCD display. It also sets up the pin modes for the sensors and LED.
- **Reading Sensors:** Continuously reads the analog values from the temperature sensor and flex sensor. It then calculates the temperature in Celsius and maps the flex sensor resistance to an angle as shown in figure 5.12.
- **Displaying Values:** The temperature and body position are displayed on the LCD. If the temperature exceeds 37.2°C, the LCD shows a message indicating the patient needs attention, and the LED lights up.
- **Monitoring Body Position:** If the angle changes significantly (by 40 degrees or more), it counts the occurrences. If the angle change occurs three times in a row, the LCD shows a message, and the LED lights up.

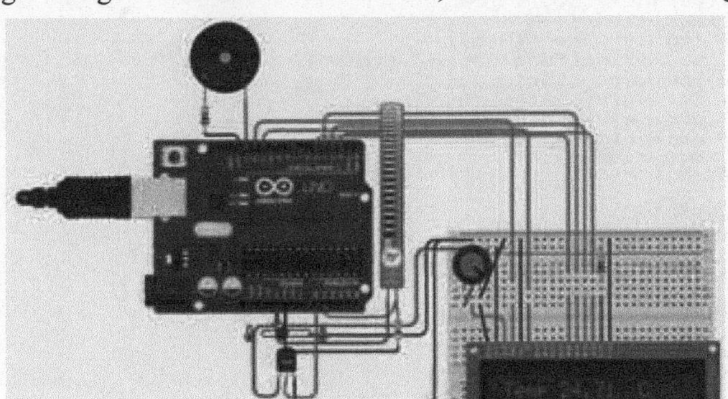

Figure 5.11: Working of the circuit.

```
#include <LiquidCrystal.h>
const float R_DIV = 47000.0;     // resistor used to create a vol
const float flatResistance = 30000.0;    // resistance when flat
const float bendResistance = 163000.0;//resistance when flexis t
float flexADC=0;
float tempADC=0;
float tempC=0;
float prevAngle=0;
int count=0;

LiquidCrystal lcd(12, 11, 5, 4, 3, 2);
void setup()
{
  pinMode(A0, INPUT);
  pinMode(A1, INPUT);
  pinMode(13,OUTPUT);
  Serial.begin(9600);
  lcd.begin(16,2);
}
void loop()
{
  lcd.setCursor(0,0);
  lcd.print("Patient");
  tempADC=analogRead(A0);
  flexADC=analogRead(A1);
  float flexV=(flexADC*5)/1024;
  float flexR= R_DIV * (5 /flexV - 1.0);
  float angle=map(flexR,flatResistance, bendResistance,0, 180);
  tempC=(tempADC*5)/1024;
  tempC=(tempC - 0.5)*100;
  lcd.setCursor(0,0);
  lcd.print("Temp ");
  lcd.print(tempC);
  lcd.setCursor(12,0);
  lcd.print("C");
  lcd.setCursor(0,1);
  lcd.print("Body Pos ");
  lcd.print(angle);

  if (tempC>=37.2){
    lcd.clear();
    lcd.setCursor(0,0);
    lcd.print("Patient needsthe");
    lcd.setCursor(0,1);
    lcd.print("attention");
   // lcd.clear();
  //  lcd.print("Temp ");
    //lcd.print(tempC);
    digitalWrite(13,HIGH);
    delay(1000);
  }
  if( abs(prevAngle - angle)>=40){
    count+=1;
    if(count>=3){
      lcd.clear();
      lcd.setCursor(0,0);
      lcd.print("Patient needsthe");
      lcd.setCursor(0,1);
      lcd.print("attention");
      digitalWrite(13,HIGH);
      delay(1000);
      lcd.clear();
    }
  }
  else{
    count=0;
  }
  digitalWrite(13,LOW);
  prevAngle=angle;
  Serial.println("Temp= "+String(tempC));
  Serial.println("angle= "+String(angle));
  delay(1500);
  lcd.clear();
}
```

Figure 5.12: Code for patient monitoring system.

5.5 Activity Monitoring

5.5.1 Flood Monitoring System in Tinkercad

This flood monitoring system uses a PIR sensor to detect motion and an ultrasonic sensor to measure the distance to the water level. When the PIR sensor detects motion, it lights up an LED. The ultrasonic sensor continuously measures the distance to the water surface. If the water level rises to a point where the distance is less than or equal to 100 cm, the system activates a buzzer to alert for potential flooding.

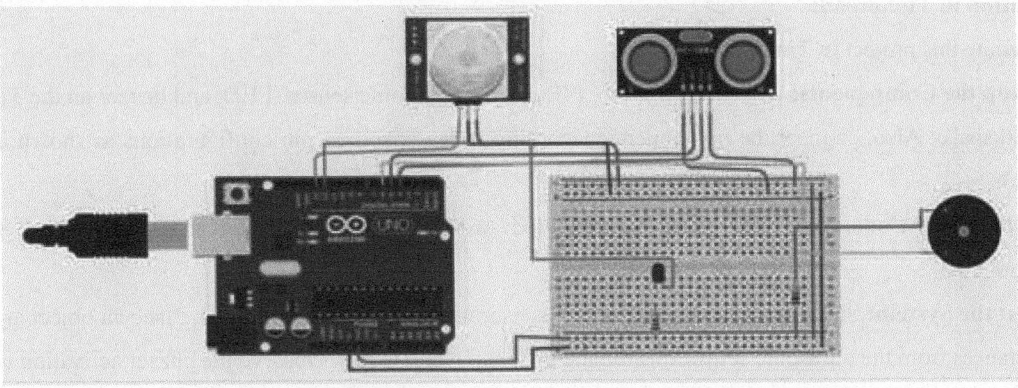

Figure 5.13: The circuit diagram for the flood monitoring system.

Components Required:

- Arduino Uno
- PIR sensor (Passive Infrared Sensor)
- Ultrasonic sensor (HC-SR04)
- Buzzer
- LED
- Breadboard and connecting wires

Arduino Connections:

1. **PIR Sensor:**
   - **VCC:** Connect to 5V
   - **GND:** Connect to GND
   - **OUT:** Connect to digital pin 13
2. **Ultrasonic Sensor (HC-SR04):**
   - **Trig Pin:** Connect to digital pin 5
   - **Echo Pin:** Connect to digital pin 4
   - **VCC:** Connect to 5V
   - **GND:** Connect to GND

3. **Buzzer:**
   - **Positive Terminal:** Connect to digital pin 6
   - **Negative Terminal:** Connect to GND
4. **LED:**
   - **Anode:** Connect to digital pin 12 through a resistor
   - **Cathode:** Connect to GND

Simulation in Tinkercad:

To simulate this project in Tinkercad:

1. **Setup the Components:** Place the Arduino, PIR sensor, ultrasonic sensor, LED, and buzzer on the Tinkercad workspace. Also, connect the components according to the specified pin configurations as shown in figure 5.13.
2. **Upload the Code:** Copy and paste the provided Arduino code into Tinkercad's code editor. Start the simulation.
3. **Test the System:** Simulate motion near the PIR sensor to see if the LED lights up. Place an object at varying distances from the ultrasonic sensor to simulate different water levels. Observe the buzzer activation when the distance is less than or equal to 100 cm.

Code Operation:

- **Initialization:** The system initializes the pin modes for the PIR sensor, LED, and buzzer.
- **Reading PIR Sensor**: Continuously reads the digital value from the PIR sensor. If motion is detected (PIR is HIGH), the LED is turned on. Otherwise, it is turned off.
- **Measuring Distance with Ultrasonic Sensor:** Uses the read Ultrasonic Distance function to measure the distance by sending an ultrasonic pulse and reading the echo. It also converts the travel time of the pulse to a distance in centimeters.
- **Activating Buzzer:** If the measured distance is less than or equal to 100 cm (indicating a high water level), the buzzer is activated with a specific tone. If the distance is greater than 100 cm, the buzzer is turned off as mentioned in the code shown in figure 5.14.

Scan for more case studies

```
int PIR = 0;

int Distance = 0;

long readUltrasonicDistance(int triggerPin, int echoPin)
{
  pinMode(triggerPin, OUTPUT);  // Clear the trigger
  digitalWrite(triggerPin, LOW);
  delayMicroseconds(2);
  // Sets the trigger pin to HIGH state for 10 microseconds
  digitalWrite(triggerPin, HIGH);
  delayMicroseconds(10);
  digitalWrite(triggerPin, LOW);
  pinMode(echoPin, INPUT);
  // Reads the echo pin, and returns the sound wave travel time
  return pulseIn(echoPin, HIGH);
}

void setup()
{
  pinMode(13, INPUT);
  pinMode(12, OUTPUT);
  pinMode(6, OUTPUT);
}

void loop()
{
  PIR = digitalRead(13);
  delay(10); // Wait for 10 millisecond(s)
  if (PIR == HIGH) {
    digitalWrite(12, HIGH);
    delay(1); // Wait for 1 millisecond(s)
  } else {
    digitalWrite(12, LOW);
  }

  Distance = 0.01723 * readUltrasonicDistance(5, 4);
  if (Distance <= 100) {
    tone(6, 880, 125); // play tone 69 (A5 = 880 Hz)
    delay(125); // Wait for 125 millisecond(s)
  } else {
    noTone(6);
  }
}
```

Figure 5.14: Code for flood monitoring system

5.6 Summary

This unit focuses on real-world IoT applications in many fields such as agriculture, healthcare, smart cities, and industrial systems. It includes extensive case studies that demonstrate how IoT devices solve specific difficulties and give novel solutions. Students learn how to use tools like Tinkercad to develop, simulate, and test IoT-based systems, putting their theoretical understanding into practice. The unit also assesses IoT systems for efficiency, scalability, and sustainability, providing insights into their real-world impact and potential to address societal concerns. This hands-on, case-study-driven approach equips students to effectively address practical IoT concerns.

5.7 Exercise

A. Long answer questions

1. Explain how the Internet of Things is altering agricultural practices, focusing on grape management in California.
2. Explain the implementation and benefits of IoT in remote healthcare monitoring, focusing on its use in chronic illness management.
3. Describe the IoT-based traffic management system that was installed in Singapore and how it has improved urban efficiency.
4. Explain predictive maintenance in industrial IoT, using the manufacturing plant efficiency case study as an example.
5. Explain Tinkercad's function in IoT teaching and prototyping. Explain its characteristics, such as circuit simulation, code integration, and component library.
6. Use Tinkercad to describe the implementation, components, and functioning of a smart irrigation system.
7. Discuss the BMI assessment system's design, operation, and applications as simulated in Tinkercad.
8. Examine the use of IoT components in Tinkercad to construct a patient monitoring system. What obstacles could develop with a real-world deployment?
9. Explain how the flood monitoring system in Tinkercad works and the importance of such systems in disaster management.
10. Compare and contrast various IoT applications (agricultural, healthcare, smart cities, and industrial IoT) based on their implementation obstacles and benefits.

B. Short Answer Questions

1. Define IoT and its role in increasing agricultural productivity.
2. What distinguishes the IoT-based vineyard management system in California?
3. Identify three advantages of IoT in healthcare.
4. What obstacles did the vineyard confront during the IoT deployment process, and how were they addressed?
5. Identify three vital indicators monitored by wearable devices in chronic disease management.
6. Explain the significance of real-time monitoring in traffic management systems.
7. What role does machine learning play in IoT-based predictive maintenance?
8. Describe the significance of Tinkercad's drag-and-drop feature.
9. Name the key components of the Tinkercad-simulated smart irrigation system.
10. How does the BMI measurement system determine weight status?
11. What function do ultrasonic sensors serve in the patient monitoring system?

C. Multiple Choice Question

1. What is the primary goal of IoT in agriculture?

a) Reduce soil quality

b) Increase crop yield and sustainability

c) Decrease water usage efficiency

d) Eliminate manual labor

2. In the vineyard management case study, which technology was used to monitor crop health?

a) PIR Sensors

b) Multispectral cameras on drones

c) Force Sensors

d) Temperature Sensors

3. What key benefit did the IoT-based healthcare system provide in chronic disease management?

a) Reduced patient compliance

b) Increased hospital readmissions

c) Real-time health monitoring

d) Delayed treatments

4. Which IoT component was central to the predictive maintenance system?

a) Force sensors

b) Vibration and temperature sensors

c) PIR sensors

d) Pressure regulators

5. What is the primary function of Tinkercad?

a) Create database management systems

b) Simulate electronic circuits and Arduino programming

c) Analyze large data sets

d) Perform real-time traffic analysis

6. Which component simulates soil temperature in the Tinkercad irrigation system?

a) Ultrasonic sensor

b) Potentiometer

c) PIR sensor

d) DC Motor

7. What is the BMI measurement formula used in the Tinkercad healthcare system?

a) Height (m) / Weight (kg)^2

b) Weight (kg) / Height (m)^2

c) Height (cm) / Weight (kg)

d) Weight (kg)^2 / Height (m)

8. In the Singapore traffic management system, what was used to detect traffic incidents?

a) PIR sensors

b) Cameras and sensors

c) Ultrasonic sensors

d) GPS devices

9. What was the major challenge faced in IoT implementation in the vineyard management case study?

a) High equipment durability

b) Lack of farmer interest

c) Connectivity issues in remote areas

d) Overuse of water resources

10. Which of the following is NOT a feature of Tinkercad?

a) Circuit simulation

b) Real-time IoT device prototyping

c) Physical hardware testing

d) Block-based programming

11. What triggers the buzzer in the flood monitoring system?

a) Soil moisture above threshold

b) Water level less than or equal to 100 cm

c) Motion detected by PIR sensor

d) Temperature exceeding 37°C

12. Which protocol is used to secure patient health data in IoT healthcare systems?

a) MQTT

b) HTTP

c) HIPAA regulations

d) FTP

13. How does the smart irrigation system indicate that soil requires water?

a) By turning on the motor, red LED, and buzzer

b) By activating the ultrasonic sensor

c) By adjusting the potentiometer automatically

d) By sending a message to a mobile app

14. What was a significant environmental benefit of Singapore's IoT-based traffic management system?

a) Increased vehicle emissions

b) Improved road accidents

c) Reduced vehicle emissions

d) Higher traffic congestion

15. Which Tinkercad feature supports beginners in programming?

a) Text-based coding

b) Pre-written code templates

c) Block-based visual programming

d) Machine learning algorithms

16. What parameter is NOT monitored in the Tinkercad irrigation control system?

a) Soil moisture

b) Temperature

c) Humidity

d) Atmospheric pressure

17. What is the purpose of LEDs in the BMI measurement system?

a) To measure height

b) To indicate BMI category

c) To monitor heart rate

d) To act as temperature indicators

18. Which IoT component measures the distance to the water level in the flood monitoring system?

a) PIR sensor

b) Ultrasonic sensor

c) Flex sensor

d) Force sensor

19. What is a key benefit of predictive maintenance in industrial IoT?

a) Increased equipment downtime

b) Condition-based maintenance

c) Reduced data reliability

d) Manual monitoring of systems

20. How does the patient monitoring system in Tinkercad alert for abnormal body positions?

a) By turning off the LED

b) By activating the flex sensor

c) By lighting an LED and displaying a message on the LCD

d) By adjusting the potentiometer

Answers for MCQ's

1. b) - Increase crop yield and sustainability
2. b) - Multispectral cameras on drones
3. c) - Real-time health monitoring
4. b) - Vibration and temperature sensors

5. b) - Simulate electronic circuits and Arduino programming
6. b) - Potentiometer
7. b) - Weight (kg) / Height (m)^2
8. b) - Cameras and sensors
9. c) - Connectivity issues in remote areas
10. c) - Physical hardware testing
11. b) - Water level less than or equal to 100 cm
12. c) - HIPAA regulations
13. a) - By turning on the motor, red LED, and buzzer
14. c) - Reduced vehicle emissions
15. c) - Block-based visual programming
16. d) - Atmospheric pressure
17. b) - To indicate BMI category
18. b) - Ultrasonic sensor
19. b) - Condition-based maintenance
20. c) - By lighting an LED and displaying a message on the LCD

CO AND PO ATTAINMENT TABLE

Course outcomes (COs) for this course can be mapped with the program outcomes (POs) after the completion of the course and a correlation can be made for the attainment of POs to analyze the gap. After proper analysis of the gap in the attainment of POs necessary measures can be taken to overcome the gaps.

Table for CO and PO attainment

Course Outcomes	Attainment of Programme Outcomes (1- Weak Correlation; 2- Medium correlation; 3- Strong Correlation)						
	PO-1	PO-2	PO-3	PO-4	PO-5	PO-6	PO-7
CO-1							
CO-2							
CO-3							
CO-4							
CO-5							

The data filled in the above table can be used for gap analysis.

INDEX